# THE
# SECRETS
# OF THE FBI

**Center Point
Large Print**

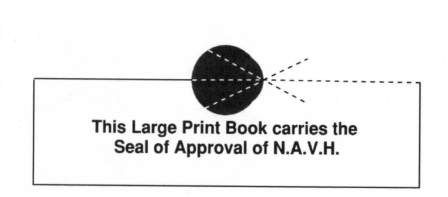

# THE
# SECRETS
# OF THE FBI

# RONALD KESSLER

CENTER POINT LARGE PRINT
THORNDIKE, MAINE

This Center Point Large Print edition is published
in the year 2011 by arrangement with
Crown Publishers, an imprint of Crown Publishing Group,
a division of Random House, Inc., New York.

The text of this Large Print edition is unabridged.
In other aspects, this book may
vary from the original edition.
Printed in the United States of America.
Set in 16-point Times New Roman type.

ISBN: 978-1-61173-184-2

Library of Congress Cataloging-in-Publication Data

Kessler, Ronald, 1943–
The secrets of the FBI / Ronald Kessler.
    p. cm.
ISBN 978-1-61173-184-2 (lib. bdg. : alk. paper)
1. United States. Federal Bureau of Investigation.
    2. Official secrets—United States. 3. Large type books. I. Title.
HV8144.F43K475 2011b
363.250973—dc23
                                              2011022287

For Pam,
Rachel, and Greg Kessler

# Contents

|  | Prologue | 9 |
| 1 | TacOps | 13 |
| 2 | Omerta | 31 |
| 3 | Red Dress | 48 |
| 4 | Secret Files | 58 |
| 5 | Break-in at the Watergate | 70 |
| 6 | Deep Throat | 78 |
| 7 | Profiling | 86 |
| 8 | Threesomes | 97 |
| 9 | Mole in the CIA | 103 |
| 10 | More Roast Beef | 111 |
| 11 | Waco | 122 |
| 12 | The Co-Director Wife | 133 |
| 13 | Behind Vince Foster's Suicide | 148 |
| 14 | Brick Agent | 155 |
| 15 | Catching Hanssen | 165 |
| 16 | "Breach" | 186 |
| 17 | Unexplained Cash | 200 |
| 18 | "Mueller, Homicide" | 210 |
| 19 | Intelligence Mind-set | 221 |
| 20 | The Center | 237 |
| 21 | The Hunt | 253 |

22   Armed and Dangerous . . . . . . . . . . . . .266
23   Preaching Jihad . . . . . . . . . . . . . . . . . . .275
24   Year of the Ponzi Scheme . . . . . . . . . .287
25   Trip Wires . . . . . . . . . . . . . . . . . . . . . .297
26   Yacht Party . . . . . . . . . . . . . . . . . . . . . .308
27   Christmas Day . . . . . . . . . . . . . . . . . . .325
28   Suitcase Nuke . . . . . . . . . . . . . . . . . . .336
29   CSI . . . . . . . . . . . . . . . . . . . . . . . . . . . .343
30   Spy Swap . . . . . . . . . . . . . . . . . . . . . . .356
31   Geronimo . . . . . . . . . . . . . . . . . . . . . . .369
32   The Biggest Threat . . . . . . . . . . . . . . .379
     Acknowledgments . . . . . . . . . . . . . . . .390

# Prologue

It was Christmas Day, just before noon. The turkey was in the oven, and the aroma was beginning to fill the house, when Arthur M. "Art" Cummings II received a call on his BlackBerry.

The FBI command center told him to call back on his secure phone. When he did, he learned that a passenger aboard Northwest Airlines Flight 253, which was on its final approach to Detroit from Amsterdam, had tried to detonate explosives as the airliner entered U.S. airspace.

As the FBI's executive assistant director for national security, Cummings, fifty, ran both counterterrorism and counterintelligence for the bureau. He was the official directly responsible for detecting and thwarting terrorist plots and espionage by other countries. Few in the U.S. government knew as many secrets.

For Cummings, hunting terrorists was a battle of wits. He was the predator, the terrorists his prey. Had a terrorist eluded him? Could he trust the information he was getting? Had he missed a clue? These were the things that kept him awake at night as he directed the FBI's transformation from an agency that emphasizes prosecutions to one that focuses on prevention of plots before they happen.

To ping in on terrorists, Cummings talked daily with Tactical Operations, a supersecret unit of FBI break-in artists who conduct court-authorized burglaries in homes, offices, and embassies to plant hidden microphones and video cameras and snoop into computers. Besides terrorists, the targets may be Mafia figures, corrupt members of Congress, spies, or intelligence officers of Russia and China.

When conducting covert entries, TacOps tranquilizes guard dogs and may stage fake traffic accidents, traffic stops, or utility breakdowns to waylay occupants and security personnel. To conceal agents as they defeat locks and alarm systems, it creates false fronts to houses and fake bushes that hide agents. If caught breaking in, TacOps agents are in danger of being shot by occupants who think they are burglars.

Besides hunting down al Qaeda, Cummings had to contend with bureaucratic rivalries. The New York City police broke a promise to the FBI and jumped the gun in the case of Najibullah Zazi, who had plotted to blow up New York City subways for al Qaeda. The Department of Homeland Security could not manage its own immigration responsibilities, yet it tried to become involved in a range of counterterrorism decisions that were the purview of the FBI. Then there was the Office of the Director of National Intelligence, an agency that often got in the way and produced little of value to the FBI.

In addition to bureaucratic infighting, Cummings had to deal with requests that could compromise the independence of the FBI. After announcing its decision to try Khalid Sheikh Mohammed in New York City, the Justice Department asked Cummings to prepare an assessment of the security threat that such a trial would pose there. Cummings resisted. He figured such an assessment from the FBI would be used for political purposes by both Democrats and Republicans. In any case, he thought the New York idea, which he believed was irresponsible, would never be carried out.

The effort by Obama administration officials to publicly use euphemisms such as "man-caused disasters" to refer to terrorism or to avoid the terms "Islamists" or "jihadists" in describing the enemy galled Cummings. "Terrible, terrible" is the way Cummings described those ideas. "Of course Islamists dominate the terrorism of today," he says.

On the other hand, Cummings had no problem with the desire of both the Obama and Bush administrations to read terrorists their rights. He believed that in most cases, the FBI could obtain the intelligence it needed to stop future plots by remaining within the framework of the legal system, including by administering Miranda warnings. The trick was to confront suspects before they were in custody, give them incentives to talk, and establish rapport.

Cummings himself was a genius at getting bad people to incriminate themselves. A master of eye contact, Cummings has a receding hairline that emphasizes the intensity of his gaze. His magnetic blue eyes direct energy toward his listener.

"It's all about parrying with the adversary," Cummings says. "How many crumbs did he leave, and how many can I pick up? How do I get to the answer, how do I get to what's really happening? There are so many different ways to do it, but the best way by far is sitting across the table from someone. The best thing is when you're sinking your fangs into his neck, and he's smiling while you do it because you convince him that what he's doing is in his best interest—when in fact it absolutely is not."

Having been told about the Christmas Day bomber, Cummings grabbed a Snickers bar and a Coke. That would be his Christmas dinner in 2009. His wife, Ellen, and three teenagers would enjoy turkey and cranberry sauce by themselves.

Cummings was now in charge of the case of Umar Farouk Abdulmutallab, one of the FBI's most controversial and potentially most damaging terrorist cases.

Cummings jumped in his FBI car, a Dodge Charger. He turned on the sirens and the flashing blue and red lights and raced toward FBI headquarters.

# TacOps

When breaking into homes and offices to plant bugging devices, TacOps agents try to avoid using rear doors. Since they are rarely used, rear doors could be booby-trapped. So when TacOps agents needed to plant bugs in a Philadelphia electronics supply company that was a front for an organized crime drug gang's hangout, they decided to walk in through the front door.

Agents decided the best time for entry would be between midnight and two in the morning. After that, trash collectors began their pickups and could see agents breaking in. The only problem was that across the street was a bar with outside seating. Patrons of the bar would spot the FBI team defeating the locks and disarming the alarm system at the front door.

So TacOps agents borrowed a city bus and rode to the electronics supply company. They parked the bus at the front door and pretended that the bus had broken down. As the FBI agent who was driving the bus lifted the hood, agents scrambled out to work on the locks and break in. Onlookers across the street could not see them behind the bus.

Once the agents were in the target building, the bus drove off. When the agents had finished installing electronic bugs, the bus returned to pick them up. But the bus whizzed past two inebriated customers from the bar who were waiting at a nearby bus stop. When the bus stopped in front of the business, the two angry patrons ran for the bus and jumped in. Since many of the agents were from different offices, everyone assumed at first that the two men were part of their operation.

"We get a couple blocks away, we start peeling off our equipment," says FBI agent Louis E. Grever, who was on the TacOps teams for twelve years. "We've all got weapons on and radio gear, and these two guys are kind of sitting there going, 'What the hell?' They start ringing the bell. *Ding, ding!* They want to get off. *Ding, ding!* Now the bus driver, who was from the local office, was not a very good bus driver. I think he practiced for like twenty minutes driving this bus. He was knocking over garbage cans when he made turns. He yells back, 'Hey, quit playing with the bell! I'm having a hard enough time driving the bus!' "

Other agents on the bus began to realize that the two men ringing to get off were not with the FBI after all. Before each job, all the agents meet each other, and now it seemed clear that these two were unwitting imposters.

"One of our guys got up, and he just happened to have a shotgun hanging on the strap on his back," Grever says. "He walks over to them and goes, 'Do we know you?' "

Now, Grever says, "They're really ringing that bell. *Ding ding ding ding ding!* And we realize these guys are not with us. So we yell up, 'Hey Phil, stop the bus! We've got a couple of riders here!' "

The driver turned around, took one look at the patrons, and realized they were not agents. Swearing, he pulled over and opened the doors.

"They get out, and we never hear a word from them," Grever says. "They had no clue what was going on. They just happened to get on the wrong bus."

Back in 1992, Grever, who has blue eyes and a reddish buzz cut, had never heard of the Tactical Operations Section. But his supervisor in the Jackson, Mississippi, field office, Billups "Bill" Allen, asked if he would like to join it. At the time, Grever had been in the FBI four years. He was expecting to be transferred to New York or Los Angeles.

About what TacOps does, Allen was cagey. Instead, he put him in touch with Mike McDevitt, a fellow former Marine, who was already on the team.

"How's your family life?" McDevitt asked him.

15

Surprised by the question, Grever answered, "Fine."

"You have any kids?"

"Yes."

"You mind spending time away from them on the road?" McDevitt asked.

"No," Grever said. "Anything for the mission."

"Good, we already got the book on you," McDevitt said. "If you are willing, can stand up to the demands, and can beat out the competition, you might have a future here in TacOps."

When Grever met with the TacOps team on the FBI Academy grounds in Quantico, Virginia, he learned that it conducts supersecret, court-authorized burglaries to implant hidden microphones and video cameras and to snoop into computers and desks in homes, offices, cars, yachts, airplanes, and embassies. In any given year, TacOps conducts as many as four hundred of what the FBI calls covert entries. Eighty percent are conducted in national security cases relating to terrorism or counterintelligence. The rest are carried out in criminal cases involving organized crime, white-collar fraud, and political corruption.

As it turned out, Grever had been recruited in part because during college he worked for an engineering company on access control and electronic security. A member of the field office's SWAT team, he had once been a police officer.

16

Before recruiting him through Allen, TacOps had checked him out thoroughly.

"Above all, they wanted to find out if I would be able to work as part of a team," Grever says. "When you spend most of your life with a very close-knit crew like TacOps, they want to make sure you can stand up to the challenges. You may be confined with them for extended periods, locked inside storage containers or on the top of an elevator. You lead a double life and are required to not talk work with family and friends. You do what might best be described as crazy."

Working as what he calls a "government-sanctioned burglar," Grever was on one of seven teams of about ten agents each that travel around the country conducting court-authorized break-ins. He conducted or supervised about a thousand covert entries.

Because of his background, Grever initially became a supervisory agent focusing on defeating alarm systems. He rose to head Tactical Operations, an FBI section with a purposely vague name. In his bio on the FBI website, the section is described only as "a deployment team chartered to provide technical support to national priority programs." In October 2008, FBI director Robert S. Mueller III named Grever the FBI's executive assistant director for the Science and Technology Branch. That put him in charge of the FBI Laboratory, fingerprints and biometrics, and the Operational Technology Division.

Consisting of a thousand people, including contract employees, the Operational Technology Division includes both TacOps and the Engineering Research Facility at Quantico. There, the FBI makes custom-designed bugging devices, tracking devices, sensors, and surveillance cameras to watch and record the bad guys. It also develops ways to penetrate computers and defeat locks, surveillance cameras, and alarm and access control systems.

On a daily basis, Art Cummings consulted with the fifty-year-old Grever to discuss innovative ways to intercept the conversations of tough targets and to lay out his priorities in national security cases.

"Before he is going to spend a hundred thousand dollars on a solution, I let him know we have a court order, and I help him prioritize based on our needs," Cummings says.

Cummings considered TacOps critical to preventing terrorism. "TacOps collects against terrorists while they are in the planning stages, while they have their guard down, allowing us to see what's really going on," Cummings says. "Combined with other collection techniques like the development of sources, scrutiny of other records, and physical surveillance, TacOps is a critical piece of an integrated collection plan that allows for a deep, multidimensional understanding of the threat."

If the FBI needs a simple wiretap of a landline phone or cell phone, or an intercept of an email account, Grever's technicians in the Operational Technology Division deal directly with the provider. Usually, the phone company can install a court-ordered wiretap within minutes by entering the target number in its computers and transmitting the conversation over an encrypted broadband link to any FBI field office. But if a physical entry is required, TacOps takes over.

In interviews with Grever and other agents currently and formerly assigned to TacOps, the FBI revealed for the first time in its history how it conducts covert entries, the bureau's most secret, most closely guarded technique. Even to members of Congress and administration officials with top-secret clearances, the operation is off-limits.

In some cases, the FBI can eavesdrop on conversations without breaking in, using parabolic microphones or laser beams to pick up sound vibrations off windows. To guard against similar intrusions, Grever's office on the seventh floor of FBI headquarters faces an inner courtyard so that no one outside can pick up his conversations. Such a remote effort to eavesdrop is referred to as a "standoff" collection. Both that technique and covert entries to plant bugs and snoop into computers and records are called "close-access attacks."

The FBI may also recruit a surrogate, who is a party to a conversation or who works in an office or home, to introduce a Trojan—an almost invisible listening device implanted in a lamp, for example, which is switched for the original. Using photos taken through a window or by an agent posing as an exterminator, a health inspector, or a telephone repairman, TacOps will have fashioned an exact replica of the lamp in the targeted office or home.

However, in most cases, a covert entry is required, offering the greatest gain but also posing the greatest risk of being caught and possibly shot by a homeowner, security guard, police officer, or foreign intelligence officer who thinks the agent is a burglar.

In selecting agents for TacOps teams, the FBI looks for men and women who have relevant experience and have worked undercover, since those agents are good at maintaining a façade. The teams include agents from all ethnic backgrounds to blend into particular neighborhoods.

Of the FBI's 13,807 agents, about 20 percent are female. They participate in the full panoply of TacOps activities, including conducting covert entries, serving on perimeter surveillance teams, and participating in "quick-react contingency teams" that will rush in to bring a dangerous situation under control.

To give agents plausible cover, male and female agents may walk together, holding hands. However, "Contrary to the James Bond movies, our female agents aren't allowed nor asked to use sex to manipulate or control a subject," Grever says. "Flirting and a smile at the right time are perfectly fine, but nothing physical."

In conducting surveillance, agents may use any type of vehicle—a bucket truck, a Rolls-Royce, or a U.S. Postal Service truck.

Agents are assigned to jobs randomly. "You could be on the Robert Hanssen case, you could be on the Aldrich Ames case, you could be on the John Gotti case, you could be on the Umar Abdulmutallab case or the Zacarias Moussaoui case," Grever says.

Over the years, the FBI has conducted successful covert entries at the Russian and Chinese embassies or their other official diplomatic establishments, as well as at the homes of their diplomats and intelligence officers. Because of the obvious sensitivity, Grever and other current FBI officials would not discuss these operations. In breaking into an embassy, the FBI may try to develop an insider to help with the entry. Once an entry has taken place, code books or electronic encryption keys used by foreign embassies are the greatest prize.

Agents on the TacOps teams have what are called deep aliases, meaning that if someone runs a check on their driver's license or social security number, the appropriate agencies would confirm their fictional identity.

"When our operators are home with family, they are simply Special Agent John or Jane Doe, but as soon as they leave the house and particularly when on a job, they become Jim Brown, Hector Garcia, or Andrea Simmons, complete with all the right documents, including alias driver's license, passport, and credit cards, and all the right stories, including fake family, fake job, and fake history—all fully backstopped," Grever says.

When returning home, undercover agents make sure they are not being followed. If pulled over for a speeding violation, they would not reveal that they are agents.

Arrangements for undercover operations are made by an FBI program code-named Stagehand. If $2 million in cash is needed as front money, Stagehand provides it. If a yacht or airplane is needed as a prop, Stagehand can provide one that was confiscated in a criminal case.

Stagehand sets up front companies so agents can hand out business cards showing they work there. The companies have real offices staffed by personnel who actually work for the FBI. Stagehand also creates front companies so agents can gain access to a target.

"One day we will be Joe's Plumbing, complete with a white work truck, company label, uniforms, and telephone number," Grever says. "If called, FBI personnel will say, 'Joe's Plumbing, can I help you?' Another day it will be Joe's Survey and Excavation Services, with the same level of backstopping."

A full wardrobe of about fifty assorted uniforms hangs on racks at the TacOps Support Center. A graphics expert designs custom-made uniforms, fake ID and badges, and wraps with fake signs for trucks. Agents will pose as elevator inspectors, firefighters, or utility workers. Alternatively, they could pose as tourists, wearing shorts and taking snapshots. They could be homeless people wearing tattered clothes. Agents select oversize clothes where they can secrete their tools for breaking in. And they go in with guns drawn.

"Usually we practice cover stories beforehand," Grever says. "If they confront you, and you give them one cover story, and then they confront me, I may give them something different."

To avoid ethical issues, TacOps agents won't impersonate a member of the clergy or a journalist. They may pose as telephone repairpeople or FedEx or UPS delivery people. But they try to avoid posing as an employee of a real company because if they are challenged, "our cover story can quickly break down if someone calls his local FedEx or UPS outlet and asks if we really work there," Grever says.

If a TacOps agent's identity is exposed because he or she is called to testify in court about an entry, that agent can no longer serve on the covert entry teams.

The strategy and contingency plans for each break-in are laid out in operations orders. Agents are required to read the court order authorizing the intrusion so they know exactly what they may and may not do.

A successful "job," as TacOps agents call it, takes weeks of planning—to determine the schedule and habits of occupants, to study the alarms and surveillance systems that need to be defeated, and to plot escape strategies.

Agents from TacOps and from the local field office fall into four groups: a survey group, which scopes out and controls the site; a mechanical group, which picks locks and opens safes and mail; an electronics group, which focuses on computers and BlackBerrys; and a "flaps and seals" group, which concentrates on special techniques the occupants may use to detect intruders. That group is also responsible for "target recovery," making sure the team leaves behind no sign that agents were there. For one job, more than a hundred agents may be involved.

"We will send agents in, and they will spend

days looking at the target, the patterns of life around it, day and night, weekends and weekdays," Grever says. "We are interested in people's sleep habits, and when they will be in a deep sleep cycle when a loud noise will not necessarily wake them up. We will track everything because—I'm not being melodramatic—our lives depend on it."

Sometimes the FBI offers bogus prizes to get occupants to leave the targeted home.

"We give people opportunities to travel and do exotic things," Grever says. " 'You've won the lottery! You've won a trip, a free dinner! Congratulations, we picked your business card out of a bucket.' That wasn't luck. That was us, trying to present an opportunity."

To cover up noises or divert attention, the FBI may drive garbage trucks through the streets and bang the garbage cans around. They may start up a wood chipper or use a jackhammer to attack a piece of concrete that has been delivered to the location and dumped on the street. They may use high-pressure water jets to clean the sidewalks, sending passersby scurrying. Agents may enlist local police to park their cruisers with lights flashing nearby. Seeing a police car, passersby will assume that the person climbing a ladder to enter an apartment or office can't be a burglar.

Agents may remotely freeze the view on closed-circuit television so security guards watching for intruders will not see them enter. During the operation, at least one of the agents does nothing but watch out windows or doors to make sure no one is approaching. TacOps agents refer to the period when they are inside an installation or defeating lock systems as the "exposure time."

While security guards are a problem, "our biggest fear, quite frankly, is innocent third parties such as a neighbor with a key to the premises and a gun," Grever says. Perhaps a suspect is away for the weekend and leaves his key with a neighbor.

"The neighbor may be nosy and sit around the home," Grever says. "If he hears something unusual, instead of calling the police, he tries to defend the neighbor's property with a gun. That's when your tennis shoes for running away fast can come in very handy."

If the neighbor calls the police, that is not necessarily considered a bad thing: The FBI scans police dispatches and usually enlists the aid of local police assigned to joint task forces. Instead of a dispatched police car showing up, an officer in league with the FBI will arrive on the scene and pretend to take a police report. By that time, the agents are long gone.

As a safety precaution, agents bring with them devices that peer under doors. They check for explosives and radiological or biological hazards. In some cases, the purpose of the entry is to determine if suspects are making bombs or developing weapons of mass destruction, as happened during the investigation of anthrax mailings.

Drug dealers will booby-trap their buildings to guard against competitors and thieves. They may rig a lightbulb so that if it's turned on, it will explode and ignite gasoline or dynamite.

Instead of breaking into an office building or government facility at night, agents may stage what they call a "lock-in." They hide inside the office building until occupants have left for the evening, then break into the targeted office. They may hide in a telephone utility closet or on top of an elevator. In one such case involving terrorism, TacOps agents rode up and down on top of an elevator for hours.

"The building finally closed up for the night," Grever recalls. "Surveillance teams outside and in neighboring high-rises where we had rented space could watch and report movements of the night security staff. When the time was right, we called our elevator to the floor just below our target, using controls we can operate remotely by plugging into the elevator command-and-control circuits. Using elevator control keys we have, we opened the doors from the inside and went to work on our targeted suite of offices undetected."

After the work was done, the agents positioned themselves on top of the elevator again and waited for the building to open in the morning.

"After changing back into our business attire, we walked out with the rest of the people who were visiting that building that morning," Grever says.

In some cases, agents are delivered to a compound inside a sealed shipping carton. In the middle of the night, like soldiers in a Trojan horse, they emerge and break into the target facility. To break into a home, an agent sealed in a refrigerator carton may be delivered to the front door, where the carton shields him from passersby as he works on the locks.

"We typically construct containers that even the most suspicious freight workers or longshoremen couldn't open without a lot of effort and time," Grever says. "Even if they did try to open our container, our emergency action team—FBI agents rushing in with raid jackets on—would be there in time to avoid a confrontation."

To make sure they are not caught, TacOps assigns field office agents or special surveillance teams to follow occupants of homes or offices—called "keyholders"—to watch them to see if they start to return. If they do, agents tailing them radio that they are heading back and estimate the time it will take them to return. Agents working the premises know their own "breakdown time," how long it will take them to gather their equipment and leave without a trace.

"If the breakdown time is fifteen minutes and the target is five minutes away, we'll have a plan in place to slow them down," Grever says. "Since we're in our own backyard, we can involve the police, fire department, public health and public safety officials, the sanitation department, the U.S. Postal Service."

Perhaps there is a "sudden traffic jam," Grever says. Or there could be an "accident in front of them, or police could pull them over. There could be a little local natural disaster—a fire hydrant is turned on and is flooding the street, and they have to go around the back way." Letting the air out of tires is another stratagem.

During an entry, one agent is in charge of making sure everything is returned to normal. At the beginning of the operation, he photographs the rooms so everything can be put back in place. If a chair or sofa is to be moved, agents first place tape on the floor to mark where the legs are.

"Trained foreign intelligence officers set traps to warn them of an intrusion by leaving a door ajar a certain degree or arranging magazines a certain way," Grever notes. The owner of a desk may never open one drawer but sets up an item inside to fall over, tipping him off if an intruder opens the drawer.

Working with the CIA, the FBI interviews defectors to learn tradecraft used by adversaries to detect FBI intrusions. Every other week, Grever meets with his counterparts at the CIA to compare notes on the latest bugging and surveillance devices.

So that nothing is left behind, each tool used during an operation is numbered and marked to identify it with the agent using it. Before leaving, agents take an inventory to make sure they have all their tools. To smooth out marks their shoes may have left on carpets, agents carry a small rake.

"We have a light that we'll use to see whether or not dust marks have been disturbed," Grever says. "We carry a supply of dust. We can throw a little bit of additional dust on if needed to make everything look as it was."

# Omerta

For TacOps agents breaking into homes, offices, and embassies, the greatest threat is dogs. They could be guard dogs or household pets. All spell trouble.

"A barking dog is as much a problem as an alarm going off," Louis Grever says. "There are several ways to deal with animals, the first being you avoid them, if you can avoid them."

Agents may befriend dogs over a period of weeks, feeding them. During a job, they may place them in soundproof crates outfitted with food and water. Or they may tranquilize them with a sedative dart from a tranquilizer gun. When the job is finished, they will give them a shot to wake them. The dosages are determined beforehand by a veterinarian on contract.

"We will provide the vet with pictures and a description of the dog in question," Grever says. "He'll look at their size and age, and he will tell us the potion to mix for them. We carry a kit with all of the narcotics and the sedatives. The point is certainly not to kill the dog, because that poses a risk of being found out."

Agents may train a fire extinguisher on a particularly aggressive dog. The blast scares it and freezes its nose. After a few blasts, simply showing the dog the fire extinguisher will make it run away, tail between its legs. In one entry at a Mafia social club in New York, the fire extinguisher ran out. A quick-thinking agent made a swooshing sound like a fire extinguisher, and that was enough to keep the dog at bay.

Another ferocious dog became docile after repeated blasts from a fire extinguisher. Later in the night, he wound up playing with the agents, bringing them toys and stuffed animals that they would throw back at him as they did their work.

"The only problem was that he tore up one of his little stuffed animals, and we had to vacuum all of that up before we left," Grever says. "We carry a quite expensive, very quiet vacuum cleaner in a backpack, and we will clean up while we're there. But we don't clean up too much, because we want to make the place look lived in."

When agents had to plant bugs in one major drug dealer's apartment, they found it had a French Fichet lock, which has a four-inch-long key and would take some time to pick. Meanwhile, nearby tenants could come out of their apartments and spot the agents. So under cover of night, both McDevitt and his partner Mike Uttaro went up on the roof of the four-story building and rappelled down. They landed on the drug dealer's balcony on the top floor.

Having been on the roof, the two TacOps agents —who were referred to as "the two Mikes"— were dirty, and the drug dealer's apartment had a white carpet. So before entering the apartment, they began removing their sneakers. In the process, Uttaro accidentally dropped one of his sneakers, which tumbled four stories to the ground.

"A dog went crazy, and a security guard came on the scene," says McDevitt, who conducted more than two thousand covert entries and later headed TacOps. "One of our surveillance agents saw that and began rustling some bushes, then took off. The security guard assumed the dog had been barking at the person in the bushes."

In another incident, agents came prepared to snare a dog inside the home of a major organized crime figure, but as soon as they caught the dog, a cat ran out.

"Cat just left exit, running west through the alley," an agent radioed. "Described as gray in color, about fifteen pounds."

"Roger, we're on it," an agent radioed back.

TacOps agents are equipped with night vision goggles, and they kept looking out the windows to see if other agents had found the cat. If the cat was not caught, the target could realize that the FBI had broken in, compromising the entire case. After an hour, an agent radioed, "Cat's in custody."

The agents placed the cat in the house. But the dog began barking, while the cat hissed. The agents thought the two were upset about the intrusion.

"The entry team goes back to the hotel and goes to bed," Grever says. "You've been working all night, and you've got to get some sleep. The worst thing that can happen is you get a phone call saying there's a problem. Usually it's the next day, when the morning team comes in, and the mics are up and running, the camera's running. One of their first jobs is to detect whether or not somebody found a wallet inside their house or thinks a chair is out of order."

In this case, the entry team was called in and told there was a problem.

"You all did everything perfectly," an agent monitoring the house told them. "With one exception: wrong cat."

"This cat immediately climbed some drapes and was hanging on the top of the drapes, and the dog was circling at the bottom waiting for the cat to eventually tire and fall down so he could go after it again," Grever says.

When the occupants returned from a trip the next day, they discovered a strange cat in their house.

"The last thing these people think is that someone broke into their house, let their cat out, put another cat in there, and then left without taking anything," Grever points out. "So they explained it to themselves by saying their cat must have gotten out through a small door that allowed the dog to go outside. They thought this other cat must have gotten in the house the same way, and they wrote it off as pretty normal."

In a case in Tampa, the best time to enter the target's home was in the afternoon between two-thirty and three-thirty. Since the agents could easily be seen, they drove a tractor trailer to the home to shield them from the neighbors across the street. But as the tractor trailer rolled into the development, telephone wires became tangled on top of the trailer. The agent who was driving radioed to the surveillance team on duty. Those agents ran to try to free the tractor trailer. Just then, a school bus full of kids showed up.

Meanwhile, a neighbor down the street who was a friend of the target was trying to drive out of the development. He saw five agents at a side entrance to the target's home, which was for sale. The friend stopped and asked what they were doing. When told by TacOps agent Mike Uttaro that they were interested in buying the home, he said, "It takes five guys to look at a house?"

"This house is in lousy condition, and we have engineers and housing inspectors here to examine it," Uttaro said. "We have an appointment with the Realtor at three."

While still suspicious, the man left, and the

agents were able to break in and search the house.

When breaking into homes, agents have encountered poisonous snakes and caged wild animals. "I walked in one place, I had my gun out, and there's two cages of orangutans, and they're going nuts," Uttaro's partner, Mike McDevitt, says. "I hear all this noise, and I have a penlight in my mouth, and I turn my head towards that, and all I see are these orange eyes looking at me. It was a jaguar in a cage."

In another case, agents found a man sleeping on a couch with a pistol on his stomach and a rifle and a whiskey bottle on the floor.

"He'd passed out," says McDevitt. "I remember laying there that night, looking at this, trying to figure out exactly what I would have done if he had awakened," McDevitt says. "I wasn't going to be able to identify myself. Since he was drunk, hopefully I'd be able to push him, and he would fall back down."

Uttaro, who conducted more than four thousand covert entries, was once installing wires in ceiling tiles while walking around on twelve-foot-high stilts. He slipped and almost went crashing through a window on the top floor of the Chrysler Building in New York. Another time, McDevitt accidentally cut into electrical wires in the Bronx, sending sparks flying.

In another New York case, McDevitt broke into

the apartment of a Mafia figure who was setting up a hit job. Pistols, rifles, and shotguns were lying on a sofa. As McDevitt and a technical agent from the field office were doing their work, they heard a noise outside the apartment door. As it turned out, the person outside the apartment was the hit man, and he soon entered the apartment using a key.

There was no place to hide, so McDevitt and the other agent ran into the bathroom and closed the door. They decided they would act as if they belonged there.

To create that impression, the technical agent took off his shirt and turned on the water in the sink. McDevitt jumped in the bathtub and pulled the shower curtain closed. Peeking through an opening in the curtain, he watched what was happening by looking in the bathroom mirror, his gun at the ready.

Hearing the water, the hit man knocked on the bathroom door. The other agent opened the door a crack.

"Who are you?" the man asked.

"Who the f—— are you?" the field agent said.

"I brought the shotgun shells," the hit man said.

"The guy turns around and he says, 'Can you lock up when you leave?' " McDevitt says.

"Sure," the technical agent replied. The hit man left, and the two agents continued their work, installing surveillance cameras and bugs.

Rather than introducing items with bugs in them, agents may install a tiny microphone or camera in a wall, leaving a pinhole in the wall for the device. Then they paint over the area with a special fast-drying paint, matching the paint perfectly.

"We have a paint-matching algorithm in one of our computers so we can mix paint right there to repaint an area," Grever says.

In installing microphones or cameras, the FBI may transmit sound or pictures through beamed light in fiber-optic strands as fine as human hair. As a result, no stray electronic emissions can be detected by debugging experts. Elevator shafts are a favorite place for running wires to transmit intercepted conversations.

Bugging devices may be made by the Engineering Research Facility or contracted out to such facilities as Sandia National Laboratories, which develops new technology to eavesdrop on communications.

Audio and video are monitored remotely over encrypted wireless transmissions. Besides photographing money changing hands, video can record keystrokes on a computer keyboard. TacOps agents may also install hidden software on a target's computer to defeat future encryption. Usually bugging devices can be controlled remotely. Sometimes agents hear debugging experts sweeping an office or home. The experts almost never find anything.

"If you know a sweep is coming, it's easy to avoid it," Grever says. "They're looking for the telltale signs of electronics—radio waves, for example. You turn off the device remotely or you bury it very deeply, where they'd almost have to do a destructive search to find it."

When a job is finished, agents brief colleagues back at the support center, and everyone picks apart the operation.

In the early days of the program, resources were scarce. Even the purchase of lock-picking kits faced a bureaucratic struggle. Agent James Kallstrom fought with headquarters to obtain the necessary funding, both when he was in New York and later when he headed the engineering section in Washington.

"Tell me what you need, and we'll do it," Kallstrom would tell agents, according to McDevitt.

In the early 1980s, the New York field office needed to quickly install a bug at the home of a Mafia figure, but no bugging device was available. So agents decided to remove a bug that already had been implanted in a Times Square hotel room of another Mafia figure, a member of the Bonanno family.

The problem: the Mafia used the hotel room as a safe sanctuary, so a bad guy was always in the room. Supervisory agent Joe Cantamessa came up with a ruse. He told Uttaro, who became McDevitt's assistant heading TacOps, to pretend to be a mob guy and to knock on the door of the mafioso. Sure enough, the man opened the door, shirtless.

Uttaro claimed he owed him money. Coming from a Sicilian background, he was able to throw in some Sicilian words for effect.

"I told him I was there to get my money, mentioning names of Italian neighbors I had grown up with," Uttaro says. "He said he didn't know what I was talking about, but he asked if I had talked with Tony about it. He was actually trying to be helpful."

After a few minutes, Uttaro left. Then Agent Cantamessa knocked on the man's door. He displayed his FBI credentials and said he needed the mafioso to identify the man who had just knocked on his door.

The mafioso agreed, and Cantamessa escorted him outside to the street, where agents made a show of pretending to arrest Uttaro, even roughing him up a bit.

"They threw me against a wall and kicked my shins," Uttaro says. "I screamed about police brutality and said they should all be sent to prison."

Meanwhile, other agents snuck into the man's apartment and retrieved the needed bugging device.

When TacOps agents entered the home of CIA officer Aldrich Ames at two in the morning, they found that the end of a key blank was stuck in the lock of a door to the basement, apparently to prevent entry. They were able to remove it and defeat his alarm system. In contrast to Ames' precautions, FBI agent Robert Hanssen had an alarm system, but when TacOps agents entered during the day, they found he had not set it before going out. The only problem was keeping track of his kids' comings and goings.

Often a covert entry is the turning point in a case.

"With some of the organized crime figures, we would work for years to develop enough probable cause to get court approval for a close-access opportunity," Grever says. "We would install microphones, and usually they feel so secure in their conversations that they will say anything and reveal themselves. They'll portray themselves in court as these law-abiding, friendly citizens. But then you start listening to those conversations or you see the meetings, and you quickly see what their intent is."

After waiting years to develop probable cause, the FBI was able to plant microphones in the Ravenite Social Club in Manhattan, where Gambino crime boss John Gotti hung out.

"In that case, I remember the night the calls started coming in: 'The target's opening up,' "

Grever says. "We had people racing to get into position."

Agents installed microphones in electrical wall fixtures near a table in a back room of the social club, in a hallway, and in an upstairs apartment. The beauty of turning an electrical outlet or light fixture into a bugging device is that it supplies its own power, so there is no need to reenter the premises to replace batteries.

Gotti was heard on the tapes talking to other mobsters about his power and people he had "whacked." Explaining why he ordered the murder of Louis DiBono, a Gambino soldier, Gotti said on the tapes that the Mafia member had made a simple mistake: he didn't respect the boss.

"Know why he's dying?" Gotti, known as the "Dapper Don" because of his expensive clothes, asked his consigliere in a taped conversation that foreshadowed DiBono's 1990 murder. "He's gonna die because he refused to come in when I called," Gotti said. "He didn't do nothing else wrong."

Shortly after that, DiBono was found dead, with three bullet holes in his head.

"Within thirty days, we had enough conversation to sink the Teflon Don," Grever says. "The one thing about the FBI is we can be patient."

On December 11, 1990, FBI agents and New York City detectives raided the Ravenite Social

Club and arrested Gotti. Gotti died of cancer in a federal prison hospital in 2002.

Conversely, Grever says, "Every now and then we get indications that somebody is doing something illegal, but our surveillance of them reveals that it's not based on valid, good information. It allows us to get them off the radar really quickly, and we will absolutely move on."

One of the FBI's greatest achievements was bugging a Mafia induction ceremony on October 29, 1989, demonstrating in graphic detail that organized crime does, in fact, exist.

"I got a phone call on a Saturday morning about nine-thirty from a tech agent in the Boston area," McDevitt says. "He said, 'Mike, is there any way you can get a couple of your guys to come up here? We have source information that there will be an induction ceremony tonight.' "

McDevitt and Uttaro got on a bureau plane and flew to Boston. The ceremony by the Patriarca crime family was to take place the next night in the basement of a house on Guild Street in Medford, Massachusetts.

The homes on the street were close together, making it difficult to enter the house through a side door without being spotted. One agent kept an eye on a couple next door who could see the side door clearly out their window.

Picking a lock can be time-consuming. Moreover, when a lock is picked, it remains unlocked until picked again, so a security guard who tries the door would find it unlocked, possibly tipping him off to a break-in. In addition, if an occupant such as an embassy later suspects a break-in, a forensic examination of the lock would reveal that it had been picked. After the entry, agents have to pick it again to restore it to a locked position. Because of these problems, agents developed a device not available to the commercial world that decodes the lock, allowing them to make an impression of the lock so that the required key can be made. So that a location can be reentered to fix a problem or replace a battery, agents leave the key they make with the local field office.

After installing bugs in the house where the induction ceremony was to take place, McDevitt and Uttaro ran the sound through existing telephone wires. The day after the ceremony, they learned from local agents that the operation picked up the induction of four men under the direction of Raymond L. "Junior" Patriarca, the organized crime boss based in Rhode Island.

Four times, Biagio DiGiacomo administered the oath: "I . . . want to enter into this organization to protect my family and to protect all my friends. I swear not to divulge this secret and to obey, with love and omerta."

Omerta is the code of silence a "made man" lives by. Punishment for violation of omerta is death.

"We get in this organization, and the only way

we're going to get out is dead, no matter what," DiGiacomo said on the FBI tape. "It's no hope, no Jesus, no Madonna, nobody can help us if we ever give up this secret to anybody."

After blood was drawn from each of the inductees' trigger fingers, a holy card with the image of the Patriarca family saint was burned. The tapes brought jail time for all seventeen participants in the induction ceremony.

During his assignment to TacOps, Grever traveled as much as 170 days a year. Often he had to work on Thanksgiving, Christmas, New Year's Eve, or Easter because those holidays—along with Ramadan—are some of the best times to enter homes or offices without being caught. On the other hand, he had a flexible schedule and could take off in between jobs. He got incentive awards for pulling off particularly sensitive jobs. Agents hate the paperwork often associated with what they do. There is little of that in the business of conducting covert entries.

"I've been to every state in the Union except two, and you get to preview all the best vacation spots, because that's often where the work is," Grever says. "You love getting the phone call at home, grabbing your bag, and telling your family, 'I gotta go! They need me! The country needs me!'"

Agents often travel on FBI or Defense Department planes.

"You land, and there's people waiting for you: 'Thank God you're here!' " Grever says. "You're like, the cape is blowing in the wind, here we go! You're like James Bond who can break into this bad guy's office on a secret mission and poke around."

The downside is that an agent breaking into a home or office could be shot. So far, it has never happened. But that is why only armed agents participate in the entries.

"Knock on wood, we have not been discovered and shot inside," Grever says. "We have been on surveillance tape before. But if nothing's out of place, nothing got disturbed, there's no alarm. Typically, the owners never ever look at their tapes."

"If discovered, running away is our first option," Grever says. "The second option is to try to talk them down, explaining who we are." However, it's unlikely a burglar claiming to be an FBI agent will be believed, so, in case they are discovered, agents bring along Taser electro-shock weapons.

While agents can elect to wear protective body armor, "most TacOps guys think that the out-line of a vest might alert an observer or would restrict their movements, or both," Grever says. "Most of us rationalize that the idea is to not get caught and thus avoid an armed confrontation."

However, if worst comes to worst, TacOps agents are authorized to use deadly force.

"You have a court order that gives the government a legal right to be there on that property," Grever says. "If threatened with deadly force, an agent can use deadly force against someone who thinks he is protecting his own property. Although the U.S. government may have a lot of liability, the individual agent, as long as we acted in good faith, won't be held liable. But that is absolutely the last option."

# Red Dress

In the early days when J. Edgar Hoover was director, the FBI considered break-ins at embassies so sensitive that no one would dare ask the director for permission to undertake them. If something went wrong, the agents and their supervisors would be blamed. So agents broke into embassies, placed bugs or stole code books, then wrote a memo to Hoover asking for permission. At the end of the memo, they wrote, "Security guaranteed." To FBI officials, that meant the job had already been pulled off without a hitch. They could then sign off on the memo and forward it to Hoover without fear of a slipup.

The charade was a metaphor for the way Hoover ran the FBI. On one hand, he was a perfectionist. When he was growing up, a maid would prepare him a poached egg on toast for breakfast at his home on Seward Square in southeast Washington. If the egg was broken, he wouldn't eat it, and it had to be done over. Hoover would offer the offending egg to his Airedale, Spee Dee Bozo.

Hoover's penchant for perfection led him to

pioneer use of technology to solve crimes in the laboratory. Before computers, he created a filing and indexing system that effectively kept track of massive amounts of information. He established a fingerprint registry. In essence, the FBI was Hoover's creation.

But Hoover's blind spots and quirks were legendary. If an agent conducted himself poorly, Hoover felt it reflected on him personally. He codified his philosophy in the phrase "Don't embarrass the bureau." By that he also meant, "Don't embarrass me." As far as Hoover was concerned, he was the bureau. His agents were his family.

Hoover so intimidated agents that when he wrote on a memo, "Watch the borders!" headquarters officials began trying to determine if there was a problem on the Mexican or Canadian borders.

"Somebody said, 'Why don't you just ask Hoover what he knows that we don't know?' " Hoover's top aide Cartha D. "Deke" DeLoach recalls. "But no one wanted to show his ignorance."

So, he says, FBI agents checked with Customs, which knew nothing of any developments on the borders. A few days later, a supervisor was reviewing the memo when he noticed it had been typed with the narrowest possible margins. Always fastidious, Hoover had picked up his pen and had scrawled on the memo, "Watch the borders!"

Hoover's quirks included a ban on drinking coffee on the job and on wearing colored shirts. Drinking coffee conflicted with the image of hardworking supermen who never took a break. As a result of Hoover's dictum, agents would take time off from work to search for a coffee shop instead of drinking coffee at their desks.

More important, Hoover turned a blind eye to the Mafia. Because of Prohibition, the Mafia took control of the liquor business, paying off police to look the other way. By instilling fear through gangland killings, the Mafia took over labor unions such as the Teamsters and major industries, from construction and garbage collecting to garment making and trucking, in most major cities. As organized crime grew in power, it penetrated politics. The Mafia could dictate appointments of judges and police chiefs. Because of those alliances, organized crime was considered untouchable. Yet as the Mafia tightened its grip on the country, Hoover consistently denied what everyone else knew: that organized crime was the single greatest criminal threat to the United States. He insisted that Mafia figures were local hoodlums who were not part of a national syndicate.

But on November 14, 1957, New York State Police found that sixty-three Mafia leaders from a number of states were meeting at the secluded estate of Joseph Barbara Sr. in the hills outside the village of Apalachin, New York. No longer able to claim that organized crime was a local matter, Hoover reluctantly began to attack it. Yet in Hoover's FBI, statistics, not quality of cases, demonstrated success.

"Back then, the FBI still had this nonsense that all cases are equal," says Dan Reilly, an agent who worked organized crime in New York. "If you caught two hubcap thieves, it was better than catching Bernie Madoff. Also the FBI had a lot of rough, tough ex-military guys. Their theory was that if anybody robs with a fountain pen, they're kind of a sissy. They liked armored-car robbers, bank robbers, kidnappers. Even within the New York FBI office, in the late 1960s, going after the Mafia was considered junk work."

At the time, the New York field office had two organized crime squads, one that went after numbers racketeering and another that focused on bookmaking. In the late 1970s, five squads of fifteen or twenty agents were formed to go after the five New York Mafia families. Agents worked on developing the backgrounds of Mafia members—when they were born, whether they were illegal aliens from Sicily, whether they had criminal records, who their relatives were.

"Slowly, through contacts with cooperating,

top-of-the-line New York City Police Department detectives, the FBI found out who the key figures were and started to focus on them," Reilly says. "And when they interviewed these people, the FBI had a great deal of credibility. The knowledge the FBI had about these figures was in itself frightening to people in a secret criminal society."

Police corruption was rampant.

"I was told to my face by top figures in the police department, they bragged to me openly that they themselves only took clean graft from gambling operations, and that they would never touch the evil money from drug operations," Reilly says. "And I, horrified internally, felt like slapping them in the face and telling them that the same guys who run drugs run gambling."

Every day, the boss of the Colombo crime family parked his white Rolls-Royce at a bus stop in front of a firehouse in Brooklyn.

"That was his parking spot," Reilly says. "No one else could park a car there. And the local precinct was notified in person by FBI agents that this was going on, and never did I see a parking ticket or a tow on that car."

Corruption reached high into political circles. One member of the Colombo family told Reilly that during Prohibition, he competed against the bootlegging operation of Joseph P. Kennedy, the father of President John F. Kennedy. The founder of the Kennedy dynasty owned an entire fleet of boats for importing liquor illegally.

In a move that later became standard practice, the FBI decided in 1972 to start its own garbage collection company in the Bronx to catch Mafia figures trying to shake it down. Meanwhile, the FBI developed Mafia informants, including a member of the Colombo crime family named Gregory Scarpa.

"Scarpa was an encyclopedia as an informant," Reilly says. "You could run any imaginable question involving organized crime by the agent who handled Scarpa on a given day, and within minutes the answer was on your desk or you had a phone call, and the information was always completely correct."

Another informant told the FBI that the Genovese crime family was considering murdering an FBI agent. Reilly walked up to the boss of the Genovese crime family in front of his home and gave him a message. Using his nickname, Reilly said to him, "Funzi, we keep hearing these crazy rumors that you folks are considering killing an FBI agent. Right now, the FBI only works half a day. The agents from Arkansas and Oregon spend their other half of the day figuring out how to get back to Arkansas or Oregon. You kill an FBI agent, and we'll start working not only full days, we'll start working overtime. You people will see so many arrests and so many convictions in the next few months you won't believe it."

Not until Hoover died in 1972 did the FBI begin to develop long-term strategies for taking out the entire leadership of Mafia families. By then, the Mafia was so powerful it was difficult to eradicate.

Many theories have been advanced to explain Hoover's aversion to attacking organized crime. Anthony Summers, in his book *Official and Confidential: The Secret Life of J. Edgar Hoover*, claimed that Hoover did not pursue organized crime because the Mafia had blackmail material on him. Summers quoted Susan L. Rosenstiel, a former wife of Lewis S. Rosenstiel, chairman of Schenley Industries Inc., as saying that in 1958, she was at a party at the Plaza Hotel where Hoover engaged in cross-dressing in front of her then-husband and Roy Cohn, former counsel to Senator Joe McCarthy.

"He [Hoover] was wearing a fluffy black dress, very fluffy, with flounces and lace stockings and high heels, and a black curly wig," Summers quoted Susan as saying. "He had makeup on and false eyelashes."

A year later, Susan claimed, she again saw Hoover at the Plaza. This time, the director was wearing a red dress. Around his neck was a black feather boa. He was holding a Bible, and he asked one of the blond boys to read a passage as another boy fondled him.

A former bootlegger, Lewis Rosenstiel was

well acquainted with Mafia figures. But Susan, who died in 2009, was not exactly a credible witness. In fact, she served time at Rikers Island for perjuring herself in a 1971 case.

"Susie Rosenstiel had a total ax to grind," says William G. Hundley, who headed organized crime prosecutions at the Justice Department. "Somebody who worked for me talked to her. It [the cross-dressing story] was made up out of whole cloth. She hated Hoover for some alleged wrong he had done. Plus the story was beyond belief."

While there was always speculation about Hoover's relationship with his deputy Clyde Tolson, there were never any rumors within the FBI or outside it about Hoover cross-dressing. Oliver "Buck" Revell, a former associate director of the FBI, observes that if the Mafia had had anything on Hoover, it would have been picked up in wiretaps mounted against organized crime after Apalachin. There was never a hint of such a claim, Revell says.

Hoover was more familiar to Americans than most presidents. The director of the FBI simply could not have engaged in such activity at the Plaza, with a number of witnesses present, without having it leak out.

On the other hand, Hoover and Tolson, both bachelors, were inseparable. They ate lunch together every day and dinner together almost every night. They vacationed together, staying in adjoining rooms, and they took adoring photos of each other.

Beginning in the 1950s, the FBI regularly assigned agents from the Washington field office to discreetly follow Hoover and Tolson as a security precaution. R. Jean Gray, one of the agents assigned to what was called HOOWATCH, says the surveillance consisted of agents in two bureau cars who would tail Hoover and Tolson as they left the Justice Department at the end of the day. While the two knew that agents watched over them, they usually did not spot them.

"We followed them to Harvey's or to the Mayflower, where they had dinner," Gray says. "Then we took them to Tolson's apartment on Cathedral Avenue, where Tolson got out. Then we went to Hoover's home. We stayed overnight. The next morning, agents would follow Hoover as he picked up Tolson and went through Rock Creek Park and down Constitution Avenue to the Justice Department," Gray says.

"We speculated about Edgar and Clyde," Gray says. "But if anything scandalous had happened with the director, it would have gone coast to coast within the bureau in thirty minutes."

Still, the fact that Hoover spent his leisure time with a man and that they took adoring photos of each other points to Hoover's being homosexual. He lived with his mother in the family home until she died when he was forty-three. He left his estate to Tolson. While he could have been in denial about his sexual orientation or was aware of it but suppressed it, he also conceivably could have had sexual relations with Tolson when the two were alone together in each other's homes, as they often were. Given their emotional attachment, Hoover and Tolson had a spousal relationship, as the term is broadly defined.

# Secret Files

Complex man that he was, Hoover left nothing to chance. The director shrewdly recognized that building what became known as the world's greatest law enforcement agency would not necessarily keep him in office. So after Hoover became director, he began to maintain a special Official and Confidential file in his office. The "secret files," as they became widely known, would guarantee that Hoover would remain director as long as he wished.

Defenders of Hoover—a dwindling number of older former agents who still refer to him as "Mr. Hoover"—have claimed his Official and Confidential files were not used to blackmail members of Congress or presidents. They say Hoover kept the files with sensitive information about political leaders in his suite so that young file clerks would not peruse them and spread gossip. The files were no more secret than any other bureau files, Hoover supporters say.

While the files may well have been kept in Hoover's office to protect them from curious clerks, it was also true that far more sensitive files containing top-secret information on pending espionage cases were kept in the central files. If Hoover truly was concerned about information getting out, he should have been more worried about the highly classified information in those files.

Moreover, the Official and Confidential files were secret in the sense that Hoover never referred to them publicly, as he did the rest of the bureau's files. He distinguished them from other bureau files by calling them "confidential," denoting secrecy. But whether they were secret or not and where they were kept was irrelevant. What was important was how Hoover used the information from those files and from other bureau files.

"The moment [Hoover] would get something on a senator," said William Sullivan, who became the number three official in the bureau under Hoover, "he'd send one of the errand boys up and advise the senator that 'we're in the course of an investigation, and we by chance happened to come up with this data on your daughter. But we wanted you to know this. We realize you'd want to know it.' Well, Jesus, what does that tell the senator? From that time on, the senator's right in his pocket."

Lawrence J. Heim, who was in the Crime Records Division, confirmed to me that the bureau sent agents to tell members of Congress that Hoover had picked up derogatory information on them.

"He [Hoover] would send someone over on a very confidential basis," Heim said. As an example, if the Metropolitan Police in Washington had picked up evidence of homosexuality, "he [Hoover] would have him say, 'This activity is known by the Metropolitan Police Department and some of our informants, and it is in your best interests to know this.' But nobody has ever claimed to have been blackmailed. You can deduce what you want from that."

Of course, the reason no one publicly claimed to have been blackmailed is that blackmail, by definition, entails collecting embarrassing information that people do not want public. But not everyone was intimidated.

Roy L. Elson, the administrative assistant to Senator Carl T. Hayden, will never forget an encounter he had with DeLoach, the FBI's liaison with Congress. For twenty years, Hayden headed the Senate Rules and Administration Committee and later the Senate Appropriations Committee, which had jurisdiction over the FBI's budget. He was one of the most powerful members of Congress. As Hayden, an Arizona Democrat, suffered hearing loss and some dementia in his later years, Elson became known as the "101st senator" because he made many of the senator's decisions for him.

In the early 1960s, DeLoach wanted an additional appropriation for the new FBI head-

quarters building, which Congress approved in April 1962.

"The senator supported the building," Elson said. "He always gave the bureau more money than they needed. This was a request for an additional appropriation. I had reservations about it. DeLoach was persistent."

DeLoach "hinted" that he had "information that was unflattering and detrimental to my marital situation and that the senator might be disturbed," said Elson, who was then married to his second wife. "I was certainly vulnerable that way," Elson said. "There was more than one girl [he was seeing]. . . . The implication was there was information about my sex life. There was no doubt in my mind what he was talking about."

Elson said to DeLoach: "Let's talk to him [the senator] about it. I think he's heard about everything there is to hear about me. Bring the photos if you have them." At that point, Elson said, "He started backing off. . . . He said, 'I'm only joking.' Bullshit," Elson said. "I interpreted it as attempted blackmail."

Commenting on Elson's allegation, DeLoach says, "It never happened."

Reading the Official and Confidential files that survived makes it clear they could have been gathered for no other purpose than blackmail. For example, on June 13, 1958, the head of the

Washington field office informed Hoover that, prior to marrying a member of Congress, the member's wife had been "having an affair with a Negro [and] also at one time carried on an affair with a House Post Office employee." More recently, the report said, the congressman's wife "endeavored to have an affair with [an] Indonesian, who declined."

In response to this tidbit, Hoover wrote back on June 25 that it was "certainly thoughtful of you to advise me of matters of current interest, and I am glad to have the benefit of this information."

"This was a way of putting congressmen on notice that we had something on them and therefore they would be more disposed to meeting the bureau's needs and keeping Hoover in power," says John J. McDermott, who headed the Washington field office and eventually became deputy associate FBI director.

Hoover let presidents know that he had dirt on them as well. For example, on March 22, 1962, Hoover had lunch with President Kennedy. Hoover told him that through bugs and wiretaps, the FBI had learned that Jack was having an affair with Judith Campbell Exner, a twenty-five-year-old divorcée. Hoover informed the president that Exner was also having an affair with Chicago mob boss Sam Giancana. Because Hoover knew such tidbits, no president would fire him.

As President Lyndon B. Johnson said, "I would rather have him [Hoover] inside the tent pissing out than outside the tent pissing in."

Many of the confidential files were destroyed after Hoover's death. One such item that never came out previously was a teletype sent to headquarters from William Simon, who headed the Los Angeles field office, just after the August 5, 1962, death of Marilyn Monroe at her Brentwood, California home. According to DeLoach, who saw the teletype, it said that then Attorney General Robert Kennedy had borrowed Simon's personal car to see Monroe just before her death.

Confirming this, Simon's son Greg says, "My father said Robert Kennedy would borrow his white Lincoln convertible. That's why we didn't have it on many weekends." Simon's daughter Stephanie Branon also confirmed that her father lent his car to Kennedy and remembered that the attorney general once left his Ray-Ban sunglasses in the glove compartment.

As attorney general, Kennedy was entitled to be driven by an FBI security detail. The fact that he chose to use Simon's personal car is consistent with William Simon's report to headquarters that he lent his car to Kennedy for the purpose of clandestine meetings with Monroe. Whether his last meeting with her, possibly to break up with her, may have contributed to her suicide is legitimate speculation.

While there is ample evidence that Hoover used the information in his files for blackmail, there was usually no need for it. Simply the perception that he had such information was enough to keep politicians in line.

In the end, the answer to why Hoover did not go after organized crime until he was forced into it is the same reason he maintained files on members of Congress. Above all, Hoover wanted to keep his job. Many members of Congress—not to mention powerful local politicians—had ties to organized crime and might try to unseat him if he went after the Mafia. The Mafia was as powerful as the president. Moreover, as a perfectionist, Hoover did not want to risk losing a case against a powerful figure.

For the same reasons, for purposes of prosecution, Hoover would not investigate corrupt politicians. As FBI director, Hoover had an obligation to go after both Mafia figures and corrupt politicians. Yet until he was pressured into investigating organized crime, those two targets were sacrosanct.

On May 1, 1972, Helen Gandy, Hoover's personal secretary, handed him the first in a series of exposés by Jack Anderson, whose column appeared in the *Washington Post.* Previously, Anderson had enraged Hoover by assigning a reporter to rummage through his trash at home. The resulting column revealed that on Sundays,

Hoover ate a hearty breakfast of poached eggs and hotcakes. It also revealed that he brushed his teeth with Ultra Brite, washed with Palmolive, and shaved with Noxzema shaving cream. Now, in his latest column, Anderson revealed that the FBI had conducted surveillance of Martin Luther King Jr.'s sex life.

Besides attending sex orgies, King was having an affair with a young woman in his office, says an agent who monitored wiretaps on King's office and home phones.

"Besides his home, King had an apartment," the former agent says. "On Tuesdays, he'd go to the apartment, ostensibly to meditate and write sermons." In fact, King's girlfriend would meet him there for sex.

For a man whose lifelong mantra had been "Don't embarrass the bureau," the continuing stream of unfavorable disclosures had to be unnerving. Yet Hoover rarely revealed his true personal feelings. Sphinx-like, he projected the same persona to his friends and family as he did to the general public. The only difference was that in person, he showed a sense of humor.

Occasionally Hoover cracked a smile or played a prank. James H. Geer, who would later head the Intelligence Division, recalled the time when a nervous new agent went to shake Hoover's hand after graduating from training, and mistakenly introduced himself as "Mr. Hoover."

"Very nice to meet you, Mr. Hoover," the director responded, smiling.

Shortly before six in the afternoon of May 1, 1972, Tom Moton, Hoover's FBI chauffeur, drove him to Tolson's apartment, where the two had dinner. Moton drove Hoover home at 10:15 p.m.

By eight-fifteen the next morning, Annie Fields, Hoover's housekeeper, became concerned. By then, she should have heard the sound of the shower. Hoover's toast, soft-boiled eggs, and coffee were getting cold. James Crawford, Hoover's previous FBI chauffeur, had come over to plant some roses. Checking on him, he found Hoover's body sprawled on the oriental rug next to his bed. He touched one of his hands; it was cold.

After examining Hoover's nude body and consulting with his doctor, the District of Columbia medical examiner, Dr. James L. Luke, attributed the director's death to "hypertensive cardiovascular disease." As part of the speculation about his love life, a rumor had gone around that Hoover had an underdeveloped sex organ. That was not true, Dr. Luke tells me.

When Hoover's will was probated, it turned out that Tolson received his estate, estimated at $560,000, including his home. It was the equivalent of $2.9 million today. Gandy received $5,000, Annie Fields $3,000, and James Crawford $2,000. The bequest to Tolson was the final word on the closeness of their relationship.

Hoover preached that even the appearance of impropriety must be avoided. He disciplined agents for losing their handcuffs. Yet after the death of the imperious FBI director, a Justice Department and FBI investigation found that over the years, Hoover had FBI employees build a front portico and a rear deck on his home at 4936 30th Place, NW, in Washington. They installed a fish pond, equipped with water pump and lights, and they constructed shelves and other conveniences for him. They painted his house, maintained his yard, replaced the sod, installed artificial turf, and planted and moved shrubbery. They built a redwood garden fence and installed a flagstone court and sidewalks.

FBI employees also reset Hoover's clocks, retouched his wallpaper, and prepared his tax returns. Many of the gifts Hoover received from FBI employees, such as cabinets and bars, had been built by them on government time. Hoover also ordered FBI employees to write *Masters of Deceit* for him under his name. He pocketed part of the proceeds.

When the FBI and Justice Department finally investigated the abuses in the mid-1970s at the direction of FBI director Clarence M. Kelley, "a number of these agents had already retired from the bureau, and we were running all over the country interviewing them," says Richard H. Ash, who headed the FBI task force. "The agent being interviewed would say, 'Wait a minute.' And he would go over to his files, pull out a log about all these things they had done, because it was eating at them that they were being used that way."

"Hoover [and some of his aides] would be prosecuted under today's standards. No question of it. And should have been," Buck Revell, formerly the bureau's associate deputy director over investigations, says. "Hoover for the money he kept from the books he supposedly wrote but didn't write. Using government funds and resources for personal gain. And use of government employees to maintain his residence. Again, that is fraud against the government. Taking vacations and putting in vouchers for expenses. Agents have been prosecuted for that. Those things that were somewhat taken for granted back then would be prosecuted today."

"Hoover did a good job for many years," says John McDermott, the former Washington field office special agent in charge who became deputy associate FBI director. "He went wrong along the way. He became a martinet. In seeking to prevent embarrassment to the bureau, he equated the bureau with himself. Everyone told him how good he was. He came to believe the exorbitant praise he was receiving. Anybody who can be conned by a flatterer has a character weakness."

Hoover ran the FBI for forty-eight years. Never again would one man so dominate the bureau.

In 1975 and 1976, the Select Committee to Study Governmental Operations with Respect to Intelligence Activities, headed by Senator Frank Church, held hearings on FBI and CIA abuses. These included surveillance of Martin Luther King Jr., illegal wiretapping and mail openings, and surreptitious entries or "black-bag jobs."

Prior to that, members of Congress took the position they did not want to know what the FBI and CIA were doing. The Church Committee hearings, as they became known, exposed real abuses and a lack of focus that undercut the mission of those agencies. The hearings ultimately improved both agencies and established an effective oversight mechanism.

When creating the FBI on June 29, 1908, as an unnamed investigative bureau of thirty-four special agents within the Justice Department, Congress had been leery of creating a national police force. Because of that, agents initially were not even empowered to carry weapons.

Despite limitations on its power, questions arose very quickly about the extent of the bureau's authority and methods. Yet whenever a new threat arose, those questions would be set aside, and Congress would entrust the bureau with new powers.

# Break-in at the Watergate

Six weeks after Hoover's death, a supervisor at the Washington field office (WFO) called FBI agent Jerry Pangburn at home at seven in the morning on June 17, 1972.

WFO said the Metropolitan Police Department had arrested five men who had broken into Democratic National Committee headquarters at the Watergate office building during the night. The police found a device with wires sticking out of it that could be a bomb. As the supervisor of the bomb squad, Pangburn needed to check it out.

Pangburn called two agents on his squad and told them to take a look at the device. An hour later, one of the agents called from Second District police headquarters to say he wanted to bring the device into WFO to have Pangburn examine it. Pangburn reminded him that rule number one in the training manual is don't bring a bomb into the office.

"Don't worry about it, it's not going to hurt anything," the agent said.

Pangburn took one look at it and realized it was

not a bomb. It was a listening device, concealed in the plastic cover of an electric door chime that had been attached to a wall near a secretary's desk at the DNC.

Pangburn called Robert G. Kunkel, the special agent in charge (SAC) of WFO, and told him the device was an electronic bug. Kunkel asked a supervisor to call Angelo J. Lano at his home in Hyattsville, Maryland. Thinking the break-in was a burglary, the supervisor told Lano that international jewel thieves had broken into the Watergate.

A man of average height with black hair and a mustache, Lano, thirty-three, was assigned to a miscellaneous crimes squad. One of Lano's duties was to keep track of thefts from the Watergate complex, which included a hotel and condominiums where some of Washington's toniest residents lived. It was Lano's day off, and he was about to leave for his son's Little League practice. On weekends, the field office assigned both a criminal agent and a counterintelligence agent to be on duty.

"I'm not going down there," Lano said to the supervisor. "You already have a criminal guy working. I have Little League practice."

Almost immediately, Kunkel called him.

"What's the problem?" Kunkel asked.

"There is a criminal guy working down there," Lano said. "I have Little League practice."

"You're the only person who knows the place," Kunkel said. "You won't be there long. Just check it out and come right back."

For the next three years, Lano would work on nothing but the Watergate break-in. As the case agent, he was the individual most responsible for breaking the case and bringing to justice those who attempted to cover up the involvement of the White House and Committee for the Re-Election of the President.

Lano called Peter Paul, another agent on his squad, to ask if he would ride with him to the Metropolitan Police Department's Second District headquarters, then at Twenty-third and L Streets, NW. The police said the burglars had been caught in the sixth-floor offices of the Democratic National Committee. They had two Minolta 35-millimeter cameras, rolls of high-speed film, walkie-talkies, Mace, and Playtex rubber surgical gloves.

Two of the suspects had given police the same phony name. The police were checking their identities through fingerprints. Eventually, the burglars were identified as Bernard L. Barker, Virgilio R. Gonzalez, Eugenio Martinez, Frank A. Sturgis, and James W. McCord Jr. All had some connection to the CIA. Two years earlier, for example, McCord had retired from the CIA's Office of Security.

At the police station, Lano emptied a carry-on

bag containing the items the police had seized from the suspects. He found additional bugging devices concealed in rolls of toilet paper. The police had not yet noticed the devices. Instead of a jewel theft, the agents were looking at an interception of communications case.

After searching two of the burglars' rooms at the Watergate Hotel, the police found four packets of hundred-dollar bills and two address books, one listing E. Howard Hunt as working at "WH." To savvy Washingtonians, that stood for White House. It later turned out Hunt had also been involved in the break-in.

Developing more evidence, Lano realized that while the Watergate break-in had begun as an effort by Nixon's "Plumbers" to obtain political intelligence, it was now a massive attempted cover-up. He requested more help. Within two days, two dozen agents from his squad—known as C-2, for Criminal Squad Number Two—had been assigned to work the case.

Agents quickly focused on the White House, but they found themselves stymied because the Hoover bureau had a rule that no one in the White House could be interviewed without permission from headquarters. It would take four or five days for headquarters to give approval. Lano urgently told headquarters he needed to conduct interviews at the White House without prior approval, and he received permission to do so.

Nearly every field office in the FBI became involved in checking leads. Lano wanted agents familiar with the case to conduct critical interviews anywhere in the country. Again, the Hoover bureau required agents to obtain approval from headquarters to travel into the jurisdiction of another field office. Lano obtained approval for agents on his squad to interview key subjects anywhere without getting the go-ahead from headquarters.

Two weeks after the break-in, agent Paul P. Magallanes interviewed a secretary to McCord at the Committee to Re-elect the President, popularly referred to with the acronym CREEP. The White House assigned a lawyer to sit in on all the interviews. In this case, the young woman was not forthcoming.

"The next morning I get a call from the office indicating that the young lady we interviewed the day before was on the phone and wanted to talk with me," Magallanes says. "They patched her through to my home, and she said, 'Listen, I'm the girl you interviewed. I really have a lot to say. I couldn't say anything in front of the White House lawyer. I want to talk with you.' "

The woman specified two conditions: She wanted Magallanes to pick her up in his personal vehicle, not an FBI car, and she wanted him to bring along a different partner. For some reason, she felt uncomfortable with the other agent who had participated in the interview with her.

Magallanes asked agent John W. Mindermann to go with him. They picked her up in Magallanes' personal car and talked with her while they drove around downtown Washington.

"She proceeded to furnish us all kinds of information in terms of what happened after the burglary was discovered," Magallanes says. "She said that McCord and G. Gordon Liddy, because McCord was then released on bail, came back to the office and started shredding documents and all kinds of things."

It was a hot Saturday in Washington, and the car began to overheat. Magallanes called Kunkel.

"Hey, get a hotel room and debrief her as much and as long as it takes," the SAC instructed.

They checked into a room at the Mayflower Hotel, the closest hotel. After several hours, the agents were wrapping up the interview, and the young woman said. "You know, you think I have a lot of valuable information. My friend has even more information."

"Who's your friend?" Magallanes asked.

"Well, she is the accountant for CREEP, and she is really frustrated as to what is happening here, and she has all this information that you guys would be very interested in," the woman said.

When Magallanes asked if she would arrange to have her friend talk with the agents, the woman said she would ask her and call Magallanes on Monday.

"Monday came along. No call," Magallanes says. "I couldn't call her. She was still working at CREEP. In those days, we didn't have cell phones or anything. Tuesday came along. No call. Wednesday, no call." Finally on Thursday, the woman called.

"Listen, my friend said that she's willing to meet with you and your partner, but she wants to get to know you first," she said. "She wants to know if she can trust you."

The accountant wanted to meet the agents at the Key Bridge Marriott in Rosslyn, Virginia. She suggested having dinner with them.

The next evening, the agents met the two women at the lounge at the Marriott. After small talk about their families, the accountant said, "I trust you guys. You know, I'll talk to you about Watergate. I'll tell you everything you want to know."

The accountant—who later publicly identified herself as Judy Hoback—suggested they go to her house in Bethesda, Maryland.

"All four of us went out there, and that was the first time in the investigation that we discovered that the CIA was not involved and that the White House was involved with a lot of shenanigans, a lot of illegal activities," Magallanes says. "She said that CREEP had something like three million in cash gathered by White House aides, in the safe."

Hoback said the money was used for unlawful activities, such as the Watergate break-in.

The interview continued until four in the morning.

"She laid the whole thing out at her house," Mindermann says. "We met her at the Key Bridge Marriott in the lounge there, even had a drink, against FBI rules. We followed her out at her request to her home in suburban Maryland. And the reason why I have so much respect for her, she was a young woman in her early thirties, she'd been widowed, her husband had dropped dead of a heart attack. She was a single mom with a little tiny house in suburban Maryland with a kid. And she desperately needed this assistant bookkeeper's job. And yet she had the courage to lay it all out."

# Deep Throat

The FBI had never before taken on a president. In fact, it had rarely investigated any branch of the government. In Hoover's FBI, local sheriffs and members of Congress were off-limits, not to mention sitting presidents, cabinet officers, and White House aides.

But Hoover was gone now, and only once did bureau headquarters try to put the brakes on the agents as they investigated the Watergate break-in and cover-up. That was when L. Patrick Gray, as acting FBI director, deferred to the Nixon White House to avoid delving into money funneled through Mexico for the break-in. Nixon claimed he was trying to protect CIA operations in Mexico. In fact, he had invented the excuse to help cover up the involvement of his own reelection committee. The delay lasted only a week.

"They didn't try to suppress what I did," says Daniel C. Mahan, another agent on the Watergate case. "It was one of the FBI's finest hours."

As leaks from the FBI's investigation of Watergate appeared in *Washington Post* stories by Bob Woodward and Carl Bernstein and elsewhere, Gray called in twenty-six agents on Angie Lano's squad on June 24, 1973, and accused them of "suffering from flap jaw."

"Somebody is leaking to the press," Gray said. "And I want that agent or those agents who are doing the leaking to step forward. I want them to put their credentials on the table, and I want them to resign, or I'll fire them."

There was dead silence.

Gray continued to berate the agents. His face turning crimson, he stood screaming at the top of his lungs, "I will get to the bottom of this. I am a former Navy captain. I have commanded a nuclear submarine. I am a graduate of Georgetown University Law School. I have conducted many investigations in the Navy, and I know how to conduct an investigation."

Gray then turned abruptly and left the conference room.

"I couldn't believe what I was hearing," Magallanes says. "Nobody could believe what he was hearing."

As it turned out, Gray himself had been improperly passing on the FBI's form FD-302 reports of interviews from the Watergate investigation to John Dean, the White House counsel. On June 21, 1972, White House aides Dean and John Ehrlichman met with Gray and told him to destroy political sabotage files from Hunt's safe in the Executive Office Building. They told him the material consisted of "national security documents" unrelated to Watergate, Gray later revealed. Six months later, Gray burned some of the documents in his family's incinerator.

After learning from Ehrlichman that Dean was cooperating with the U.S. attorney and would be revealing what had transpired on June 21, Gray told his congressional supporter, Senator Lowell Weicker, so that Weicker would be prepared for that revelation. Weicker leaked the item about the destruction of documents to the press.

On April 23, 1973, Leonard M. "Bucky" Walters, an assistant FBI director, was carpooling to work with William Soyars, another assistant director. Walters told Soyars that he planned to resign that day over Gray's destruction of evidence. Soyars pledged to do the same. At nine in the morning, Walters met with W. Mark Felt, the top FBI official under Gray.

"I told Felt that I would not work for a director who had destroyed evidence in a case the FBI was investigating," Walters says. "I told him I would retire by the end of the day. I also told him I would ask the other assistant directors to do the same."

In the next half hour, Walters called each of the other assistant directors. To a man, they all agreed to resign. Walters gave the news to Felt, who said he would tell Gray. An hour later, at ten-thirty in the morning, Gray called a meeting of the executive conference and announced that he would leave that day.

Later, when Gray was subpoenaed to appear before the grand jury investigating Watergate, Agent Lano, who was one of those Gray had accused of leaking to Woodward and Bernstein, made sure he personally served Gray with the subpoena.

In addition to seven Watergate burglars and accomplices, forty government officials were eventually indicted on charges of conspiracy, obstruction of justice, and perjury. Among those ultimately convicted were Attorney General John N. Mitchell, White House counsel Dean, White House chief of staff H. R. Haldeman, and domestic policy advisor John Ehrlichman. Nixon himself was named an unindicted co-conspirator and driven from office.

The fact that Bob Woodward and Carl Bernstein of the *Washington Post* were breaking stories on the investigation, portraying a coordinated campaign and cover-up of political espionage carried out by top Nixon aides, helped to ensure that the FBI probe would not be suppressed. But it still grates on Lano and some other agents that the two reporters obtained leaks from the FBI and that the public thinks they solved the Watergate case.

On the other hand, Mindermann says, "Their stories actually really, really helped us, because it kept the investigation going. It was critical to have that silent public support out there. You can only keep an investigation like this going if you have the kind of publicity that the *Washington Post* provided through Woodward and Bernstein, because lacking that, you're going to be shut down, one way or the other."

"The media served a significant purpose," says Edward R. Leary, another agent on the case. "On the one hand, it was a pain in the neck to us because what would be published in the paper was generally one day to two months behind where we were. We would have to go up the chain with information to explain or critique what was on the street. Why should we be bothered telling whoever wanted to know whether an article was accurate? On the other hand, through media involvement, clearly public focus was placed on the incident, and the glare of the public spotlight eventually opened some doors that would have been closed to us."

Each of the agents on the squad had different theories about the identity of Deep Throat. In discussing the stories with his editors, Woodward would refer to one of his sources, who was knowledgeable but not always forthcoming, as "my friend." Possessed of a wry sense of humor, Howard Simons, then the managing editor of the *Washington Post*, dubbed the source "Deep Throat" after an X-rated movie then in the news. Because of the notoriety attached to the name, this Watergate source acquired a status far beyond that of other sources who were also important and to this day remain anonymous.

Some FBI agents thought Deep Throat was a composite meant to fuzz up the identities of Woodward and Bernstein's sources. That was a misunderstanding of how the name evolved. As a *Washington Post* reporter during Watergate, I sat next to Bernstein. Each evening, Woodward would stand over Bernstein, who was the better writer, and Bernstein would type out their stories as they discussed their information and sources.

It was clear from those conversations that they had a number of legitimate sources. They had directories of White House and CREEP personnel and were running down the list, knocking on doors in the middle of the night. In some cases, the FBI thought they had obtained reports of FBI interviews, when in fact the reporters—as in the case of bookkeeper Judy Hoback—had conducted their own interviews with the same individuals. There was no reason to conflate sources.

It would turn out to be ironic that Gray had assigned W. Mark Felt, who was Deep Throat, to investigate the leaks. Felt and Edward Miller were later prosecuted for signing off on illegal break-ins that Miller says Gray approved. In preparation for that case, the FBI in 1979 asked agent Paul V. Daly to look into the Watergate investigation to determine if anything troublesome might surface. Daly talked with Dick Long, who headed the white-collar crime section at headquarters and supervised the Watergate investigation.

"We were just trying to find out exactly what might come out, and Long told me, 'Well, you know, Mark [Felt] was Deep Throat,' " Daly says.

Long, who has since died, never said how he claimed to know who Deep Throat was.

"He never got into how he knew it," Daly says, "other than to say, 'We would brief Felt, and Felt would leak.' "

For my book *The Bureau: The Secret History of the FBI*, I interviewed Felt in August 2001 at the Santa Rosa, California, home where he was living with his daughter, Joan. Joan told me that a year earlier, Woodward had shown up unexpectedly at their home and had taken Felt to lunch. Joan said her father greeted Woodward like an old friend, and their mysterious meeting appeared to be more of a celebration than an interview.

"Woodward just showed up at the door and said he was in the area," Joan Felt said. "He came in a white limousine, which parked at a schoolyard about ten blocks away. He walked to the house. He asked if it was okay to have a martini with my father at lunch, and I said it would be fine."

After Woodward left the house to get the limousine, which was parked almost three-quarters of a mile east at Comstock Junior High School, Joan Felt went out and caught up with him to give him further instructions about what her father could eat for lunch, she told me. They walked together to the limo, and Joan Felt rode back with Woodward to pick up her father.

Having suffered the effects of a stroke, Felt was in no position to provide credible information. When I interviewed him, he could not remember having had lunch with Woodward and confused Woodward with a government attorney. But Felt was compos mentis enough to tell me firmly, "I was definitely not Deep Throat."

There was no way Woodward would have gone to such lengths to conceal his visit unless Felt was Deep Throat. In the 2002 book, I wrote that the circumstances lent support to the notion that Felt was indeed Deep Throat, who subsequently revealed himself in 2005.

"Without Felt's feeding, confirming, and guiding those reporters who published information which stoked the public and drove political and public demands to keep the investigation alive, it is quite possible that we would not have made it as far as we eventually did," Mindermann says. "Mark Felt is a real, genuine American hero."

# Profiling

Clarence M. Kelley, who became FBI director on July 9, 1973, was well aware of the bureau's failings from the Hoover era. A former FBI agent and police chief, Kelley quickly stopped the fixation with statistics and emphasized quality over quantity in pursuing cases. The burly, square-jawed Kelley demanded that investigations be opened only when there was reason to believe a violation of law had occurred. He encouraged pursuit of public corruption cases. He began a push to hire females and minorities. And he was open to modernizing the bureau.

While the FBI during Hoover's early years was a pioneer in applying science to solve crimes, Hoover later often vetoed innovations. So when agent Howard D. Teten began teaching police officers who attended the FBI National Academy, which is strictly for police, the rudiments of what became known as criminal profiling in the early 1970s, he and his supervisors never told the director what they were doing.

The father of criminal profiling, Teten began to see a correlation between the crime scene and the person who committed the crime. In carrying out any action, criminals and noncriminals act in particular ways. For example, some writers use a computer, others pen and paper. Some write in the morning, some at night. Each writer has a unique style, with variations in grammar, sentence structure, and voice.

In the same way, criminals carry out their crimes in distinctly personal ways. What they do, rather than what they say, betrays who they are. By reading those signs, profilers can often determine from the crime scene the kind of person who committed the crime and the fantasies that propelled him or her—in effect, the perpetrator's signature. While profiling can be used to help solve any crime, it is especially useful in helping to solve the most vicious and emotional crimes—murder and rape.

Profilers look at every aspect of the crime, including interviews, photographs, investigative reports, autopsy reports, and laboratory reports. What sets profiling apart from good police work is that the conclusions are based on patterns that emerge by matching the characteristics of thousands of crime scenes found in similar cases with the characteristics of the actual perpetrators who are later apprehended.

Besides forensics and information gleaned from witnesses and other interviews, profilers look at motivation.

"Why was this particular victim the target of

this crime at this particular time?" says Mark A. Hilts, who heads the FBI's unit that develops profiles to help solve crimes against adults. "We kind of get into the mind of the offender. And not in any kind of psychic manner, but just through understanding criminals and why they commit the crimes they do. How does the criminal gain control of his victim? How does he manipulate the victim? How does he maintain control? How does he select his victim in the first place?"

With a profile, investigators can narrow a search and begin focusing on one or two individuals. At times, profiles are so uncannily accurate as to seem clairvoyant. When police found the mutilated torsos of two teenagers floating in a river, they identified them as a boy and girl who had been missing. The FBI profiled the killer as a male in his forties who knew the children. He probably led a macho lifestyle, wore western boots, often hunted and fished, and drove a four-wheel vehicle. He was self-employed, had been divorced several times, and had a minor criminal record.

With the profile, the police focused on the children's stepfather, who fit the description perfectly but had not previously been a suspect. They were able to develop enough additional information from witnesses to convict him of the murders the following year.

The FBI had found that a murderer careful enough to dispose of a body in a river is usually more sophisticated and often an older person. If the body is dumped in a remote area, the killer is probably an outdoors person with knowledge of the area. When the slashes on the victim's body are vicious and directed at the sex organs, the assailant often knows the person.

If there is no sign of forced entry and the assailant stayed around at the crime scene to have a snack after killing the victim, he likely lived in the neighborhood and knew the victim. In contrast, killers who don't feel comfortable in an apartment leave immediately.

Thus, based on a few elementary facts, the FBI can draw a profile of the killer as an older man who likes the outdoors, is familiar with the area where the body was left, knows the victim, and lived in the neighborhood.

Using such analysis, the FBI over the years has helped solve thousands of cases so that serial murderers and serial rapists could not strike again.

To supplement their knowledge, FBI profilers in the early years of the program interviewed offenders in prison. They began with assassins—Sirhan Sirhan, Sara Jane Moore, and Lynette "Squeaky" Fromme.

At one point, Robert K. Ressler was interviewing Edmund E. Kemper III, who had killed his mother, grandparents, and six other people. Kemper was serving multiple life sentences in California. Hannibal Lecter, the serial killer played by Anthony Hopkins in *The Silence of the Lambs*, was actually a composite of serial killers such as Kemper, who removed people's heads and saved them as trophies; Edward Gein, who decorated his home with human skin; and Richard T. Chase, who ate the organs of his victims.

When he was finished talking with Kemper in his cell just off death row, Ressler rang a buzzer to summon a guard to let him out. When the guard didn't come, the 295-pound prisoner told Ressler to "relax." He said the guards were changing shifts and delivering meals.

"If I went ape-shit in here, you'd be in a lot of trouble, wouldn't you?" said Kemper menacingly. "I could screw your head off and place it on the table to greet the guard."

Ressler was able to cool Kemper off by suggesting that he might have a concealed weapon. After that incident, agents interviewing inmates would take along a partner. And contrary to the impression created by Jodie Foster's role in *The Silence of the Lambs*, the FBI would never send a trainee to interview anyone.

A clear pattern emerged from the interviews. Most of the perpetrators lived a fantasy life that included enacting the types of crimes they had committed. The crime allowed them to realize their fantasies. Now that they knew what was inside their heads, the agents could better match what they saw at the crime scene with the way suspects carried out their crimes. How did suspects case an area before choosing a victim? What did they look for in a rape victim? Could a victim have said anything that would have dissuaded them from committing a rape? Did they keep trophies to remind them of their victims? If so, what were they? Did they tell anyone about their crimes or contact the victim after the crime?

Roger Depue, who began working with Teten in 1973 and later headed the profiling unit at the FBI Academy, made profiling part of the FBI's operations, assigning agents exclusively to develop profiles to help both the police and the bureau solve crimes.

The profilers divided killers into two broad categories: organized and disorganized. Each type of killer has a different kind of fantasy. Each leaves his distinctive characteristics at the crime scene. And each has a set of personal characteristics that can help identify him.

"The disorganized killer is the least sophisticated," Depue says. "At the crime scene, agents see signs of rage and poor planning because he commits the crime spontaneously. He says nothing or very little to the victim. Suddenly he engages in violence. The weapon is a weapon of opportunity. For example, the killer may use a rock to beat a victim. He will leave the weapon at the crime scene. The scene has a lot of evidence, including blood, fibers, and hair. The body is found where the murder took place. No effort is made to conceal where it is."

The disorganized killer generally has below-average intelligence and is socially inadequate. "He prefers unskilled work and is sexually incompetent," Depue says. "He tends to be a younger sibling in his family. His father's work was unstable, and he often received harsh discipline as a child. He lives alone. Before the crime, he appears anxious. He usually does not use alcohol before committing the crime. He has minimal interest in news of the crime. After the crime, his behavior changes significantly. He may go on a drinking or drug binge or become highly religious."

The organized killer is the typical serial killer. He has average to above-average intelligence. He prefers skilled work and is sexually competent. His father had stable work, but he experienced inconsistent childhood discipline. He is usually an older sibling. Edmund E. Kemper III, John Wayne Gacy Jr., David "Son of Sam" Berkowitz, Ted Bundy, and Henry Lee Lucas were examples of organized serial killers.

"The organized killer enjoys the predatory

aspect of killing—hunting, manipulating, and gaining control of the victim," Depue says. "He may select a certain kind of weapon, and he learns from experience. He often drinks before committing the crime and possesses social skills. He usually lives with someone. His car is in good condition. He follows the crime in the news media. After the crime, he may change jobs or leave town. He interacts with victims. Because he is so skilled, it is difficult to catch him. And when he is caught, everyone says, 'I can't believe he did it.' "

An organized killer has a fantasy that drives him. "For example, Edmund Kemper told us he needed to have particular experiences with people. In order to do that, he had to 'evict them from their bodies.' In other words, he had to kill them," Depue says.

Many serial killers revisit the scene just to rekindle their fantasy. When he decided killing a particular woman was too risky, Berkowitz would return to the scene of a previous crime and reenact the murder, aiming his gun just as he had aimed it when he killed his victim. Jeffrey L. Dahmer kept photographs of his dismembered victims.

Most perpetrators engage in ritualistic behavior that never changes. For example, after entering a home, a rapist might confront the victim in a particular way, while she is sleeping. He may stand over her and watch her as she sleeps, enjoying the sense of control he feels. He derives pleasure from the victim's feeling of helplessness when she wakes up and sees him standing there, perhaps nude. As he improves his methods and becomes more organized, his ritual will remain the same because he commits the crime in order to enjoy the ritual.

Besides bureau cases, FBI profilers work cases brought to them by local police. Sometimes police who have ignored the profilers' advice have done so to their regret. When profilers advised police from an Illinois town that an unknown murderer might visit the cemetery of his victim on the anniversary of his crime, they staked out the cemetery all day, hoping the assailant would show up. Because the weather was nasty, they finally gave up. They left their video cameras in place, rigged to start when detecting motion. Sure enough, the killer showed up. But the police were not there to identify him. They have a videotape of a man, but they have no idea who he is.

When I interviewed profilers in 1984 in the basement of the FBI Academy at Quantico, Virginia, there were just four of them—Roger Depue, John Douglas, Roy Hazelwood, and Robert Ressler. Now the FBI has twenty-eight such agents housed in an unmarked office building near Quantico in Stafford, Virginia.

Besides profiling, the agents began working on a number of other techniques for helping FBI agents solve crimes, such as how to confront suspects during interviews and how to evaluate their language. Based on an evaluation of the suspect, the profilers tell agents whether they should interview a suspect in the morning or at night, whether to use a hard or a soft approach.

"If someone says, 'My wife and I and our children went out shopping, and the kids got a little bit unruly'—in other words, he went from 'our kids' to 'the kids'—a suspect is unconsciously distancing himself from the kids," Teten says. "You would listen for that where there was no logical reason for distancing, perhaps suggesting that the father killed his own children."

The same kinds of observations led profilers to conclude that when a right-handed person looks to his left when asked a question, it may mean he is genuinely trying to remember the answer and attempting to tell the truth. If such a person looks to his right, he may be trying to create information—in other words, to lie. Conversely, left-handed people usually look to the left when they are lying.

"If we are talking about memory, you shouldn't be creating," Teten observes.

Since Teten began developing profiling, the term has taken on a sinister meaning, referring to singling out suspects solely because of their race. That kind of clumsy detective work is considered neither good profiling nor good law enforcement.

# Threesomes

On Sunday morning, May 23, 1976, the Washington field office called agent Joseph Judge at home. The command center wanted him to investigate whether federal money was being used improperly to pay a congressional aide who was performing no work.

Elizabeth Ray, a voluptuous, thirty-three-year-old blonde from North Carolina, made the claim herself in a page-one *Washington Post* story that had appeared that morning. She said she was on the payroll of a congressman for the sole purpose of having sex with him. The sixty-five-year-old congressman in question was not just any member of Congress. He was Wayne L. Hays, an Ohio Democrat who was chairman of the powerful House Administration Committee. The committee controlled perks that are dear to congressmen's hearts, from Capitol Police protection to parking.

"I can't type, I can't file, I can't even answer the phone," the *Washington Post* story quoted Ray as saying. She began working for Hays in April 1974 as a clerk. Since then, she had not been asked to do any Congress-related work.

Instead, she appeared at her Capitol Hill office behind a blank door in the Longworth House Office Building once or twice a week for a few hours.

"Supposedly," she said, "I'm on the oversight committee. But I call it the Out-of-Sight Committee."

Ray said she would have sex with Hays once or twice a week. Typically, Hays would take her to dinner at one of the Key Bridge Marriott restaurants in Virginia around 7:00 p.m., then they would adjourn to her Arlington apartment.

Hays denied all, saying, "Hell's fire! I'm a very happily married man." Indeed, he had just divorced his wife of thirty-eight years and married his personal secretary but expected Liz Ray to continue as his mistress.

Hays specifically denied ever having had dinner with Ray, but Marion Clark and Rudy Maxa, the two *Post* reporters who broke the story, were present on different occasions when Hays dined with Ray at the Hot Shoppes and Chapparral restaurants in the Key Bridge Marriott. They also listened in on phone calls between Hays and Ray, confirming their intimate relationship.

The *Post*'s story had described Ray's apartment as being in a high-rise building with colored fountains banking its entrance in Arlington. Agent Judge immediately realized that that described the apartment house where he lived.

Having been assigned to investigate, Judge flashed his FBI credentials and confirmed with the manager that Ray lived in the apartment house. He got her apartment number. At ten-thirty in the morning, Judge knocked on Ray's door, but she was not home. Two days later, he and a partner arranged through her lawyer to interview her in her apartment.

"That was a circus because every kind of news media was out there in front of the apartment, and we were going in to interview her, and she was a captive," Judge says. "We actually brought some groceries—lunch meat, bread, and milk—because she couldn't leave."

In several interviews, Ray told the agents that she went to work at the Longworth House Office Building irregularly. If she decided to go in, she would arrive at ten in the morning and leave by two in the afternoon.

"She was the only one who was able to bring her little dog to work," Judge recalls. "And the little dog had toys and a water bowl in her little office. She had hair appointments and manicures, and she would talk on the phone. She never had any work to do."

What never came out until now is that Ray would arrange threesomes with Hays.

"Elizabeth had to recruit other girls," Judge says. "That was part of her job. I don't think she ever had to get more than one other girl. Then

Hays would put them on the payroll. He had virtually unregulated power, so he could get them a job anywhere on the Hill."

Judge found that such arrangements were not that uncommon on the Hill.

"We ended up interviewing a lot of females up there on Capitol Hill on how everything worked," he says. "You had these young girls coming and getting hired on Capitol Hill, and they were pretty and starry-eyed, and these are pretty powerful men. The best aphrodisiac in the world is power, and these guys had it."

A former congressional aide recalled how, in the pre-AIDS days, he participated in a monthly "gang bang" with a shapely twenty-five-year-old blonde who worked for Senator Alan Cranston, the California Democrat. "The Dirksen Senate Office Building has an attic," the aide says. "The word would spread that the girl was out, and guys would go. You'd go up there and join the end of the line. She was very pretty." The woman, who sometimes took on two staffers at once, became known affectionately as the "Attic Girl."

Eventually Liz Ray was given immunity from prosecution, and because the laws at the time were vague, "we eventually came to a plea agreement, and he [Hays] agreed to resign his chairmanship," Judge says.

One of Washington's great scandals, the episode marked the end of Hays' political career.

He had hoped to be Ohio governor or Speaker of the House. Instead, he did not run for reelection. Hays died in 1989 at the age of seventy-seven.

Freed from Hoover's constraints on investigating politicians, the FBI in 1976 began a probe of bribes allegedly paid by South Korean influence peddler Tongsun Park to members of Congress. In what became known as Koreagate, the Justice Department indicted Park on federal charges that included money laundering, racketeering, and acting as an unregistered agent of the Korean Central Intelligence Agency.

Park was never convicted of wrongdoing in a U.S. court. He fled to South Korea, and charges were dropped after he agreed to return to the United States and testify before Congress. Park told a House hearing that he distributed cash in exchange for favors to thirty members of Congress. Only two, Otto Passman, a Democrat from Louisiana, and Richard Hanna, a Democrat from California, were indicted. Passman was acquitted, while Hanna was convicted.

"Congressmen would receive envelopes from Park periodically with ten thousand-dollar bills in them," says Allan E. Meyer, the FBI case agent.

In the end, according to Paul R. Michel, the Justice Department prosecutor in charge of the case, Park's claims to have paid off dozens of congressmen, as indicated by his own financial records, constituted "puffing" so he could receive the money from the Korean Central Intelligence Agency himself.

"He was bragging to South Korea that there were a number of congressmen receiving money from him, and he was just pocketing the sums that supposedly had been paid to congressmen," Michel says.

As part of a plea agreement brokered by the South Korean government, "Park agreed to essentially endless polygraphing," Michel says. "He would show up at eight in the morning in Seoul and undergo FBI polygraphing on the testimony he gave us the day before. We would walk him through every entry for three and a half weeks."

Because Park passed polygraph tests on what he told Michel, Michel says, "I had confidence that Park's account ultimately was correct."

# Mole in the CIA

Having become FBI director on February 23, 1978, William H. Webster began appointing agents to develop sophisticated techniques to combat spying. Under Webster, a former federal judge and U.S. attorney, the focus of the bureau's Intelligence Division shifted from going after assorted anti-war protesters and former Communists to chasing real spies from other nations and the American traitors who helped them.

Instead of merely conducting surveillance of KGB officers assigned to the United States as diplomats, the FBI took what it likes to call a proactive approach. The FBI operated double agents to eat up the KGB officers' time, to learn what they were after, and to eventually help expel them.

In what became known as the foreign counter-intelligence program, the FBI's Intelligence Division engaged in a secret and highly effective dance with the KGB and the GRU—Soviet military intelligence—watching, learning, and moving in when necessary to thwart a spy operation.

Because the largest contingents of KGB operatives were in Washington and New York, those were the main cities where counterintelligence operations took place. Under the nose of the press, the FBI kept secret the fact that many utility boxes contained video cameras for watching KGB operations. The FBI operated some stereo equipment stores so agents working undercover could befriend KGB officers. Neighbors of KGB officers would invite them to parties where the rest of the guests were undercover FBI agents. A nondescript office in Springfield, Virginia, was in fact headquarters for a highly effective joint FBI-CIA operation known as Courtship that resulted in the recruitment of at least one KGB officer within the Soviet embassy in Washington.

Many of the cars that KGB officers drove in Washington were equipped with FBI bugging devices. Through sensors implanted in the cars, agents could track the location of KGB officers. An artificial intelligence program signaled when an officer had departed from his daily routine.

Once caught, however, spies were not necessarily prosecuted. Because it was embarrassing to acknowledge traitors in their midst, the CIA, Defense Department, and other national security agencies had succeeded over the years in convincing the Justice Department not to prosecute espionage cases. Instead, Americans who spied for foreign countries would be allowed to quietly resign from jobs that gave them access to sensitive information.

A year before Webster became director, Attorney General Griffin Bell changed the policy and began prosecuting spies to deter espionage. John L. Martin, a former FBI agent who took over espionage prosecutions in 1973 and became chief of the Justice Department's counter-espionage section in 1980, was the architect of the new policy. Before Martin took over the job, no spies had been successfully prosecuted in federal courts for nearly a decade. By the time he retired in August 1997, Martin had supervised the prosecution of seventy-six spies. Only one of the prosecutions resulted in an acquittal.

"I'm a firm believer in giving them their full constitutional rights and then sending them to jail for a lifetime," Martin, a handsome, perpetually tanned man, would say.

The climax to the bureau's effort to perfect its counterintelligence program came in 1985, known as the Year of the Spy, when the FBI arrested eleven spies. They included John A. Walker Jr., a Navy warrant officer; Jonathan J. Pollard, a spy for Israel; Ronald Pelton, a former National Security Agency employee; and Larry Wu-Tai Chin, a spy for the Chinese. All pled guilty or were convicted.

While the Walker case was one of the FBI's biggest spy cases, none was more bizarre than that of Karl and Hana Koecher. In 1962, the Czech Intelligence Service began training Karel

Frantisek Köcher—his original name—to become a mole. While not formally part of intelligence terminology, "mole" is commonly used to describe an agent or spy who obtains a job with an opposing intelligence service to provide classified information on a continuing basis to his own intelligence service.

At a party in Prague in 1963, Koecher met Hana Pardamcova, a nineteen-year-old translator who was also a member of the Communist Party. Five feet two inches tall, Hana was gorgeous, warm, and outgoing. Three months later, they married.

A brilliant Renaissance man, Karl entered the United States in 1965 and developed an elaborate legend or cover story. Pretending to be a rabid anti-Communist, he claimed that Czechoslovakia Radio in Prague fired him because of his biting commentary about life under the Communists. Karl obtained excellent recommendations from professors at Columbia University and used them in applying to the CIA.

On February 5, 1973, Koecher became a CIA translator with a top-secret clearance. The first known mole in the CIA, Koecher translated written or tape-recorded reports from CIA assets. Because of Koecher's knowledge of science and engineering terms, the CIA gave him some of its most sensitive material to translate from Russian or Czech.

Karl reported directly to the KGB. For his

efforts, Koecher won multiple decorations from the KGB and the Czech Intelligence Service. Hana helped by engaging in "brush contacts" and filling "dead drops" to receive cash or pass along information.

Through his translation duties, Karl was able to piece together the identity of Aleksandr D. Ogorodnik, a critically important CIA asset. Ogorodnik—code-named Trigon—worked for the Soviet Ministry of Foreign Affairs in Moscow. He provided the CIA with microfilms of hundreds of classified Soviet documents, including reports from Soviet ambassadors. The information was so valuable that it was circulated within the White House.

The KGB arrested Ogorodnik in 1977. He agreed to confess and asked his interrogators for pen and paper. "By the way, for some years, I have written with the same pen, a Mont Blanc pen," he said. "I think it's on top of my desk. If one of your people happens to go near my apartment in the next few days, I'd like to have it."

The KGB delivered the pen, which contained a poison pill carefully concealed by the CIA. Ogorodnik opened the pen and swallowed the pill. Within ten seconds, he was dead.

Aside from his translation duties, Koecher had an unusual way of obtaining classified information: attending sex parties. A redheaded man of slight build with a graying mustache, Koecher introduced his wife to mate-swapping. Hana liked it so well that she became a far more avid swinger than he was.

Karl and Hana regularly attended sex parties and orgies in Washington and New York. They frequented Plato's Retreat and the Hellfire, two sex emporiums in New York open to anyone with the price of admission. They also enjoyed Capitol Couples in the Exchange, a bar in Washington, and the Swinging Gate in Jessup, Maryland. Known as the Gate, it was a country home outfitted with wall-to-wall mattresses and equipment for engaging in acrobatic threesomes.

Karl and Hana had a wide circle of married friends with whom they swapped spouses. For example, they met a couple from New Paltz, New York, at a swinging party. With white hair and a tanned face, the husband looks like Cary Grant. His wife has blond hair cropped short, with skin like something from an Ivory Soap commercial. When they met, Hana, fully clothed, was sitting on a sofa. He sat down beside her. After introducing himself, they went up to a bedroom and engaged in sex, he told me.

Because of her extreme sexual proclivities, Hana quickly became a favorite on the orgy circuit. A sexy blonde with enormous blue eyes, Hana liked to accompany Karl to Virginia's In Place, an elite private club organized in 1972 by a suburban Virginia real estate man who was bored with his wife.

For the club, the man rented a spacious home in Fairfax, Virginia, just minutes from Koecher's CIA office in Rosslyn, Virginia, across the Potomac River from Washington. The home had a large circular driveway and was framed by four tall white pillars. It was a rendezvous for weekend sex parties.

Hana was one of the most active partygoers. Described by one of her partners as "strikingly beautiful" and "incredibly orgasmic," Hana loved having sex with three or four men on the double bed. While Karl participated, he often retreated to the living room and chatted.

If both spies enjoyed swinging, they also found the orgies a good way to meet others who worked for the CIA or other sensitive Washington agencies. Because security rules at agencies such as the CIA banned such activities, participants placed themselves in a compromising position in more ways than one. The Koechers took full advantage and picked up valuable information from other partygoers who were officials of the Defense Department, the White House, and the CIA.

In early 1982, the FBI learned about the Koechers from a defector and began conducting surveillance of them. The FBI arrested both Koechers. After Koecher pleaded guilty in a secret court proceeding in New York, the Koechers —with spy prosecutor John Martin there observing—were included in a prisoner exchange that included Natan Sharansky, the Soviet dissident, in February 1986. The exchange took place on a snowy day over the Glienicker Bridge, which joined East Germany and West Berlin. It was the same bridge where the United States had exchanged U-2 pilot Gary Powers for KGB officer Rudolf Abel more than twenty years earlier.

Under the terms of an agreement, the Koechers were barred from ever entering the United States again. They had to surrender their fraudulently obtained U.S. citizenship.

During five days of interviews that began on April 29, 1987, in Prague, Karl Koecher told me that attending the orgies was useful. "Even knowing that somebody attends parties like that —maybe a GS-17 in the CIA—is interesting stuff," Koecher said. "Or you just pass it on to someone else [another intelligence officer], who takes over. That's the way it's done."

The group sex was "just the thing to do at that time," Hana Koecher told me matter-of-factly. "All our friends somehow went to a little club or something. So we went there too, to see how things are."

I asked Koecher how he felt about Ogorodnik's death.

"I'm deeply sorry about that," Koecher said. "But the people who did him in were the CIA and he himself. They recruited him in such a clumsy manner."

# More Roast Beef

Hoover's need for control led him to mistrust undercover operations. The idea of an agent blending into a neighborhood where Mafia figures or terrorists lived by sporting a beard and casual clothes horrified him. Agents had to report to the office every day and drive only bureau cars, known as Bu-cars. Easily spotted, they were full-size Ford sedans sprouting antennas for their two-way radios.

In contrast to that approach, William Webster gave the go-ahead for long-term undercover work and stings.

"It was after Hoover where this expansion occurred, allowing long-term undercover operations, assigning agents no cases except to develop top-echelon criminal informants, Mafia guys themselves," says Sean McWeeney, who headed the organized crime section at headquarters from 1979 to 1986.

In the mid-1990s, the FBI established an undercover group code-named Shortstack just to handle the secret arrangements.

"We provided agents with everything from phony social security, driver's licenses, and passports to a business cover," says Michael Reith, who headed the group for nine years until 2003.

Now the FBI has gone so far as to tell agents working undercover roles that if they are in a situation where their cover would be blown if they did not participate in taking drugs, they may do so. Once they report taking drugs, they are tested for months to make sure they have not developed a habit. If Hoover knew about that, he would have turned over in his grave.

To track suspects and conduct surveillance, the FBI in the mid-1970s created the Special Support Group (SSG). Known as Gs, they are lower-paid, unarmed surveillance employees used in counterintelligence cases. They might pose as joggers, derelicts, in-line skaters, priests, ice cream vendors, mail carriers, or secretaries. As they or agents follow suspects on a street, they are in constant communication with one another. When driving, they may pass the suspect or move with him along parallel streets. They may switch vehicles to further trick a suspect. The vehicles may be Corvettes, old rattletraps, bull-dozers, buses, or ice cream trucks.

Long before caller ID was introduced, Reith was instrumental in pushing telephone com-panies to hand over records of incoming local calls when needed in a pressing case. Such records were the key to solving a number of cases, including the murders of Joseph and Beverly Gibson. On December 24, 1987, the Gibsons were found shot to death in their mobile home in Hazlettville, Delaware. Their son Matthew, born just nine days earlier, was missing.

Just before the shootings, Joseph Gibson's parents, who lived near their trailer, received at least two calls from a woman asking for directions to the trailer. The caller said she had met the couple at the hospital where the baby was born and wanted to visit them.

Reith asked the phone company if it could turn over records of calls made to the grandparents from any phone within the 302 area code.

"They said, 'We don't conduct that kind of a search,'" Reith says. "I said, 'I know you have that information as part of your billing records.'"

After much prodding, the phone company agreed to design a computer program that would spit out the information. Calls to the grandparents had come from the home of Richard W. Lynch and Joyce Lynch. The FBI discovered that Joyce Lynch had told her family she was pregnant when she was not. Just before Christmas, Richard Lynch told friends and family that his wife had given birth to a boy. The Lynches had kidnapped Matthew because they wanted a baby boy.

Two weeks after the shootings, the Lynches

were arrested and charged with the murders. Matthew was given to his grateful grandparents.

Under Webster, the FBI even went after Congress in the late 1970s and early 1980s. In a two-story house rented in Washington, undercover agents who conducted what was named the Abscam case would tell members of Congress they represented a sheik looking for political favors. Agents then videotaped congressmen receiving cash in exchange for promised legislative goodies. Seven members of Congress, including Senator Harrison A. Williams Jr. of New Jersey, were convicted. Instead of threatening members of Congress, as happened under Hoover, the FBI was sending them to jail.

Besides going after members of Congress, the FBI took on powerful officials in Las Vegas, including Harry E. Claiborne, chief judge of the U.S. District Court in Nevada. In December 1983, he was indicted for taking bribes, obstructing justice, and filing false income tax returns. He was eventually convicted of income tax evasion. As the FBI investigation of Claiborne proceeded, Harry Reid, then a congressman from Nevada and later Senate majority leader, demanded to meet with Webster to ask why the FBI was going after Claiborne.

FBI Agent Walter B. Stowe Jr., who was assigned to Congressional and Public Affairs, handled the request and set up a meeting.

"The actual meeting was totally anticlimactic, with Reid raising perfunctory questions about the Claiborne investigation and Webster explaining that it would not be appropriate to discuss the details even with a congressman," Stowe says. "My impression of the meeting is that Webster very subtly gave Reid a lesson in power and made the message crystal clear that the director of the FBI is not subject to political influence."

However, when Webster was later nominated to be director of Central Intelligence (DCI), Reid cast the only vote against his confirmation. Claiborne was convicted in 1984 of tax evasion and was sentenced to two years in prison. He became the first sitting federal judge to be removed from office in half a century.

Webster, who had an ageless face, thin lips, and a high forehead, turned out to be a skilled administrator. He chose exceptionally talented managers and let them run the bureau but always kept them subject to his sharp questioning. Webster made it clear that agents would be in trouble if they kept problems from him. If Webster thought an agent was not giving him the full story or had not done his homework, the tone of his voice became taut and his eyes steely.

"At one of the first executive conferences, they started to give Webster the dance," says William A. Gavin, who became an assistant director under Webster. "He didn't let them dance more than seventeen seconds before he was all over them. He would let you know with a crisp, terse statement with the blue sparks coming out of his eyes. I wouldn't want that happening to me more than once. It was like your dad when he took you to task. You didn't want to upset him again. He saw through the bureaucratic horse manure. All of a sudden, people realized, 'If we don't know the answer, say we don't know the answer.' "

Despite the progress under Webster, now that Hoover was no longer around, discipline within the FBI began to break down. According to bureau legend, a New York FBI agent went to lunch at a deli around the corner from the field office, then on Sixty-ninth Street at Third Avenue. The agent thought the deli was an establishment that offered a discount or more food to FBI agents and police officers. He ordered a roast beef sandwich and watched as the counterman piled on the slices. The deli man slid the plate toward the agent. To the agent's chagrin, the sandwich looked no bigger than any other roast beef sandwich. Showing the deli man his credentials, the agent said, "FBI! More roast beef."

The story soon spread throughout the FBI. No story is more widely known within the bureau. When they are dissatisfied, agents say, "More roast beef!" When they report to their bosses that they showed their credentials, they say, "I roast-beefed him."

The story—which is basically true—is appealing to agents because it goes to the heart of what it means to be an agent. FBI agents have awesome power. They are authorized to carry weapons and can shoot to kill. They can deprive a suspect of his freedom and send him to jail for life. They can eavesdrop on private phone conversations, videotape what goes on in bedrooms, subpoena witnesses to testify before a grand jury, open mailboxes and read mail, obtain email and telephone records, and review income tax returns.

By consulting their files, they can find out the most damaging personal information. By showing their credentials, they can bypass airport security, take their weapons on airplanes, enter movie theaters free of charge, and park illegally without getting a ticket. But unless an agent is on bureau business, has proper authorization, and, in many cases, has a court order, he has no more power than any other citizen. Showing "creds," as they are called, to obtain more food at the local deli violates the most basic credo of the FBI.

When deciding whether agents should be fired, Webster had a lenient approach, tending to look for extenuating circumstances. Considering how much trust the public places in agents, it was dismaying that during his tenure falsifying reports of interviews, obtaining information from bureau files for friends, and lying during administrative inquiries were not by themselves firing offenses.

When it comes to integrity, standards should not be compromised, says Buck Revell, the former associate deputy director under Webster. "There should be a bright line that you simply don't cross. You don't make false statements. You do not lie. You do not give false testimony. If you do, you will not be employed."

Over time, the more lenient approach had its consequences.

At 5:30 p.m. on April 16, 1980, Earl Thornton, an FBI janitor, opened the door to the Federal Credit Union on the eighth floor of FBI headquarters. The FBI building is a skewed tetrahedron, not quite a square. To conform to local restrictions, the building is seven stories along Pennsylvania Avenue but, to the rear, rises eleven stories. From the side, the grotesque overhang at the rear gives the impression that the building is poised to topple on pedestrians— no doubt the image Hoover desired when he designed the building.

Once in the credit union, Thornton turned on the lights. He was about to start vacuuming when he saw a stocky man with brown hair behind the counter in front of an open safe. After a pause, the man behind the counter jumped up.

"FBI! Freeze!" he said.

The janitor quickly recognized the intruder as H. Edward Tickel Jr., the FBI's top break-in artist. Tickel could pick almost any lock, crack any safe, and enter any home or embassy without creating suspicion. Because of his specialty, the bureau entrusted some of its most precious secrets to him.

Tickel told Thornton he had been called to the credit union, which had $260,000 in cash in the safe, because of a report the door was unlocked. He placed Thornton under arrest. But Tickel's story unraveled when he could not identify who had called him to the credit union.

An investigation determined that, aside from his activities in the credit union, Tickel had been selling stolen rings and loose diamonds. He also was involved in selling stolen cars and stealing two-way FBI radios for friends.

Tickel was acquitted in federal court in Washington of breaking into the credit union. However, he pleaded guilty to having taken the radios. After a nine-day trial, Tickel also was convicted in Alexandria, Virginia, of charges connected with jewelry theft—interstate transportation of stolen goods, making false statements, obstruction of justice, and tax evasion.

If the Tickel case was bizarre, it was nothing compared with the case of FBI agents Frank and

Suzanne Monserrate. Married to each other, the Monserrates were held up at gunpoint after leaving the Playhouse in Perrine, a suburb south of Miami, on January 4, 1987. The Monserrates had left the club just after two in the morning when Chester Williams confronted them and demanded their money.

Williams, who had an extensive criminal record, began ripping the gold chains off agent Sue Monserrate's neck. Williams had chosen the wrong victims. Agent Frank Monserrate did not have his gun on him, but he knew his wife carried hers in her purse. When Williams demanded money, Suzanne Monserrate reached into her purse to get her wallet. At that point, her husband grabbed his wife's .38 caliber revolver and shot Williams several times, fatally wounding him. Meanwhile, Williams had shot and wounded Sue Monserrate in the back.

As is standard with any shooting, the bureau's inspectors began an investigation. At first, the couple lied about their activities, but their stories fell apart. Eventually, Frank "disclosed that he and his wife did, in fact, fully participate in sexual activities at [the club], to include swapping spouses," according to the report by the FBI's Office of Professional Responsibility. The swapping was both with another couple who had been interviewed by inspectors the night before and with "several other couples whose identities he does not know and whose names he could not now recall."

After several interviews, Suzanne Monserrate, a respected agent who had a fresh midwestern look, admitted for the first time that she and Frank "engaged in sexual intercourse with other people" at the club during their two years of membership. Retracting information she had given previously, she said that she "also participated in oral sex and engaged in sexual activity with other females at the club."

In July 1987, the FBI fired both Monserrates. What it came down to was that FBI agents simply don't go to sex clubs. The Monserrates might have received only suspensions, except that they lied about their activities. Moreover, Suzanne Monserrate had committed a sin almost as bad as going to a sex club—checking her hand-gun and FBI credentials with a club employee. It would be difficult to have sex while wearing a gun and a badge, but FBI agents are never supposed to relinquish them.

Many agents believe Hoover, who opposed allowing females to become agents, is lurking in the basement of FBI headquarters, waiting for his chance to return to power. If ever there was a need for him to come back, the Monserrate case was it.

# Waco

As a former judge, William Webster brought a sense of probity to the FBI. So President Reagan thought when he chose Webster to be director of Central Intelligence in May 1987 that replacing him at the FBI with another judge would be a splendid idea.

Reagan selected William S. Sessions, the chief judge of the U.S. District Court in San Antonio, who became FBI director on November 2, 1987. With white hair that framed his face, Sessions had a wide smile and riveting eyes that looked through glasses with large round lenses. He looked like a country boy, farm-raised, with enough of a Texas twang to make the stories he liked to tell sound authentic.

Sessions loved the perquisites of his job. He wore his brass FBI badge pinned to his shirt at all times. Even when talking to retired agents, Sessions referred to himself in the third person as "your director." These idiosyncrasies annoyed some agents, who pointed out that unless agents are going on an arrest, they pin the badge to the inside of their credentials case.

Sessions quickly developed a reputation among

agents as a cheerleader who engaged in what they called "Sessions-speak."

"He just babbled," says Larry Lawler, a special agent in charge under Sessions. "At the SAC conferences, there was the gibberish meter. Sessions would get up, and the meter would start beeping. He thought he was a very good orator. He talked, and everyone looked at each other and said, 'What the hell is he saying?' "

Agents reported trying to brief him on important subjects in his office, only to find him looking past them to his television set. His most memorable contribution was offering them cookies. When traveling, he would interrupt a briefing on a spy or Mafia case to ask about the sights.

Sessions kept a neat office. He was proud of the fact that he emptied his in-box each day. But the way he ran the bureau was frenetic. A fan of technology, he peppered assistant directors with questions by email, requiring them to conduct research that was often pointless because Sessions did not remember having asked the questions.

At one point, Sessions asked a question of Joe Stehr, the head of Sessions' security detail. When Stehr came back with the answer, instead of listening, Sessions began whistling "The Yellow Rose of Texas" as he walked away.

In December 1990, Sessions traveled to Atlantic

City to publicly announce, with then Attorney General Dick Thornburgh, that based on an FBI investigation, the Justice Department was filing a civil suit against the city's largest union of casino workers. On the way, Sessions asked agents from the Newark field office to brief him on the case. In the middle of the briefing, he began singing a commercial: "Brylcreem, a little dab will do you. Brylcreem, you'll look so debonair."

Unlike Webster, Sessions saw no reason to learn the details of investigations, and he displayed little interest in them. Instead, he focused on the personnel, technical, and systems aspects of the bureau, trying to improve advancement opportunities for women and minorities and pushing the FBI to become a pioneer in DNA typing. He gave lower-level managers responsibility for investigations.

In the standoffs at Waco and Ruby Ridge, that proved to be disastrous. Both incidents started with abortive arrests by other agencies. The Ruby Ridge debacle was set in motion on August 21, 1992, when U.S. marshals approached the property of Randall "Randy" Weaver, a self-proclaimed Christian white separatist who lived with his family in a remote mountain cabin near Ruby Ridge in northern Idaho. After his release on bond, Weaver had failed to appear for a pretrial hearing on a charge of selling unregistered firearms—two sawed-off shotguns he bought for

$450 from a Bureau of Alcohol, Tobacco, and Firearms (ATF) informant.

As four marshals were checking out Weaver's property, his dog started barking and gave them away. A gunfight ensued, leaving Marshal William F. Degan and Weaver's fourteen-year-old son Sammy dead. The rest of his family remained in the cabin.

When the marshals asked for assistance from the FBI, a Hostage Rescue Team (HRT) headed by Richard M. Rogers arrived on August 22 in two Air Force C-130s. Instead of waiting to arrest suspects when they left the compound, the HRT deployed eleven agents to surround Weaver's cabin. Because a marshal had already been killed and Weaver was thought to be extremely dangerous, Larry A. Potts, the assistant director in charge of the Criminal Investigative Division under Sessions, approved special rules of engagement for the incident stating that agents "can and should" shoot any of the armed adults in Weaver's cabin.

In firearms training at Quantico, every agent is taught the FBI's deadly force policy: an agent may shoot only when he believes that he or another person is in imminent danger of being killed or seriously injured by a suspect. Opening fire for any other reason amounts to "wartime rules [that] are patently unconstitutional for a police action," as an appeals court said.

The other policy the FBI drums into the heads of new agents is that sometimes the best thing to do is to do nothing. Over time, suspects will get tired, hungry, and bored and eventually give up peacefully. When dealing with what the FBI calls crisis management, agents are taught at Quantico to "isolate, contain, and negotiate."

Both policies were violated at Ruby Ridge. In fact, Rogers came up with an assault plan that called for dismantling the house with two armored personnel carriers if Weaver and his family did not come out within two days.

Just after 5:00 p.m., the Hostage Rescue Team snipers began taking positions around the cabin. It had started to sleet. An hour later, an FBI helicopter took off for a reconnaissance run around the cabin. As the helicopter clattered overhead, Weaver, his sixteen-year-old daughter, Sara, and his adopted son, Kevin Harris, stepped out of the cabin carrying rifles. FBI Agent Lon Horiuchi thought one of the men looked as if he were about to shoot at the helicopter, and Horiuchi fired at him. Because Horiuchi believed the man was preparing to shoot, his shot fell within the FBI's standard deadly force policy. The man he wounded was Randy Weaver.

As all three ran back toward the cabin, Horiuchi fired again at the same man. He figured the man would continue to threaten the heli-copter from inside the house, where it would be difficult, with women and children around, for Horiuchi to get a clear shot. As it turned out, Horiuchi's second shot blasted through the cabin's wooden door and into the face of Vicki Weaver, Randy's wife. The round exited the other side of her head and struck Harris in the arm. Vicki Weaver died almost instantly. Not until the bodies were recovered did Horiuchi realize he had killed her.

Since Horiuchi thought he was firing at a man he believed was endangering an FBI helicopter, the second shot also fell within the FBI's original deadly force policy. Weaver continued to hold off the FBI from his cabin until he surrendered ten days later.

A state prosecutor filed criminal charges against Horiuchi, but a federal judge agreed with the agent that because he had been acting in an official capacity, a federal court should hear the case. The federal court dismissed it.

Weaver was charged with the murder of U.S. Marshal Degan. In July 1993, a federal jury, believing the marshals shot first, acquitted him. He was also acquitted of the weapons charge. Ultimately, the Justice Department agreed to pay Randy Weaver $3.1 million to settle his wrongful death lawsuit.

To be sure, the FBI had made many mistakes in dealing with the siege, but in the end, Ruby Ridge came down to an accidental shooting:

Horiuchi did not intend to shoot Vicki Weaver. The more permissive rules of engagement—while abhorrent—had nothing to do with the outcome. Anyone who has fired weapons knows how easy it is to miss the target, particularly when under stress. Almost every day, police officers accidentally shoot suspects, and—unless it becomes a racial issue—there is usually little public outcry.

What made Ruby Ridge a symbol of government tyranny is that right-wing groups seized on the case and turned it into a cause célèbre. That happened again with the siege at Waco. That disaster began on February 28, 1993, when the ATF staged a calamitous raid on a ramshackle compound in Mount Carmel, Texas, ten miles east of Waco. There, thirty-three-year-old David Koresh and his group of religious fanatics had been arming themselves with illegal machine guns and explosive devices, preparing for what Koresh said would be a bloody confrontation with nonbelievers.

In the forty-five-minute gun battle during the raid, the Davidians, as they called themselves, killed four ATF agents and wounded or injured another fifteen. The ATF had to withdraw, and President Clinton ordered the FBI to take over. Under the direction of Jeffrey Jamar, the beefy FBI special agent in charge (SAC) in San Antonio, members of the HRT began surrounding the compound on the afternoon of February 28, hoping to negotiate an end to the standoff.

But after more than a month had elapsed, the FBI realized its strategy for dealing with Koresh was not working. Koresh would promise to come out but then say God had told him to wait. Meanwhile, conditions within the compound were deteriorating. From several people who had chosen to leave, FBI agents learned that the Davidians were surrounded by human waste and dead bodies from the ATF raid. Plus Koresh continued to live with his wives, who were as young as twelve, an abuse of children and a violation of statutory rape laws.

After obtaining approval from Sessions and Attorney General Janet Reno, Jamar picked the morning of April 19 to move on the compound. Just before six in the morning, when the wind had died down, the FBI warned Koresh and his followers over loudspeakers, "This is not an assault! Do not fire! Come out now and you will not be harmed!" For some, this only confirmed Koresh's predictions that the world was coming to an end. Steve Schneider, Koresh's lieutenant, broke off communication by defiantly throwing a telephone he was using out a front window.

A few minutes later, a modified M-60 tank began battering holes near the entrance to the compound and spraying a mist of CS tear gas through a boom on the tank. The Davidians began firing at the tanks, but agents held their fire. At nine in the morning, a tank bashed in the front door to make it easier for the occupants to leave. It also knocked a hole in the wall near the northwest corner of the compound. At noon, the FBI demolished whole sections of the exterior. The fifty-one-day standoff was over.

At 12:05 p.m., a wisp of smoke followed by a small tongue of flame appeared at the southwest corner of the compound. By 12:20, fire was whipping along the west side, fanned by thirty-mile-an-hour prairie winds. Two minutes later, FBI agents climbed out of their tanks and surrounded the compound. One cult member fell from the roof, engulfed in flames. As the cult member tried to wave them off, agents tore off his burning clothing and placed him inside an armored vehicle. A distraught woman emerged from the flames, her clothes smoking. An agent snatched her as she tried to run back into the burning compound. The agents entered the building and tried to find children, wading thigh-deep into a concrete pit filled with water, human excrement, floating body parts, and rats.

From the FBI officials on the ground to those back at headquarters watching the events unfold in the command center, everyone was stunned.

A local arson investigation established that the fire began with internal fires that had been set. In addition to the obvious evidence—billowing black clouds of smoke, signifying the use of an accelerant—the FBI's infrared aerial video photography showed at least four fires, separated by half a city block, starting almost simultaneously in different parts of the compound.

Beyond the infrared photography, FBI snipers peering through the windows of the compound saw Davidians pouring what appeared to be a liquid seconds before the fires started. They also saw cultists cupping their hands as if lighting matches. Kerosene and gasoline were detected on the clothes of some of the survivors, who maintained that the FBI had started the fire. After enhancing the tape recordings of electronically bugged conversations, the FBI learned that as the flames started, the Davidians were telling one another to pour more fuel around the compound.

Eighty Davidians, including twenty-five children, were identified as having been killed in the fire. Seven—including Koresh—had gunshot wounds in their heads, most likely self-inflicted. The autopsy reports showed that some of the children had been stabbed or bludgeoned to death.

Devastated by the outcome, FBI agents who had risked their lives to try to rescue the Davidians faced an onslaught of criticism from the media, Congress, the survivors, and the families. Why couldn't the FBI have waited? It was a good question. The negotiators wanted more time, while the HRT, headed by Rogers, took a more aggressive approach.

"We had waited for two months," Rogers tells me. "What is reasonable for a government agency? Four government agents were dead and sixteen wounded. They had weapons they had used on helicopters. What is the least amount of force that can be used? Tear gas. What would have been said if we had allowed it go on, and they died of disease? You want to end it on your terms."

Sessions had a similar attitude. In one meeting with Attorney General Reno on April 17 before the raid, Sessions was emotional, flailing his arms. "They're [the Davidians] making monkeys of the FBI," he said.

"A lot of pressure is coming from Rogers," Deputy Assistant FBI Director Danny O. Coulson complained in a March 23 memo nearly a month before the raid.

Given the outcome, senior FBI officials realized the bureau should have waited out the Davidians, as the bureau often does in hostage situations. While underage children were being abused, stopping that was not worth the chance that the Davidians would go on a suicide rampage.

Because the various FBI elements at the scene —the HRT, the negotiators, and the profilers— did not come under one commander, the HRT won out, and the FBI moved in.

Because of the lack of coordination, "We were our own worst enemy," says Byron Sage, the chief FBI negotiator.

e proposal. If allowed to proceed before othei
rms could bid, it would have violated govern-
ent procurement rules because of the lack of
ompetitive bidding. In addition, bureau officials
ecided it would have been improper to award
e contract to him because of his relationship to
e director's special assistant.

In the end, the FBI hired another private firm
 improve security, including installing a fence.
 intruders could be seen, the FBI wanted to
stall what is known as a security fence with
ertical iron pickets, the same kind used around
e White House and foreign embassies in
ashington. But Alice Sessions insisted on a
x-foot wooden fence with slats almost touch-
g each other. It would give her more privacy,
e said. FBI security officials objected. They
id the FBI should not pay for the fence she
anted because it would allow snipers to hide
ehind it and would not enhance security. They
elieved that Alice Sessions wanted the fence to
eep in Petey, the family dog.

William Sessions walked out of an FBI meeting
lled to discuss the issue, leaving Alice Sessions
 charge. Similarly, when Alice demanded a pass
 she could enter FBI headquarters without being
corted in, the director ordered it done. Only
mployees with a top-secret security clearance
e allowed to have the pass, yet the FBI issued
r building pass no. 14592, which entitled her to

# The Co-Director Wife

The first hint of something wrong was when John
E. Otto, the acting FBI director, called William
Sessions at home several times to discuss procedures for Sessions' swearing in as director. Each
time, Sessions' wife, Alice, would grab the
receiver from her husband and make her own
demands.

"Alice would interject and criticize the
swearing-in procedures," Otto says. "I finally
said we cannot accept having a Martha Mitchell
dictating to the bureau. He said he agreed."

As it turned out, Alice Sessions saw herself as
a co-director of the FBI. When referring to her
husband becoming FBI director, Alice Sessions
said, "When we were sworn in . . ." She called
herself her husband's "eyes and ears." Referring
to gossip she picked up, she said, "I learn things
in the elevator."

After describing how his wife helped him in
representing the FBI, Sessions said, "So I think
it's kind of a two-for-one proposition. You have
a director, and you also have a director's wife—
very important to the bureau."

But Alice Sessions had a warped view.

"We are probably being recorded," she told me ominously during a phone interview patched through the FBI headquarters switchboard for my book *The FBI: Inside the World's Most Powerful Law Enforcement Agency*. Asked in another interview if she believed the FBI was wiretapping all her calls or only those calls routed to her home through headquarters, Alice said, "My other line often gives me indications of compromise," referring to a second line to her home. "I have no idea if they are doing it on other calls." Referring to the FBI's wiretapping capabilities, Alice said, "I have consulted some other people professionally about this. In fact, I had the telephone company in a year ago."

At one point Alice Sessions told Ronald H. McCall, then the head of the director's FBI security detail, that the bureau had placed an electronic bugging device in their bedroom. Alice Sessions said she thought the bug was in a transmitter supplied to Sessions by the bureau for coded communications.

"I began thinking that the radio was kind of funny, you know," she told me.

The allegation was reported through the chain of command of the Administrative Services Division up to the level of assistant director, startling the entire bureau.

Alice Sessions freely advised her husband on matters ranging from the qualifications of bureau officials to the handling of maternity leave. H opinions were overwhelmingly negative, but s shared them freely with wives of bureau officia In her view, the bureau was full of self-servin inept officials with their own agendas.

At foreign embassy receptions, Alice wou amaze members of the FBI security detail asking for doggie bags. While attending a meeti of Interpol in Lyon, France, Alice Sessions din with Interpol officials at one of France's b restaurants. Alice complained to astonished F agents that the food was terrible.

When her husband was a judge, Alice Sessi displayed little interest in the court. Now Sessions was FBI director, she saw an opportu to enhance her own status and power. When FBI decided the director's home off Sixte Street in Washington needed improved secu Alice suggested that the security detail Donald Munford. Then the husband of S Munford, Sessions' longtime assistant, Munford was in the home security alarm bus in San Antonio, not in Washington. Becaus was the director's wife and she was determ the security detail complied with her reque: asked for an estimate.

Don Munford proposed a system that have cost $97,046—roughly a quarter $435,000 the Sessions paid for the bedroom home in 1989. Bureau officials the special privileges accorded an assistant director or above. With the special gold pass, Alice Sessions could bring in visitors without signing them in.

When headquarters employees forget their passes, their supervisors are notified in writing. But because she often forgot to bring the pass, Alice Sessions and her friends were admitted without any pass. Realizing that the director exempted his wife from such regulations, FBI security officials were afraid to challenge her.

Even this level of access was not enough for Alice Sessions, who asked for and received a four-digit code that allowed her access to the director's suite without going through receptionists. Entry is controlled in this way because of the extraordinarily sensitive information the suite contains. On an official's desk could be the name of a Mafia informant or a spy the FBI is watching, or documents from other supersecret agencies such as the CIA or NSA. In general, only those FBI officials who work in this high-security area—known as "Mahogany Row" because of its wood paneling—have a code to enter the suite.

When I asked about her special access, Alice Sessions said she did not know a top-secret clearance was required. "Why shouldn't I be able to go in and out of Bill's office?" she asked. "They better get on to investigating me for a top-secret clearance because, believe me, I hear a lot more things than the girls in the telephone room do. I'm privy to a lot more things than that."

In his own dealings, Sessions seemed to go out of his way to demonstrate his propriety. He would return FBI paper clips attached to documents sent to his home. In his courtroom, he had been a stickler for rules and procedures. In his speeches, he would talk about the importance of following regulations and laws.

But in other settings, Sessions betrayed a lack of sensitivity about the way he conducted himself. As director, he repeatedly steered his speaking engagements toward his home state of Texas. In his first four years as director, one of every five of his official trips was to his home state—an average of one trip every two months. While Sessions could justify each trip as being related to business, the pattern made it clear he was taking advantage of his position to see his family, friends, doctor, and dentist back in Texas.

At various times, most of the FBI's top officials, including Floyd Clarke, Jim Greenleaf, John Otto, and Buck Revell, warned Sessions about his abuses and the problems caused by Sessions' assistant Sarah Munford and Alice Sessions. Revell issued standing orders that any agent in his Dallas field office who received a call from

Alice Sessions or Sarah Munford was to take no action on their requests and to refer them to him. Prophetically, Revell and the other top FBI officials speculated that Sessions could lose his directorship if the abuses got out. While the FBI director can serve no longer than ten years, the president can remove him at any time.

Sessions' assistant Sarah Munford demonstrated her belief that she was above the law on December 24, 1991, when two Texas state troopers stopped her and her son Glenn one mile west of San Saba, Texas, for having tinted side windows, a violation of Texas law.

According to trooper Stephen L. Boyd, as he approached the driver's side of the car, Munford rolled down the passenger window and displayed her FBI credentials. Although she was a support employee, Munford had so-called "soft credentials" that look like an agent's and are kept in a credentials case. Apparently she thought that waving the credentials out the window would take care of the ticket. Saying she was the assistant to the director of the FBI and that her family was in law enforcement, Munford told the trooper, "You go home at night, and your kids think you are a decent person, and then you go and do something like this."

Boyd told me he ignored her and wrote her a ticket. He explained to her that the judge would probably dismiss the case if her son, who owned the car, mailed in a photo showing that the tinting had been removed.

Munford had attached her FBI business card to Boyd's copy of the ticket, and the following week, he decided to call the number on the card and complain. He was quickly transferred to the FBI's Office of Professional Responsibility, which opened an investigation into Munford's actions.

Having learned of Sessions' abuses and documented them when writing *The FBI*, I wanted to get Sessions' comment. When the public affairs office refused to arrange an interview with Sessions to go over the items, Greenleaf, the FBI's associate deputy director, suggested I itemize them in a letter to Sessions.

In the June 24, 1992, letter, I outlined many of the abuses. On the grounds that the FBI is obligated to make its Office of Professional Responsibility (OPR) aware of any specific allegations of wrongdoing by high-level FBI officials, the bureau turned over my ten-page, single-spaced letter to OPR. That office then officially gave the letter to the Justice Department's OPR.

Just after that, Attorney General William Barr received a second, anonymous letter purportedly written by a retired FBI agent. Dated June 25, 1992, it focused on Sessions' practice of disguising personal trips as official business. The fact that the second letter was dated a day after the FBI received my letter suggests that the anonymous writer was aware of my letter.

Based on the two letters, the Department of Justice's OPR opened an investigation into Sessions' actions and broadened the FBI OPR investigation into Sarah Munford's activities.

After a month and a half, Sessions decided to grant my request for an interview. When he met with me in his conference room, the FBI director declared he would not answer any of the questions raised in the letter. Instead, he launched into a half-hour tongue-lashing.

Sessions noted that he had given me unprecedented access to the FBI, making sure that everyone cooperated and waiving the usual rules requiring public affairs personnel to be present at interviews. He said he thought the book would focus exclusively on the great work the FBI does. He said he was "offended" and "disappointed" that I had delved into any FBI personnel matters, particularly issues relating to his wife.

Predictably, Alice Sessions weighed in with her own analysis. In an interview with the *San Antonio Light*, she suggested that evidence had been manufactured and that her husband was "waking up out of a stupor, realizing he's been had." Someone tacked a copy of the article to a bulletin board in FBI headquarters with the inscription "Alice in Wonderland."

Self-destructive or self-deluding, at the height of the investigation into his improper use of FBI planes, Sessions flew with Alice on the FBI's Sabreliner jet aircraft to attend a performance of the Bolshoi Ballet at the Sands Hotel and Casino in Atlantic City on November 27, 1992. The Sands picked up the $100 tab for the tickets.

When it finally came out in January 1993, the Justice Department's OPR report contained so many additional examples of Sessions' abuses and lack of judgment that it hit like a bombshell. The 161-page report disclosed what the *New York Times* called "a seemingly endless record of chiseling and expense account padding."

Besides having the FBI pay for the fence around his house even though it detracted from the security of his home, the report said Sessions abused government travel for personal gain, systematically used his security detail for personal errands, and allowed his wife an FBI building pass without the required clearance.

The report said that four times while he was director, Sessions and his wife took the FBI plane to San Francisco, where their daughter lived, for Christmas. There, in an effort to justify the trip as official business, they had the FBI generate excuses for making the trip on the government's dime. Indeed, after Alice Sessions attended a breakfast meeting to which she had not been invited, she confided to an agent that she had come to the meeting because she had to justify her trip.

Even as the report was being written, Sessions made a similar trip to San Francisco for Christmas 1992. On another trip, Sessions had FBI agents load firewood for his home into the FBI car and drive it from Salisbury, Connecticut, to Poughkeepsie, New York, then fly the firewood back to Washington.

The OPR report concluded that the issues raised by the internal investigation were so serious that the president should decide whether Sessions should remain in office. Attorney General Barr ordered Sessions to reimburse the government $9,890 for the fence around his property, pay taxes on the value of his FBI transportation to and from work, release his mortgage documents to OPR, and repay the government for travel and per diem payments for personal trips.

The OPR report came out the day before Bill Clinton became president. Asked about the report, Clinton spokesman George Stephanopoulos called it "disturbing." In an editorial entitled "Time's Up for William Sessions," the *New York Times* called for his removal.

In comments to the press, William Sessions blamed everyone but himself and mounted an impressive lobbying campaign. He convinced *Washingtonian* magazine that he was the victim of a conspiracy that included me, Hooverites, bigoted FBI agents, Michael Shaheen of Justice's Office of Professional Responsibility, and Attorney General Barr, among others. He did not respond to a request for comment for this book.

Thus Sessions emerged as an enigma, not at all a clone of Webster, who leaned over backward to avoid the appearance of impropriety. While Sessions acted as a cheerleader for the bureau, the reality was that he—like his wife—mistrusted the FBI and had disdain for its agents.

Instead of the pleasant man Sessions appeared to be, Barr and other Justice and FBI officials concluded he was, in fact, arrogant. How else to explain Sessions' position that he was not subject to the rules that governed everyone else?

The standoff over Sessions and his future paralyzed every other facet of the bureau's operations—administration, personnel, legislative, and budget. With crime increasing and the federal budget tightening, the FBI needed to enhance its technological capabilities. For months such proposals had been piling up on Sessions' desk.

Twice Sessions met with Janet Reno in a futile effort to refute the charges against him. Twice Reno refused Sessions' requests to fly on a Justice Department plane to visit his son in San Antonio and to see his daughter in San Francisco. Each time, Sessions invented business reasons for the trips. Reno, like Bill Barr, had taken to groaning each time she heard Sessions' name.

"I knew I should have stayed in Miami," she remarked one time when hearing of Sessions' latest misuse of power, saying he had "brought this all on himself."

After Reno gave a speech in the courtyard of the Justice Department on April 6, 1993, Sessions began walking toward her, apparently hoping to speak with her. Ignoring him, Reno walked in the other direction. Finally Reno asked Sessions to meet with her at the Justice Department on Saturday morning, July 17, 1993. With White House counsel Bernard Nussbaum present, Reno told Sessions that President Clinton would fire him if he did not resign by Monday.

After leaving the meeting with Reno, in full view of television and newspaper cameras, Sessions tripped on a curb outside the Justice Department. He broke an elbow. After spending the evening in a hospital, Sessions appeared outside his home. Defiantly, he told reporters that as a "matter of principle" he would not resign. Beyond promoting his own self-interest, it was not clear what principle he was upholding. By ignoring Clinton's wish that he resign gracefully, Sessions had plunged the FBI into turmoil as he battled pointlessly to keep his job.

On Monday, Clinton made the announcement he should have made six months earlier. In the White House briefing room, the president said he had telephoned Sessions to tell him he was removing him. Appearing with Clinton at the White House, Reno said she had concluded that, as outlined by the facts contained in the OPR report, Sessions had exhibited "a serious deficiency in judgment."

In the end, it came down to the question of whether Sessions would leave FBI headquarters on his own or whether he would have to be carried out by agents. To make sure he got the message when Clinton called him at 3:50 p.m. to dismiss him, Philip Heymann, the deputy attorney general, met with Sessions in his office to warn him the call was coming. Heymann explained to Sessions what the procedures would be. Like any agent removed from the rolls, the director would have to turn in his FBI credentials and badge and remove from his office only personal effects. Meanwhile, Clinton faxed Sessions a letter informing him of his removal. But Sessions was still in his office at 3:59 p.m. Clinton called him a second time, this time telling him his firing was to take effect "immediately."

Finally Sessions got the message. As instructed, he handed over his FBI credentials to Heymann. Now considered a visitor, Sessions had to be escorted through the halls by his security detail. He gave a final press conference at headquarters. Saying he had been subjected to "scurrilous attacks," Sessions vowed to continue to "speak in the strongest terms about protecting it [the FBI] from being manipulated and politicized both from the inside and out."

Sessions left FBI headquarters at six o'clock. He got one last ride home from his security detail. It was the first time an FBI director had been fired.

Within the FBI, there was jubilation, tinged with sorrow that events had taken such a tragic turn. Darlene Fitzsimmons, Sessions' secretary, began sobbing.

"Sessions is a very nice man, but he was led around by Sarah Munford and his wife," she told me.

Other secretaries on Mahogany Row broke out a bottle of champagne.

# Behind Vince Foster's Suicide

The day after William Sessions was removed as director, a man drove his white van into the parking lot at Fort Marcy Park along the Potomac River in northern Virginia to find a place to urinate. While walking through the woods just before 6:00 p.m., he discovered a dead body. He reported it to two U.S. Park Service employees, who called 911.

At 6:10 p.m. on July 20, 1993, U.S. Park Police and rescue personnel found Vincent W. Foster Jr., the deputy White House counsel, dead with a .38-caliber revolver in his right hand and gunshot-residue-like material on that hand. There was a gunshot wound through the back of his head. There were no signs of a struggle.

An autopsy determined that Foster's death was caused by a gunshot through the back of his mouth, exiting the back of his head. The police learned that Foster had called a family doctor for antidepressant medication the day before his death. Four days before his death, he had told his sister Sheila that he was depressed, and she had given him the names of three psychiatrists.

However, he expressed concern that his security clearance might be lifted if he saw a therapist.

While the U.S. Park Police and autopsy reports concluded that Foster had committed suicide, questions inevitably were raised. Some suggested that Foster had been murdered and moved to the park to conceal the location of the crime. While suicide cannot be explained rationally, the investigations as reported publicly never established what may have triggered Foster's decision to take his own life at that particular time.

As part of his broader investigation into allegations surrounding Bill and Hillary Clinton's investments in the Whitewater real estate development, independent counsel Kenneth W. Starr investigated Foster's death. One reason was that records involving Whitewater were in Foster's office. Starr retained current and former FBI agents to conduct interviews with those who dealt with Foster, both at the White House and in Little Rock.

Former FBI agent Coy Copeland was the senior investigator who read the reports of the other agents. According to Copeland, what never came out publicly was that the agents learned that about a week before his death, Hillary Clinton and Foster, who was her mentor at the Rose Law Firm in Little Rock, held a meeting with other White House aides to go over the health care legislation she was proposing. Those who were present told the FBI agents working for Starr that Hillary violently disagreed with a legal objection Foster raised at the meeting and humiliated Foster in front of aides, Copeland says.

"Hillary put him down really, really bad in a pretty good-size meeting," Copeland says. "She told him he didn't get the picture, and he would always be a little hick-town lawyer who was obviously not ready for the big time."

Based on what "dozens" of others who had contact with Foster after that meeting told the agents, "The put-down that she gave him in that big meeting just pushed him over the edge," Copeland says. "It was the final straw that broke the camel's back."

After the meeting, Foster's behavior changed dramatically. Those who knew him said his voice sounded strained, he became withdrawn and preoccupied, and his sense of humor vanished. At times, Foster teared up. He talked of feeling trapped.

On Tuesday, July 13, while having dinner with his wife, Lisa, Foster broke down and began to cry. He said he was considering resigning.

That weekend, Foster and his wife drove to the Eastern Shore of Maryland, where they saw their friends Michael Cardoza and Webster Hubbell and their wives.

"They played tennis, they swam, and they said he sat in a lawn chair, just kind of sat there in the lawn chair," Copeland says. "They said that just was not Vince. He loved to play tennis, and he was always sociable, but he just sat over in the corner by himself and stared off into space, reading a book."

Two days later, Foster left the White House parking lot at 1:10 p.m. The precise time when he shot himself could not be pinpointed. After Park Police found his body, they notified the U.S. Secret Service at 8:30 p.m.

"I think he had pretty much made up his mind that weekend what he was going to do," Copeland says.

In issuing his 114-page report, Starr exhaustively detailed a series of issues that were troubling Foster, including critical *Wall Street Journal* editorials and upcoming congressional hearings on the firings of White House Travel Office personnel.

A perfectionist, Foster placed tremendous demands on himself. In days or weeks before his death, he had written that he "was not meant for the job or the spotlight of public life in Washington. Here, ruining people is considered sport."

"I have never worked so hard in my life," Foster wrote to a friend on March 4. "The legal issues are mind-boggling, and time pressures are immense. The pressure, financial sacrifice, and family disruption are the price of public service at this level. As they say, 'The wind blows hardest at the top of the mountain.' "

Starr's report recounted how the FBI ran down even the most bizarre theories about Foster's death and conducted extensive ballistics tests that refuted assertions that Foster had not committed suicide. Starr retained Dr. Brian D. Blackbourne, a forensic pathologist who is the medical examiner for San Diego County, California, to review the case. He concluded that "Vincent Foster committed suicide on July 20, 1993 in Ft. Marcy Park by placing a .38 caliber revolver in his mouth and pulling the trigger. His death was at his own hand."

Starr also retained Dr. Henry C. Lee, an expert in physical evidence and crime scene reconstruction who then was director of the Connecticut State Police Forensic Science Laboratory. He reported that "after careful review of the crime scene photographs, reports, and reexamination of the physical evidence, the data indicate that the death of Mr. Vincent W. Foster Jr. is consistent with a suicide. The location where Mr. Foster's body was found is consistent with the primary scene," meaning the place where he committed suicide.

But in his report, Starr never referred to the meeting where Hillary humiliated Foster in front of aides, nor to the change in his disposition after that. The findings are included in the agents' reports of interviews, according to David Paynter, the archivist who read the reports when cataloguing them and making them available under the Freedom of Information Act at the National Archives. However, those reports are now missing from the appropriate files at the archives.

Starr never told Copeland why he decided to exclude the material from his report, and Copeland can only speculate on his reasoning.

"Starr was a very honorable-type guy, and if it did not pertain to our authorized investigation, he did not want to pursue it," Copeland says. "And I think he felt that Hillary's personality and her dealings with subordinates in the White House were immaterial to our investigation."

Clearly, Foster might have decided to commit suicide regardless. But based on the FBI investigation, this episode a week before his suicide triggered his decision to end his life. Asked why he excluded it from his report, Starr did not respond.

In response to a request for comment from Secretary of State Hillary Clinton, Philippe Reines, senior advisor to the secretary and deputy assistant secretary of state, said that since she is focused on "the world's problems," her advisors "spare her from baseless distractions such as your fantastical accusations." As a result, "we will neither share them with her nor have comment for you," Reines said.

Because the White House objected on the grounds of executive privilege, Starr's investigators never interviewed Hillary. However, "one of our agents got the brunt of one of her rampages," Copeland says. As he was serving a subpoena in the Eisenhower Executive Office Building adjacent to the White House, the FBI agent made the mistake of saying hello to Hillary as she passed him.

"He dared to speak to her in the hallway," Copeland says. "She had a standing rule that no one spoke to her when she was going from one location to another. In fact, anyone who would see her coming would just step into the first available office." But the agent "didn't know the ground rules," Copeland says. "As he was leaving, she got out of the elevator and was approaching him," Copeland says.

"Good morning, Mrs. Clinton," the agent said.

"She jumped all over him," Copeland says. " 'How dare you? You people are just destroying my husband.' It was that vast right-wing conspiracy rant. Then she had to tack on something to the effect of 'And where do you buy your suits? Penney's?' "

For many weeks, the agent told no one about the encounter.

"Finally, he told me about it," Copeland says. "And he said, 'I was wearing the best suit I owned.' "

# Brick Agent

Having witnessed William Sessions' abuses, FBI agents were overjoyed when President Clinton nominated Louis J. Freeh to be director on July 20, 1993. A federal judge and a former federal prosecutor, Freeh had begun his career as an FBI agent. Finally, agents thought, they would have a director who understood what they do and could manage the bureau effectively.

Unlike Sessions, who referred to himself as "your director," Freeh insisted on being called by his first name. But while Freeh bonded with street agents and dispensed with the perks that Sessions so loved, Freeh brought to the job his own idiosyncrasies.

Freeh's concept of investigations was limited to what he had done as an agent ten years earlier —knocking on doors and interviewing people. He did not understand that technology had become essential to law enforcement. He had no use for computers and did not use email.

Weldon L. Kennedy, whom Freeh appointed associate deputy director for administration, remembered that Freeh kept a computer on the credenza behind his desk.

"I never saw him use it, nor did I ever see it turned on," Kennedy says.

By the time Freeh left, just before 9/11, the FBI's personal computers were so primitive that no one would take them even as a donation to a church. They were pre-Pentium machines, incapable of using current software, reading a CD-ROM, or even working with a mouse. The FBI's internal email was so slow that agents used their personal email addresses instead. The FBI system did not allow email outside the agency. Often because of funds from the Justice Department, local police were far more technologically advanced than the bureau. Because few of the FBI's computers could handle graphics, agents would ask local police departments to email photos of suspects to their home computers.

As their primary computer, agents were expected to use something called an Automated Case Support System. Developed in the mid-1990s, it used 1980s technology. It could not connect to the Internet and did not use a mouse. The system was so slow and useless that for investigations alone, the bureau had developed forty-two additional, separate systems that agents used instead of the main system. Each of these additional systems had to be checked to make sure all references to an individual had been obtained.

"Brick agents," especially those from New York, tend to see management as the enemy. Freeh never lost that mentality. Even when he had promoted a manager himself, Freeh saw the official as a threat to his own authority and treated him or her with suspicion and hostility.

"Freeh took away from the SACs the desire to make decisions because they feared repercussions," says Anthony E. Daniels, whom Freeh named assistant FBI director to head the Washington field office. "They were terrified of him. Freeh had contempt for management."

"Freeh said he wants everything straight. The first person who told it to him straight, he cut his head off. If an agent brought him bad news, he killed the messenger and pushed him out," Weldon Kennedy says.

For all his faults, Hoover understood the importance of the press. It could enhance the power of the FBI by creating an image, albeit embellished, of his agents as supermen. If people believed in the bureau, they were more likely to cooperate with agents. As part of their training, SACs under Webster gave mock press conferences. Having been an agent fewer than six years, Freeh never got near the FBI's press operations. He saw the bureau as an arm of prosecutors—who usually speak to the media only at formal press conferences—rather than as an American institution accountable to the public.

Traditionally, the FBI had allowed reporters to interview agents about cases where convictions had been obtained. But Freeh decided that no case should be discussed until all appeals were exhausted—a process that often took decades. It meant that scarcely any FBI cases could be discussed.

Under Freeh, even favorable feature stories about the profiling program and other FBI successes were blocked. Because Freeh would not allow press officers to give the FBI's side, negative stories appeared without presenting the bureau's side.

That policy was particularly harmful when it came to the increasingly wild charges about FBI involvement at both Ruby Ridge and Waco. While both occurred under William Sessions, Freeh was director when the incidents became politically charged. Rather than letting the FBI correct false claims and place the incidents in context, Freeh, with great fanfare, called news conferences or issued statements to deplore what had happened and announce disciplinary actions. In doing so, he made himself look good at the expense of the bureau.

"We needed to respond to these outlandish accusations and put out the facts quickly," says Bob Ricks, one of the SACs in charge at Waco. "Even when we were called murderers, we were supposed to sit there and smile," he says. "I had never seen the FBI in that position before. No one was willing to defend the FBI because these problems had not happened on Freeh's watch."

As part of his jihad against headquarters, Freeh began slashing experienced headquarters personnel and sending them to the field. He referred to them as "drones." Weldon Kennedy warned Freeh that the bureau needed to keep experienced people on hand to supervise cases. Kennedy felt impelled to intervene when Freeh wanted to transfer an agent in the laboratory who was the world's foremost expert on shoe and tire treads to the Jacksonville field office to do background checks.

John W. Hicks, the assistant director in charge of the lab, also forcefully warned Freeh about the personnel cuts, saying the quality of work would suffer and backlogs would grow if he proceeded with his plan to transfer to the street half of the 130 agents who were lab examiners. It was foolish to turn experts with decades of experience in ballistics or explosives into street agents. But Freeh's animus toward headquarters would not be appeased. When Freeh ignored him, Hicks resigned from the bureau.

Because Freeh wanted the most experienced agents to leave headquarters for the field, seasoned supervisors in Chinese counterintelligence were gone. As a result, no one was in a position to direct the investigation of Wen Ho Lee, a Taiwanese-born scientist at Los Alamos National Lab who was suspected of passing intelligence secrets to China. The FBI botched the investigation through a series of decisions.

"Because Freeh did not have the evidence for a classic espionage case, he painted this as a devastating case and tried to cover up the lack of evidence by bringing a fifty-nine-count indictment citing vague and unsupportable charges," former spy prosecutor John Martin says.

At Lee's bail hearing in December 1999, the government convinced a judge that Lee was so dangerous he had to be jailed without bail. Lee spent nine months in restrictive conditions. A small light burned constantly in his cell so he could be watched. During his daily hour of exercise, Lee was required to wear leg shackles.

To show how deceitful Lee was, Robert Messemer, a new agent on the case, said at the bail hearing that Lee told a colleague he wanted to borrow his computer so he could download a "resumé." In fact, Messemer testified, Lee borrowed the computer to download classified files.

During discovery proceedings, the defense found that Messemer had testified falsely. Lee's colleague never told the FBI that Lee had said he wanted to download a resumé. Lee had told the colleague the truth—that he needed the computer to download files. At a second bail hearing on August 17, 2000, Messemer claimed he had made an honest mistake. The admission was devastating.

In 1985 alone, the FBI under Webster arrested eleven major spies without a single claim that rights had been violated or that the FBI had acted improperly. Neither Webster nor Martin, the Justice Department's chief spy prosecutor, would have approved what Martin described as an obviously flawed indictment because of lack of evidence.

Outraged that he had been "led astray . . . by the executive branch of our government," Judge James A. Parker freed the sixty-one-year-old Lee on September 13, 2000. The judge said his jailing "embarrassed our entire nation and each of us who is a citizen of it." Sobs could be heard coming from Lee's friends and family.

Lee pleaded guilty to a single felony count of illegally gathering and retaining national security data. He agreed to a sentence of time served and to sixty hours of debriefing under oath.

Freeh also was responsible for the problems with the case of Richard Jewell. When a pipe bomb exploded during the Olympics at Centennial Olympic Park in Atlanta on July 27, 1996, the FBI became interested in Jewell, a security guard who had alerted police to a suspicious green backpack just before one in the morning. Jewell appeared on TV to describe how he tried to help evacuate the area after the bombing, which killed two and injured 111.

Three days later, the *Atlanta Journal-Constitution*, citing unnamed sources, published a story saying Jewell was a suspect in the FBI's investigation. The story pointed out that sometimes those who claim to be heroes at crime scenes are the perpetrators.

Because of the story, the FBI decided to speed up its timetable for interviewing Jewell. That afternoon, agents Don Johnson and Diader Rosario drove to Jewell's apartment and asked him if he would come into the field office. If Jewell could clear up questions to the agents' satisfaction, they planned to drop their interest in him.

Jewell agreed and followed the agents to the field office in his car. An hour and fifteen minutes into the interview, the agents were still reviewing Jewell's background with him when Freeh called David W. "Woody" Johnson Jr., the FBI's SAC in Atlanta. Johnson was in his office down the hall from the room where Jewell was being questioned. With him were other SACs and Kent B. Alexander, the U.S. attorney.

Freeh said the agents should read Jewell his rights.

Any agent fresh out of the FBI Academy at Quantico knows that, under a long line of court rulings, a suspect must be read his Miranda rights if he is in custody or is about to be arrested. In Jewell's case, neither was true.

Johnson pointed this out to Freeh, and Alexander told Freeh on the speakerphone he agreed with Johnson. But the director was adamant.

Woody Johnson walked down the hallway and pulled out the two agents who were successfully interviewing Jewell and passed along Freeh's instruction. The agents went back to the conference room and read Jewell his rights. Jewell said he would like to call an attorney, and that ended the interview.

"If we could have continued with Jewell, we could have confirmed what he told us and cleared him more quickly," Woody Johnson says.

Three months later, the FBI cleared Jewell, as it could have done immediately if Freeh had not intervened. In the meantime, Jewell's reputation had been besmirched. Eventually Eric Robert Rudolph, a fugitive, was charged with the bombing.

When Eugene F. Glenn, head of the FBI's field office in Salt Lake City, complained that the bureau's inquiry into the Ruby Ridge fiasco amounted to a cover-up, Freeh's general counsel, Howard M. Shapiro, responded that to raise such charges was "absolutely irresponsible and destructive to the FBI." That was the mentality that had pervaded the bureau under J. Edgar Hoover.

Freeh's one positive contribution was expanding the FBI's presence overseas. Having prosecuted a major FBI Mafia case called the "Pizza Connection," Freeh recognized how global crime had become. By the time Freeh left, the FBI had forty-four overseas field offices, called legal attaché offices or legats, from Moscow and Panama City to Nairobi and Islamabad, compared with twenty when Freeh took over. It now has seventy-five legats or suboffices of legats. Freeh pushed the expansion despite opposition from some bureau officials who could not comprehend the need for an expanding presence overseas.

But because of Freeh's monumental missteps, it seemed the agency that Hoover had so lovingly created was self-destructing. Almost every six months, a new debacle erupted. By imposing his will in areas he knew little about, Freeh disrupted the normal deliberative processes within the FBI. His emphasis was on making himself look good in the short run. In the long term, that approach damaged the credibility and reputation of the FBI and had a far more disastrous impact on the bureau than Sessions' abuses.

# Catching Hanssen

In the movie *Breach*, an FBI supervisor tells Ryan Phillippe, who portrays FBI support employee Eric O'Neill, "That was the worst spy in American history you just brought down."

But the real-life version of how the FBI uncovered Robert Hanssen, the agent who was the spy in its midst, is quite different and has never previously come out.

Since 1986, the FBI had been trying to uncover a mole in the U.S. intelligence community. As one asset after another was arrested and executed by the KGB, both the FBI and CIA became convinced that the KGB had a high-ranking source whose revelations were leading to the compromise of American agents.

The arrest of CIA officer Aldrich Ames in 1994 explained many of the roll-ups. He is blamed for the deaths of at least nine U.S. agents in the Soviet Union and for disclosing American counterintelligence techniques. But some of the compromises remained mysteries. The suspicion that another spy was giving up American assets became a certainty after the FBI began looking into whether American diplomat Felix Bloch was working for the Soviets.

A longtime State Department employee, Bloch was deputy chief of mission in Vienna until 1987. In Paris, French counterintelligence officers conducting surveillance of Reino Gikman, a KGB officer, photographed Gikman having a drink with Bloch in the bar of the Hôtel Meurice on the rue de Rivoli on May 14, 1989. After downing whiskeys, Bloch and Gikman had dinner together in the hotel's dark-paneled restaurant. At the end of their meal, Gikman walked off with a black carry-on bag, which Bloch had left under their table. They met again in Brussels on May 28. Meanwhile, French intelligence authorities informed the FBI of the meetings.

On June 22, a man phoned Bloch and said he was calling on behalf of Pierre, the code name Gikman used with Bloch. In the intercepted conversation, the man cryptically told Bloch that Pierre could not see him in the near future because he was sick. "A contagious disease is suspected," he said. "I am worried about you. You have to take care of yourself." The warning meant that the KGB knew that Western intelligence agencies were aware of Bloch's relationship with the Soviet spy agency.

In November 1994, the FBI began a determined effort to uncover the spy who tipped off the KGB that Bloch's contact with Gikman had been detected and who gave up other assets to the Soviets. Called Graysuit, the operation consisted of sixteen senior FBI agents under the supervision of agent Mike Rochford, who led an undercover FBI counterintelligence operation and later headed the FBI's espionage section. In the end, it would be Rochford himself who recruited the Russian intelligence officer who gave up Hanssen and solved the case.

To do that, Rochford had to develop trust. Professorial-looking, Rochford talks softly. You don't quickly trust someone whose features are too regular or whose hair is parted just so. Rochford's face is slightly off balance. His salt-and-pepper hair is hopelessly flyaway. His silver-rimmed glasses slip down his nose, and so he can see you, he lowers his head, another habit that makes him seem deferential and therefore more trustworthy. Looking over his glasses with his soft blue eyes, he quietly says, "Uh-huh," projecting sincerity and making his companion want to spill his guts.

Relating the story of how Hanssen was uncovered for the first time, Rochford says, "I started a squad up, and I didn't tell the people I wanted to join it. Instead, I was told I could take anyone I wanted, so I went around and identified the folks I wanted. All of a sudden they get these strange calls from the polygraph unit asking them to show up. They would take a polygraph test, and if they passed, the next person they saw was me. I had some of the best talent in the bureau in espionage matters."

Nearly all espionage cases have been solved because someone brings in a tip. Lacking that, Rochford developed a matrix of fifty-eight items that matched the spy he was looking for. Among the items was the fact that the "unsub" or unidentified subject, had the ability to give the KGB and later the Russian Foreign Intelligence Service (SVR) reports on weekly meetings of the CIA's counterintelligence center. The spy knew about the FBI's investigation of Felix Bloch. He had access to highly classified technical penetrations of Soviet and later Russian establishments. He knew the identities of KGB officers who were spying for the CIA.

The CIA controlled nearly all the operations that had been compromised. This mistakenly led both the FBI and CIA to assume that the spy came from that agency. Beginning with 235 unsubs, the squad narrowed the list of possible spies to thirty-five, then sixteen, then eight, and finally one. He was CIA officer Brian Kelley, who had access to most of the programs that had been compromised. He had led the effort within the CIA to investigate Bloch. By coincidence, he lived near Hanssen.

"We had every reason to believe that the penetration was in the CIA," Rochford says.

"We were just blatantly wrong in not looking hard enough inside the bureau."

But Rochford points out that the CIA officers working the case also believed the penetration was in the CIA.

"We teamed up with the agency on this analysis, and their analysts were every bit as competent as ours," Rochford says. "And we'd sit around a table at the CIA's Counterintelligence Center and actually vote about who the most culpable suspect was. And to a person, everyone at the voting table pressed for individuals within the agency. So it wasn't just us."

At one point, the FBI gave Kelley a polygraph test.

"They came to me and said, 'Listen, we've got a spy, we know we have a spy,'" Kendall Shull, the FBI polygrapher, says. "They said, 'These programs have been compromised. So we know who it is, Brian Kelley, he works for the CIA.' And they'd had everything bugged in his house and his car."

However, contrary to expectations, Kelley passed the polygraph test.

"I explained to them that the test was accurate, and they basically told me that he had beaten my test," Shull says. "They just felt like, 'Well, it's impossible. It's just too much evidence to prove that this guy is the guy that did it.' I said, 'Well, I'm not changing the results of my test.' And they did not ask me to. I said, 'I'm sticking with no deception indicated. And I think you've got the wrong guy.' "

Rochford confirms that Kelley passed the polygraph test, but he says that after the test, Shull wrote in his FD-302 report about the test results that Kelley showed no deception when asked to purposely lie during what is known as a stimulation test, a pretest to get acquainted with procedures for the real test. According to Rochford, Shull wrote that meant that a polygraph test would not pick up his deception, casting doubt on the test results.

Shull says he can't recall that result or what he wrote in the still-classified document. But he says—backed up by former FBI polygrapher Richard Keifer—that the pretest is only to get subjects acquainted with the real polygraph test and has nothing to do with the validity of the final results.

While Rochford still considered Kelley the prime suspect, he continued to pursue other leads. Desperate to find the spy, Rochford decided to try cold pitches to current or former Russian intelligence officers who might have relevant information and be tempted by big bucks. Specifically, Rochford would offer a million dollars per scalp handed over. Rochford got the idea from KGB officer Vitaly Yurchenko, who revealed to Rochford when he defected to the

CIA that the KGB was trying that approach.

"Nobody likes cold pitches because they're the worst technique in the profession of intelligence," Rochford says. "It's going up to somebody whom you don't know and asking them to do the equivalent of going to bed with you. It's very intimate, and if you're not developing it from a practical interrelationship human kind of way, 99.9 percent of folks will say no."

Rochford drew up a list of two hundred potential targets, either current or former KGB or Russian Foreign Intelligence Service officers. The list updated one previously devised by Tim Caruso, Jim Holt, James Milburn, and Art McLendon and was put together with their help and the help of other case agents on Rochford's MC-43 squad.

CIA officers around the world were assigned to pitch some of the potential assets, while Rochford and other FBI agents went after others. FBI agent Wayne Barnes, for example, says he recruited an intelligence asset whom he believed to be the source who gave up Hanssen. That was a mistaken assumption, Rochford says.

Before making a pitch, the FBI agents and CIA officers studied everything about the individual. Even if they came up empty-handed, the intelligence officers who were pitched would report back on their encounters, in effect advertising to others that money was to be made by giving up the elusive spy.

Rochford made twenty-eight such pitches before he finally hit pay dirt. In that case, he had the FBI set up a phony company to lure to a friendly country a Russian SVR officer who was a businessman. The head of the phony company, who was working for the FBI, pretended to offer the Russian an opportunity to start a business enterprise. Once the Russian made the trip, the head of the company told him the deal had fallen through. As the man was leaving the meeting where he was given the bad news, Rochford stepped out of a van and walked up to him on the street.

"Hey, how are you?" Rochford said.

The intelligence officer looked at Rochford oddly and said, "Well, who are you?"

Normally Rochford would use an alias. But, breaking with his normal practice, he openly identified himself as an FBI agent, displayed his credentials, and gave him his FBI business card.

"This is a provocation!" the man said.

"I don't know what you're talking about," Rochford said. "Let's sit down and have a drink."

"No, no," the officer said. "I don't drink with strangers."

Nonetheless, the man agreed to have a glass of water with Rochford at the restaurant in the man's hotel.

"Let me tell you what I'm going to do with

this business card," the man said. "I'm going to take this to the nearest Russian establishment, I'm going to talk to the security officer, he's going to take it to a major newspaper, and your business card and your picture are going to be on the front page."

"Great, don't flatter yourself," Rochford replied. "You're not that important."

"You set me up with this business, I know you did," the officer said.

Denying that, Rochford said, "I'm not trying to hurt your business, I'm not trying to hurt you, I'm not trying to hurt your country." But, Rochford said, "Here's what I want to do. I want to make you the most successful Russian businessman who's doing business in the post-Soviet era."

The plane tickets the FBI had arranged for the man through the phony business required him to remain in town for a week before he returned to Russia. If he wanted to return sooner, he would have had to pay for a much more expensive return ticket himself, and he did not have a lot of money.

"I'm actually going to be here when you are," Rochford said. "Why don't we have dinner tonight, and we can talk more about this, because I can see you are upset. As long as you're here, I'll pick up your meals."

"I'll tell you what," the officer said. "I'll show up, but I'm going to show up with a security officer from the Russian establishment."

"Well, okay, terrific, I'd like to meet him," Rochford said. "I'll take him to dinner."

The intelligence officer began a long denunciation of America, saying Communism was a superior ideology and the Soviet Union had disintegrated only because President Reagan outspent the Soviets on defense. As the man began swearing in Russian, Rochford took out a pen and began writing down what he was saying.

"What are you doing?" the man asked, not realizing that Rochford spoke fluent Russian.

"Very colorful language," Rochford said. "I want to use some of this language." Pointing to a word he had written down in Russian, Rochford said, "Did I spell that right?"

Later, Rochford met with a group of FBI agents and analysts and CIA officers staying at another hotel and related the day's events. He was crestfallen, saying the target really did not want to see him again. Russian analysts Jim Milburn and Carolynn Gwen Fuller, who had helped formulate the original scenario for the pitch, gave Rochford additional guidance. They and the others convinced him that it was worth another shot. Rochford agreed to go ahead with another meeting with the man at six o'clock outside his hotel.

"You're paying for this?" the man said when Rochford invited him to dinner. When told he was, the man said, "Let's have a lobster dinner."

For the next several days, Rochford and the intelligence officer ate breakfast, lunch, and dinner together. The man alternated between acting friendly and being confrontational. Eventually, Rochford brought up the case of a suspected CIA spy who had never been prosecuted. He also asked if Aldrich Ames had given up more than was known. Rochford referred to them as case one and case two, respectively. The idea was to build up gradually to the unsub—case three— who was Rochford's real target.

Over drinks, the source began giving up some tidbits about the first two cases.

"You could tell he was getting comfortable with me, and I was getting comfortable with him," Rochford says.

Yet when they were walking down a street and saw an expensive car, the man would counter-pitch Rochford. "You see that person driving that Mercedes?" he would say. "If you come and visit me over in Russia, I'll get my guys to give you all that."

After their meetings, Rochford expressed more doubts to his team. It seemed that every time he took a step forward, the other guy took two steps back.

"This guy, he's not buying into any of this stuff," Rochford said. "He's playing me along; I've seen this happen before."

But they encouraged Rochford, saying he was making progress.

Eventually Rochford came out and told the SVR officer, "I'm willing to pay a million dollars for the answer to one of the cases, and I won't bother you again."

The man revealed details about case one that could have potentially resulted in a prosecution. He also revealed more about case two, Ames, and the intelligence losses that occurred because of him.

Two nights before the man was due to fly home, they were having cocktails over dinner. The man proposed a toast.

"Mike, I'm going to make you a general, and I'm going to be the most successful Russian-American businessman in the history of our country, like you suggested," the officer said. "We're going to make this work."

They clinked glasses.

Later, they were walking around the city. The man looked at Rochford and described a highly secret technical penetration of the Russians, unsettling the FBI agent. The man noticed his reaction. He told Rochford that his reaction confirmed to him that the FBI agent also was aware of the secret operation.

"If that's what my face is telling you, fine, but I'm not going to tell you I know anything about it," Rochford said.

"Do you want to know what we know, how we know it, the timing of the knowledge, and how it came to us?" the man asked.

"Well, that would be very interesting," Rochford replied, trying not to appear too eager.

The man suggested they go to Rochford's hotel room and draw up a contract.

"I need several million dollars," he said.

"You're living in a fantasy, I can't make those deals," Rochford said. "I told you a million dollars per scalp. We might be able to get you something for case one and maybe case three." Since case two—Ames—had already been prosecuted, the FBI would be interested in additional information but would not pay a million dollars, Rochford said.

"If I give you this, I'd have to be relocated into a safe Western country someplace and might need retraining for some private job," the source said.

"We can have these conversations, it's all good, but we can't do it here," Rochford said.

The man seemed to have second thoughts.

"If we go to your hotel room, you will report everything, and one of your people will get a tape of the conversation, and then I'll be compromised, and they'll kill me," the man said. But he did go to Rochford's hotel room, where Rochford wrote out a contract by hand. At first, Rochford told him that the only two people who knew about their relationship and could sign the contract were Louis Freeh, the FBI director, and George Tenet, the director of Central Intelligence.

"You're lying to me, you have a team of people," the officer said. "They're probably right next door."

"You have to trust me," Rochford said. "The director of the FBI and the DCI know, but of course others know as well."

They went to Rochford's hotel room and continued negotiations over seven hours, having lunch and dinner in the hotel. The final contract Rochford wrote up ran to five pages.

The contract provided for an immediate upfront payment of $750,000. Including the cost of resettlement, training, and annuities, the total package was worth $7 million. That included the "scalps" represented by cases one and three plus additional intelligence. The man also agreed to testify if necessary in any court proceeding. His identity would be protected in court.

"I'll get this in the hands of the FBI director," Rochford said. "He will convey it to the DCI, and they'll give me an answer by the morning."

After the contract was approved and signed, Rochford set up ways to convey the money to the source and to meet with him and communicate with him secretly in Russia through the CIA.

The Russians did not know Hanssen's real

name or where he worked. They knew him as Ramon. Like the FBI and CIA, they assumed he worked at the CIA. So the source expressed concern that the CIA would be involved. Rochford assured him that arrangements would be made by a CIA officer whom he had worked with for years and trusted.

They shook hands and set up a date when a CIA officer in disguise would pick up documents from the source in Russia. But at the appointed time, the Russian didn't show up. "The question was, did he trick us?" Rochford says. "He already had over five hundred thousand dollars. We had detractors in both agencies asking, 'Did he take us?'"

Few know as many secrets as Arthur M. "Art" Cummings II, chief of the FBI's national security investigations.
*Photo courtesy of Arthur M. Cummings II*

For twelve years, FBI executive assistant director Louis E. Grever was what he calls a "government-sanctioned burglar," planting bugs in homes and offices of Mafia figures, terrorists, corrupt members of Congress, spies, and foreign intelligence officers. If caught, he could have been shot as an intruder. *FBI photo*

At the Engineering Research Facility at Quantico, Virginia, agents arrange wiretaps of phone conversations and make custom-designed bugging and tracking devices, sensors, and surveillance cameras to watch and record targets. The facility is the heart of the FBI's TacOps program for deploying teams of agents to break into homes, offices, and embassies to plant bugs. *FBI photo*

Agent Mike Rochford, who successfully pitched a Russian Foreign Intelligence Service (SVR) source who gave up FBI spy Robert Hanssen. *FBI photo*

The FBI gave a source in the Russian Foreign Intelligence Service (SVR) a package worth seven million dollars to reveal a spy who turned out to be FBI agent Robert Hanssen. *FBI photo*

Karl Koecher, a mole in the CIA, and his wife, Hana, attended sex orgies to obtain information for the KGB until the FBI arrested them for espionage and sent them back to Prague. *Ronald Kessler photo*

To conform with local restrictions, FBI headquarters is seven stories tall on the Pennsylvania Avenue side; to the rear, it rises eleven stories. *FBI photo*

Agent Cynthia Deitle pursues Ku Klux Klan members who killed blacks as far back as the 1960s.
*FBI photo*

The swap of Russian spies was a good deal for the United States, says John L. Martin, chief of the Justice Department's counterespionage section, who prosecuted seventy-six spies. Russia tried to include Robert Hanssen and Aldrich Ames in the swap.
*Ronald Kessler photo*

At the FBI Academy in Quantico, Virginia, agent trainees undergo 116 hours of firearms training.
*FBI photo*

Agent trainees receive 176 hours of training in investigative skills at the FBI Academy. *FBI photo*

A possible "WMD attack or attacks on planes in various ways" keeps FBI director Robert S. Mueller III awake at night. *FBI photo*

# "Breach"

As it turned out, the SVR intelligence officer had not shown up for the clandestine meeting with the CIA in Russia to give up Robert Hanssen because he thought he would be spotted. He agreed to another meeting, where he turned over a package with the documents that would identify Hanssen as the spy Mike Rochford was hunting.

The CIA flew the documents back to the United States and handled the arrangements flawlessly. As specified by the FBI, the agency made records of the transfers according to the rules of criminal procedure.

At headquarters, FBI technicians processed and numbered every page of the documents obtained from the intelligence officer recruited by Mike Rochford. Both the FBI and the CIA believed the documents would finger Brian Kelley. But what they showed instead was that the spy had made significant drops of documents for his Russian handlers in northern Virginia at a time when Kelley was out of the country.

"Unless he had a co-conspirator, he couldn't have been the guy," Rochford realized.

One envelope turned over by the intelligence

officer was marked with instructions not to open it until Rochford had checked with the source. Later, the source asked Rochford if the FBI liked what he had sent. He specifically asked about the specially marked envelope.

"Did you open that envelope?" he asked.

"No," Rochford said. "You said not to open it until we talked."

"You dummies," the man said. "I was hoping you'd understand. I just meant to be careful with it. Go ahead and open it."

Inside was a tape recording of a man talking from an FBI offsite facility in New York with a KGB officer at a pay phone in Virginia. The two agreed that if they ever lost contact, they would reconnect by having the Russians put an ad in a newspaper to sell a Plymouth model that did not exist. The Russians taped the call so they could be sure that if they ever met with the spy in person, they could verify his identity.

Listening to the tape, FBI analysts Jim Milburn and Robert King immediately recognized the voice as that of their colleague, agent Robert Hanssen. In the meantime, the FBI was trying to match the fingerprints found on a plastic bag used for a dead drop picked up by the Russians. Like the tape recording, the plastic bag had been inside the envelope marked "Do Not Open." The FBI quickly identified the prints on the plastic bag as Hanssen's.

The delay in opening the envelope proved costly. On November 13, 2000, Hanssen gave the Russians the biggest dump he had ever given them. It was a week later that the FBI opened the envelope, matched fingerprints, and listened to the tape recording.

"If we had known Hanssen was the guy, we could have followed him to that drop and stopped him from giving that dump," Rochford says. "In that dump on November 13, he gave the Russians an inch and a half of documents that gave up sources in the agency and in Canada, Australia, and Great Britain."

At six-thirty in the morning on November 15, the two analysts walked into Rochford's office at the Washington Field office.

"It's not Brian," Milburn said. "It's Bob Hanssen."

"Oh shit," Rochford said.

"Somebody in my own organization—how could I have missed it?" Rochford thought. "And how could we have been so aggressive against Brian? And been so wrong? And how are we going to make this right?"

Hanssen's clearances not only allowed him access to secrets at the CIA, NSA, the White House, and the Defense Department but also allowed him to check an FBI database that would show if the FBI was investigating him. Even though Hanssen had access to most of the information Kelley had, he was not even listed as one of the suspects in the matrix.

"Nobody in the bureau was listed," Rochford says. "We screwed up, no question." But, he insists, "Nobody thought the bureau was invulnerable." Rochford says he vividly remembered the case of FBI agent Richard Miller, who turned out to be a spy. Rochford had personally worked the case of FBI agent Earl Pitts, who also spied for the Russians.

As for the fact that Kelley passed the polygraph test, "In the back of my head, I remembered that Aldrich Ames took a polygraph before his arrest, and the agency said that he passed," Rochford says. "The FBI later looked at his chart and said he failed." Beyond that, Kendall Shull, who polygraphed Kelley, told Rochford that in the pretest, "Brian beat him," Rochford says.

Noting that Shull was one of the FBI's best polygraphers, Rochford says, "So what are we supposed to think? Had he not said that, it would have been much easier to walk away. But I couldn't." At the same time, Rochford admits, "There were different folks within the bureau who thought we should be moving on to other suspects, and they were probably right. We just didn't."

On to him at last, the FBI on January 13, 2001, reassigned Hanssen to headquarters and manufactured a position so he could be watched. A little after 8:00 p.m. on February 18, 2001, ten FBI agents shivered in the cold as they observed Hanssen walk to a dead drop, a spot under a bridge in Foxstone Park in Vienna, Virginia.

As the fifty-six-year-old Hanssen emerged from under the bridge, the agents, weapons drawn, surrounded their fellow agent and placed handcuffs on him. Another team of agents found $50,000 in hundred-dollar bills left for Hanssen at a second drop site.

Charged with spying for the Russians, Hanssen pled guilty to selling to the Soviet Union and later to Russia six thousand pages of documents and twenty-seven computer diskettes cataloguing secret and top-secret programs over twenty-one years. He left more than two dozen packages in dead drops for his handlers in parks in New York City and Washington, D.C.

Hanssen had begun spying for the GRU, Soviet military intelligence, in 1979. He compromised Dmitri F. Polyakov, a Soviet general in the GRU who was code-named Top Hat. A double agent for the FBI since 1961, Polyakov considered himself a Russian patriot, dedicated to the cause of overthrowing the Communist regime. He would accept no more than $3,000 a year, provided mostly in the form of Black and Decker power tools, fishing gear, and shotguns.

In 1985, Hanssen chose to deal with the KGB, which was more prestigious and powerful than the GRU. As a sign of his bona fides, when he was in New York, Hanssen disclosed to his handlers the names of three KGB officers the United States had recruited—Valeriy Martynov, Sergey Motorin, and Boris Yuzhin. Shortly after that, they were recalled to Moscow. Yuzhin was jailed for fifteen years, and the other two were executed. Ames also had fingered them.

Besides compromising nine agents working for the United States, Hanssen gave the Russians documents that included the Continuity of Government Plan, the program to ensure the survival of the U.S. government in the event of a nuclear attack; the National Intelligence Program, which revealed everything the U.S. intelligence community planned for the coming year; and the FBI's Double Agent Program, which evaluated double agent operations worldwide.

Hanssen told the Russians how NSA intercepted the satellite communications of the Soviet Union and other countries, let them see the results of debriefings of KGB defector Vitaly Yurchenko, and provided them with a range of documents from the CIA and National Security Council.

Perhaps most intriguing, Hanssen let the Soviets know that the United States had built a secret tunnel under the Soviets' new diplomatic compound at Mount Alto along Wisconsin Avenue in Washington. The Americans had used new technology the NSA developed for drilling silently.

NSA also began developing highly advanced bugging devices that the FBI hoped a double agent might be able to place inside the embassy. The cost of the tunnel, which ran from a townhouse owned by the FBI, was nearly $1 billion, including development of the new technology.

While Ames' spying had led directly to more deaths, Hanssen gave up the crown jewels of the intelligence community.

Compared with Ames, "Hanssen was even more important to us [the KGB] because his disclosures went to the heart of Washington's intelligence infrastructure," Victor Cherkashin, a former KGB colonel, wrote in his book *Spy Handler.*

In November 1990, Felix Bloch, who was being investigated by the FBI over his meetings with a KGB officer, lost his job with the State Department, but no charges were ever brought against him. Before FBI agents interviewed Bloch, John Martin of the Justice Department went over with the agents how to establish the elements of the crime of espionage and when a Miranda warning should or should not be given. Bloch was neither in custody nor about to be arrested. He began talking to the agents and seemed on the verge of making an admission about money he had received from the Soviets. At that point, the agents stopped the interview and read Bloch his Miranda rights.

"If I have the right to remain silent, I will remain silent," Bloch said.

Martin was furious. It was, he now says, the same mistake Freeh made when he ordered agents to read Richard Jewell his rights in the middle of an interview.

"I specifically advised the agents that they were under no obligation to give Bloch his rights," Martin says. "Only if the agents had enough evidence to arrest him going into the interview and intended to arrest him, or if Bloch already was in custody, did they need to warn him of his rights. Giving him his rights in the middle of an interview was inconceivable. To this day, I don't know what they were thinking. Clearly, they had their own ideas."

When Louis Freeh announced Hanssen's arrest at a press conference in February 2001, he pointed out that while Hanssen's spying was a disaster, the FBI's impressive investigation was a success story. A reporter asked the director how much responsibility he accepted for the fact that Hanssen had evaded detection by the FBI for fifteen years.

"Well, the buck stops with me," Freeh declared. "I'm accountable, I'm responsible."

Freeh's comment was artful, but it papered over the fact that after Ames' arrest in 1994, Robert "Bear" Bryant, as head of the National Security Division, urged Freeh to approve regular polygraph tests for all counterintelligence agents. After encountering opposition from many SACs and from the FBI Agents Association, Freeh shelved the proposal.

Polygraph tests are not perfect, but if nothing else, they are a deterrent. If Freeh had approved Bryant's proposal in 1994 to polygraph counter-intelligence agents, it is highly unlikely Hanssen would have taken a chance on continuing his relationship with the Russians. The Hanssen spy case was another debacle traceable in part to Freeh.

As for the movie *Breach*, the movie never purports to depict how the FBI got on to Hanssen. Instead, it portrays Eric O'Neill as the hero who helped document the case against Hanssen once the bureau focused on him. In fact, as a member of the Special Support Group (SSG), O'Neill's job was simply to keep track of him for six weeks during the three months he was under surveillance by the FBI. In contrast, Rochford had been trying to track the spy since 1986.

To create more drama, the movie showed Hanssen firing his revolver in Rock Creek Park and almost hitting O'Neill.

"That never happened," Rochford says. "What did happen is I remember that Eric saw his gun in his briefcase one time in the office. And I remember him reporting back to the handling agent, who was a female agent, that he was a little afraid of that."

In addition to O'Neill, the FBI ran two other undercover operatives against Hanssen, Robert King and agent Rich Garcia. Their contributions to the case were equal to O'Neill's, Rochford says. To allay any suspicions the spy might have, King met several times with Hanssen over lunch at various restaurants during the month before his arrest.

"King calmed him and gave him the impression that we were not very far in finding the mole, when in fact we knew the mole was Hanssen," Rochford says.

Two days before his arrest, Hanssen showed up unexpectedly at the control center for the spy case, on the fourth floor of FBI headquarters. Because it was a room within a room to shield it from electronic emanations from within and without, it was known as "the Vault." Agents there were putting the final touches on the Washington field office's plan for his arrest. Hanssen asked to speak with King.

"King came to the only door of the Vault and talked to Hanssen in the hall," Rochford says, "while the others continued to work feverishly inside the Vault. Hanssen asked about the buzz going on inside. King allayed his suspicions and said it was just normal analytic work."

Contrary to the movie's portrayal, O'Neill

never socialized with Hanssen or his wife. He did tell the FBI where Hanssen had left his Palm III Pilot when Hanssen had left his office: in Hanssen's leather briefcase. The FBI obtained a court order under the Foreign Intelligence Surveillance Act (FISA) so that the bureau's Tactical Operations Support Center and case agent Stefan Pluta could conduct an entry. Rather than O'Neill, it was Regina Hanson, a new FBI agent, who downloaded the PalmPilot's memory card with Hanssen's stored phone numbers and other secure information.

In all, "there were well over three hundred agents, SSGs, pilots, analysts, and agency folks that worked that case," Rochford says. "Eric O'Neill didn't do 90 percent of what the movie gave him credit for. The agency and the bureau worked together over a period of time to come up with terrific resolutions to penetrations," Rochford says. "That's how you got Ames, that's how you got Harold James Nicholson, that's how you got Pitts, that's how you got Hanssen."

When asked about the disparity between his role and the movie's portrayal, O'Neill initially claimed that King had nothing to do with the case. When given the details, he said he was not aware of them. He also claimed that Regina Hanson had nothing to do with the case. "That person didn't exist," he said. Again, when given the details, he said he was not aware of her role.

But O'Neill insisted his big contribution was coming up with the idea of downloading the data from Hanssen's PalmPilot, and that that was crucial to the case.

"He [Hanssen] treated the PalmPilot like it was one of his children," O'Neill said. "I thought we really need to get this device from him." From the PalmPilot, agents learned the date and time of Hanssen's next drop of documents for the KGB. At that point, the FBI arrested him.

While Rochford says O'Neill may well have suggested it at some point, downloading the contents of such an electronic device was "standard procedure" in such a case and would have occurred no matter what. Because Hanssen was under surveillance "every minute," Rochford says, agents would have detected his next drop without needing to know of it in advance.

When it was pointed out that the real key to solving the case was developing the source who gave up Hanssen, O'Neill, who pitched the idea of a movie originally and sold the rights to his story, said, "I agree that the movie has a lot of fiction in it and overplayed my role. It's a movie, and you have to sell tickets and have a bad guy and a good guy. I didn't have control over the movie, other than providing some direction and saying this happened or this didn't happen."

Of the spy's own motives, Hanssen wrote dramatically to the KGB in March 2000, "One might propose that I am either insanely brave or quite insane. I'd answer neither. I'd say, insanely loyal."

If Hanssen was not insane, he certainly was kinky. On the surface, he seemed a devoted family man, with a wife and six kids, who lived in a four-bedroom split-level house on a cul-de-sac on Talisman Drive in Vienna, Virginia. Almost every day, he attended Mass at St. Catherine of Siena Church in Great Falls, Virginia. Coincidentally, it was the same church Freeh attended. Hanssen belonged to the church's conservative Opus Dei society, which was fiercely anti-Communist.

Yet there were many compartments concealed behind Hanssen's perpetual smirk. Besides spying for the Soviets, Hanssen befriended Priscilla Sue Galey, a well-proportioned woman Hanssen met at the Washington strip club where she worked. Hanssen bought her a used Mercedes-Benz and jewelry and paid for her trip to Hong Kong, where he went to inspect the FBI legat.

When Hanssen's high school friend Jack Hoschouer came to visit, Hanssen would rig a closed-circuit video camera so his friend could stand on a deck outside the Hanssens' bedroom and watch him have sex with his wife, Bonnie. He also posted on the Internet erotic stories about Bonnie that gave his full name and email address, along with his wife's name.

Hanssen looked down on everyone, especially women at the FBI. He told colleagues women never should have been accepted as agents. At one point, he became involved in a dispute with a female intelligence analyst. He pushed her, and she fell. In 1995, Bear Bryant transferred him to work at the State Department's Office of Foreign Missions, where he had less access to secrets.

Dressed in a green jumpsuit, Hanssen, looking gaunt, pled guilty on July 6, 2001. Soon after, he began twice-weekly debriefings. He was sentenced to life in prison without the possibility of parole.

More than the money, Hanssen seemed to enjoy getting back at the FBI, outwitting the intelligence community, and feeling he was in control. He hated uncertainty, he told the KGB. Spying gave him power and control over both the KGB and the FBI.

# 17
# Unexplained Cash

On the evening of Robert Hanssen's arrest, Kathleen McChesney, the special agent in charge in Chicago, called Walt Stowe, the associate SAC at the field office, to say she would pick him up in twenty minutes. She did not tell him why.

When Stowe got into McChesney's bureau car, she explained that Hanssen had been arrested for espionage. The FBI wanted them to tell Mark A. Wauck about the arrest. An FBI agent based in Chicago, Mark was the brother of Hanssen's wife, Bonnie.

At about eight o'clock, McChesney and Stowe pulled up to Wauck's home in Park Ridge, Illinois, and knocked on his door. Wauck's youngest son opened the door and said to his father, "Dad, there are some people here to see you."

Wauck knew McChesney, his boss at the field office of five hundred agents, but he did not know Stowe. He took the two agents into his library. Stowe recalls that as soon as they told him of his brother-in-law's arrest, Wauck brought up the fact that ten years earlier he had warned James Lyle, a Soviet counterintelligence supervisor based in Chicago, that Bonnie had found $5,000 cash in one of Hanssen's dresser drawers. Wauck said he had assumed all this time that the FBI had followed up on the warning.

In fact, it had not. Lyle recalls the conversation with Wauck but says Mark merely told him that Bonnie had found some cash in a drawer and didn't know where it came from. As a result, Lyle did not take any action or pass the information to headquarters.

"My reaction was, so what?" says Lyle, who was chief of the counterespionage group at the CIA when Hanssen was arrested. Lyle says he responded, "What's the issue, Mark? Why doesn't she ask where the money came from?" While an amount of money may have been mentioned, Lyle says, he doesn't recall how much.

But Wauck says he explicitly told Lyle that, given that Hanssen was assigned to Soviet counterintelligence, he felt he should report Bonnie's discovery—as well as two other troubling facts—because it could mean his brother-in-law was being paid by the Soviets. Stowe remembers clearly that Wauck described his conversation with Lyle ten years earlier as reporting suspicious activity possibly related to espionage.

"I remember Mark mentioning five thousand in cash his sister found," Stowe says. "I was flabbergasted. Mark said, 'Why didn't someone look into this?' He seemed to me totally open and forthcoming."

Confirming Stowe's account, McChesney says Wauck immediately brought up the $5,000 in cash and the fact that he had reported it to Lyle as being suspicious.

"That amount of cash would be suspicious for any government employee to have hidden around his or her house," McChesney says. "It is the type of situation agents are directed to bring to the attention of their supervisors, regardless of where the money may have come from."

The fact that Wauck claimed to have told the FBI about his suspicions back in 1990 has come out before. But what has not been revealed publicly until now is that, upon being told of Hanssen's arrest, Wauck immediately brought up his warning to Lyle. Given that he had no time to invent a story on the spot, his spontaneous reaction corroborates his claim that he had indeed described the discovery as a red flag of suspicious activity that should be pursued.

Without knowing that, and given that Lyle denied the claim, many in the FBI understandably dismissed Wauck's version because it seemed to fly in the face of common sense.

"If you're an FBI agent and you believe that somebody in your family is involved in something, and that person in your family happened to be an in-law, and they have equal clearance to yours, and you're an agent, you're trained as an FBI agent, what should you do?" asks Mike Rochford, who thought highly of Lyle.

"Well, you demand to be interviewed," he says. "You don't just whisper in the ear of a supervisor. And if they won't interview you, what you do is you write an investigative insert, or a teletype, and you document it. He never documented it. And so this did not make sense to me. No agent would ever handle a situation like that. It looked to me like it was post-arrest re-creation of history so as to make him look better than he was."

Stowe recalls asking Wauck that same question on the evening of Hanssen's arrest.

"Why didn't you push it?" Stowe asked him. "Wauck said he fulfilled his responsibility. He said he told Lyle, and nothing happened. Are you going to push when a supervisor decides to say nothing?"

But in the first interview Wauck has given to fully describe what happened, he offered new details to corroborate his story and to help explain why he thought Lyle had followed up on his concerns and reported them to head-quarters.

Wauck says he first began to wonder about his brother-in-law in 1985, when Wauck was about to be transferred from New York to Chicago to work Polish counterintelligence and learn Polish. When Wauck mentioned that to Bonnie, she said, "Isn't that great? Bob says we may retire in Poland."

At the time, Poland was under Soviet domination. An FBI agent would not have been allowed to live there unless he defected and cooperated with Polish and Soviet intelligence services.

"Bonnie, that's crazy," Wauck responded.

While he was troubled by her comment, Wauck says he somehow convinced himself that the thought of retiring to Poland stemmed from Hanssen's devout Catholicism and his admiration of Pope John Paul II, who was from Poland.

In 1990, Wauck spent two weeks attending a State Department seminar in Washington on the Soviet Union and Eastern Europe.

"When we got home, my wife, Mary Ellen, told me that my sister Jeanne Beglis had told her that Bonnie had come 'running up the street'—the two sisters live only a block apart—to tell her that she had found five thousand dollars in Bob's sock drawer."

That was equal to $8,340 in today's dollars. Wauck had never heard of an FBI agent having that much cash, let alone keeping it in a dresser drawer.

After Hanssen's arrest, Bonnie—who is still married to Hanssen—admitted to the FBI that she learned around 1980 that her husband was having unauthorized dealings with the Soviets. In 1980, she walked in on him in the basement of their Scarsdale, New York, home when Hanssen was writing a note to the GRU, Soviet military intelligence.

Hanssen tried to conceal the note from her, and she suspected he had a girlfriend. To allay her fears, he admitted that he had been providing the Soviets information in return for thousands in cash. He said the information was of no value and he promised to break off the relationship, consult a priest, and give the money to charities of Mother Teresa.

Bonnie denied to the FBI finding any large sums of money. But Wauck's sister Jeanne told the same story about finding cash to their older brother Greg, who also relayed it back to Wauck. Wauck's concerns were heightened by his awareness—through a colleague who had talked to an FBI supervisor in headquarters—of the FBI's hunt for a mole within the intelligence community.

After hearing of the unexplained cash, Wauck discussed the issue with his wife. If he told the FBI what he had learned, he could face repercussions, both within his family and within the FBI. To suggest that another agent was a spy might reflect on his judgment, he thought. Up to that point, only one other FBI agent—Richard W. Miller—had ever been arrested for espionage, and the material he gave up was minor.

"The FBI's mentality at that time was that

treason and espionage were things that pointy-heads at the CIA did, but not the FBI's straight shooters," Wauck says.

Ironically, while the FBI was in charge of investigating espionage, it did not then have a unit in charge of internal security where such concerns could be reported. Nor did Wauck know anyone at headquarters to whom he would feel comfortable imparting such sensitive information.

Wauck's wife urged him to do what he thought was right. He decided to report to Lyle what he had learned. Back in New York, they had worked on the same squad and had commuted to work together. Moreover, Wauck assumed Hanssen must be spying for the Soviets rather than another country. Lyle had just come out to Chicago from headquarters to supervise Soviet matters, so he would be the best person to transmit Wauck's report to headquarters.

As Wauck recalls it, he approached Lyle and said he had something to tell him that was so sensitive that he didn't want to discuss it in his office. He insisted that they go to the floor above to sit in a windowless interview room.

"I told him of the cash, the mole hunt, and the comment about retiring to Poland," Wauck says. "We went back and forth for at least a half hour, maybe more, discussing the merits of what I had to say. At one point he said to me, 'Do you realize what you're talking about?' And I responded, 'Yes, espionage.' "

While Wauck was not certain Hanssen was a spy, he believed all three points he brought up with Lyle should have triggered a preliminary inquiry.

"I'll take care of it," Lyle said, according to Wauck.

After that, Wauck assumed the matter was being investigated. Per bureau policy, information about the investigation would be shared only on a need-to-know basis.

"I felt that I'd done what I could and, in my position, had to trust the bureau to follow up," he says. "I understood that espionage investigations can run for many years and that a mole might not be continuously active, which turned out to be the case with Hanssen."

Normally, Wauck spent little time with Hanssen beyond seeing him at family weddings. Like everyone else, he considered him an oddball.

"My parents and the Hanssens and about half of the rest of my family all belonged to Opus Dei," Wauck says. "I resisted their urgings to join, and Hanssen was always being held up to me by my parents as a paragon. He belonged to Opus Dei and had a perfect marriage, or so they thought."

The only time Wauck was alone with Hanssen was in the early 1990s, when Wauck, a lawyer, spent time at Quantico training as a legal instructor. He visited with the Hanssens at their home. When they were in a car together, he remembers Bob Hanssen complaining bitterly that he was being transferred from headquarters to the Washington field office.

"I recall being very quiet and circumspect while he spoke, because what was going through my mind was, 'Holy cow, maybe they're investigating him and trying to isolate him from sensitive material,' " Wauck says.

In 1997, after he had set up his first email account on Juno.com, Wauck turned to Hanssen for advice on installing the Linux operating system on his computer, and they would email each other. If Wauck thought Hanssen was a spy, why would he email him on a friendly basis? It's a question asked by FBI agents who would like to think that Wauck made up the story about delivering a warning to Lyle.

"By that time my attitude was, it looks like they didn't find anything," Wauck says. "I realized that, in my position as a field agent in Chicago, I couldn't expect to be briefed on what was done."

Aside from the corroboration offered by Walt Stowe, Lyle's version of the conversation back in 1990 doesn't make sense. Why would anyone mention that his sister had found some cash in her husband's drawer without providing some context and giving a reason for bringing it up?

Stowe says that as soon as Wauck began talking on the night of Hanssen's arrest about his conversation with Lyle, "It was clear to me that something was missed ten years ago. I would hate to have to explain why I did not report that information up the line."

# 18

# "Mueller, Homicide"

At eight forty-five on the morning of September 11, 2001, Robert S. Mueller III was planning a brown-bag lunch with reporters when his secretary told him to turn on the TV.

The new director of the FBI rushed down the stark white corridors of headquarters from his seventh-floor office to the Strategic Information Operations Center (SIOC). It was a $20 million, twenty-room complex of phones, secure computers, and video screens used to monitor and coordinate major breaking cases. He had just moved into his office the week before, and now Mueller was hit with the double whammy of dealing with the attacks and trying to uncover plans for possible new attacks while learning what his job was all about.

Nominated by President George W. Bush, Mueller was a graduate of Princeton. He had served in the Vietnam War and was awarded the Bronze Star and the Purple Heart. After the Marines, Mueller thought he would like to become an FBI agent. With that in mind, he obtained a J.D. degree from the University of Virginia Law School in 1973. But instead of joining the FBI, Mueller became a prosecutor, first in the U.S. attorney's office in San Francisco and then in Boston. Along the way, Mueller married his high school sweetheart, Ann Standish.

In 1990, Mueller was appointed assistant attorney general in charge of the Criminal Division of the Justice Department. In that position, he supervised prosecutions of John Gotti, the Libyan suspects indicted in the Pan Am Flight 103 bombing, and Panamanian leader Manuel Noriega.

Mueller left Justice in 1993 to become a partner in the Boston law firm of Hale and Dorr. But Mueller hated private practice. One day, he called Eric H. Holder Jr., the U.S. attorney in Washington. When Mueller headed the Criminal Division, Holder had reported to him. Now Mueller was calling him to apply for a job.

"He called up out of the blue and said he wanted to try murder cases," Holder says. "I was like, 'What?' Here's this guy who was the former assistant attorney general, the head of the Criminal Division. He came to the U.S. attorney's office and tried cases as a line guy."

Having tossed aside his $400,000-a-year partnership for a government salary in May 1995, Mueller began prosecuting knifings and shootings. He answered the phone, "Mueller, Homicide."

In 1996, Mueller became chief of the Homicide

Section in the U.S. attorney's office. He went on to become U.S. attorney in San Francisco. After President Bush took office, Mueller became acting deputy attorney general, and Bush later appointed Mueller, fifty-six, FBI director.

At his confirmation hearing, Mueller was asked if he would take a polygraph test. In contrast to Freeh, who said he would take a polygraph test but never actually did, Mueller replied, "This may be my training from the Marine Corps, but you don't ask people to do that which you're unwilling to do yourself. I have already taken the polygraph."

"How did you do?" Senator Orrin Hatch asked.

"I'm sitting here; that's all I've got to say," Mueller answered to laughs from the senators.

In contrast to Freeh, Mueller was a proponent of new technology. In 1989, he bought a Gateway computer for his home so he could tally items for taxes more easily with a Quicken program. When he was U.S. attorney in San Francisco, he tasked a talented computer programmer to create new software for tracking cases. The program—called Alcatraz—was adopted by U.S. attorney offices throughout the country.

Several weeks before taking over as director, Mueller met with Bob Dies, the FBI's new computer guru. Mueller ticked off the standard software such as Microsoft Office he wanted on his computer. Dies told him he could have it installed, but none of it would work with anything else in the bureau. Mueller was flabbergasted.

Just before 9/11, Mueller began ordering thousands of new Dell computers. But the bureau's mainframe computer system was so flawed that memos sent to agents never arrived, and there was no way for the sender to know if a memo had been received. To store a single document on the FBI's Automated Case Support System required twelve separate computer commands. On these green-screen terminals, the FBI could search for the word "flight" or the word "schools"—retrieving millions of documents each time—but searching for "flight schools" was so complicated that almost no one in the FBI could do it. The CIA, in contrast, had been able to perform searches for terms such as "flight schools" on its computers since 1958.

Because flight attendants on the doomed planes had called in the seat numbers of some of the hijackers, FBI agents began matching seat assignments to the hijackers' names on flight manifests. Agents ran out leads from credit card and telephone records. Anyone who had ever shared a residence or a hotel room with a hijacker was immediately placed on a growing watch list.

Within days of the 9/11 attack, Attorney General John Ashcroft asked the FBI for a list of terrorist suspects who might be under surveillance. He was told the FBI had no such list. The files were spread over the country, and they were all paper records. When Ashcroft asked why the FBI did not have such information in computers, he was told the bureau had at least forty computer systems, but most of them could not talk to each other.

With the Automated Case Support System so primitive, agents had designed Rapid Start. This makeshift computer program kept track of investigative reports for agents working a breaking case but was never intended to manage a big case. Still, because of Freeh's contempt for technology, that was all the bureau had. As reports and leads poured in about the attacks, Rapid Start became so overloaded that documents could not be retrieved. This led to more delays.

Even worse, because Rapid Start did not connect to field offices, reports had to be downloaded and transmitted to the Automated Case Support System in each field office. Aside from the time involved, the process was unreliable, so agents at the SIOC would often call and fax leads to the field. Dozens of fax machines lined the walls, flooding SIOC with paper.

"Sometimes three teams of agents were dispatched to one house when only one team should have been sent, because we had three duplicative leads being sent out," Dies says. "Meanwhile, we needed those extra agents to work other leads."

In some cases, because the downloaded material never showed up, no follow-up calls were made or faxes sent. Leads were not covered for days.

Robert M. Blitzer, who was in charge of counterterrorism at headquarters prior to the attacks, says the bureau simply did not have the resources to deal with terrorism. Bureau officials such as Buck Revell and Bill Baker, who early on recognized terrorism as a problem, had since left the bureau. Many who remained did not have the intellect to devise new strategies for dealing with the threat. If they did, they found Freeh would not listen.

"I don't think Freeh ever trusted any of us," Blitzer says.

Before 9/11, Blitzer recalls being inundated by threats and leads coming in from the CIA, State Department, NSA, and Defense Intelligence Agency (DIA). The FBI could not analyze it all, much less follow each lead to its logical conclusion.

"The FBI, because of lack of resources, was not able to analyze and exploit all of the intelligence on Osama bin Laden," Blitzer says. "I would have reams of stuff on my desk. It was frantic. I came in on weekends. There was an ocean of work. We got thousands of threats every year. I would ask myself, 'What should we do with this? Is it real or not? Where should I send it?' We were trying to make sense of it. I don't think we ever came to grips with it."

While the terrorists communicated by code on the Internet, agents had computers that lacked CD-ROM drives. Because of the lack of analysts and computers, "we didn't know what we had," Bear Bryant, the former deputy director, says. "We didn't know what we knew."

While Mueller never publicly criticized Louis Freeh, an aide says that when Mueller took over, he expressed "shock" that Freeh had left the technological and administrative sides of the FBI in a "shambles." Mueller was dismayed by how little the FBI knew about possible terrorists in the country.

As the new director, Mueller began restructuring the bureau, emphasizing technology, analysis, and the centralization of terrorism investigations at headquarters. The changes made it clear what Mueller thought of Freeh and some of his policies. Freeh spent much of his time acting as the case agent on the bombing of the dormitory for U.S. military personnel in Dharan, Saudi Arabia, on June 25, 1996. In his last year in office just before 9/11, Freeh gave eight interviews to Elsa Walsh of the *New Yorker* portraying his starring role in the FBI's investigation of the Khobar Towers bombing and his meetings with Saudi officials to obtain their cooperation.

In contrast to Freeh, Mueller saw himself as

an administrator rather than a case agent. He read books on management and consulted business leaders such as IBM's Lou Gerstner. He brought in Harvard Business School faculty and students to do a case study of the FBI and the changes he initiated. Unlike Freeh, Mueller would not promote himself. In interviews with me, he refused to describe what he had done to earn the Bronze Star and the Purple Heart. He would say only that he "got into some firefights." He added, "You never get the medals for that which you probably deserve them. You always get the medals for that which you don't even think about doing."

However, from the Marine Corps, I obtained the citation that went with the Bronze Star. It says that on December 11, 1968, the platoon that Mueller commanded came under a heavy volume of small arms, automatic weapons, and grenade launcher fire from a North Vietnamese Army company.

"Quietly establishing a defensive perimeter, Second Lieutenant Mueller fearlessly moved from one position to another, directing the accurate counterfire of his men and shouting words of encouragement to them," the citation says.

Disregarding his own safety, Mueller then "skillfully supervised the evacuation of casualties from the hazardous area and, on one occasion, personally led a fire team across the fire-swept terrain to recover a mortally wounded Marine who had fallen in a position forward of the friendly lines," it adds.

It was a real trial by fire that steeled him for the challenges he would face as FBI director.

"I think he recognized that being the head of the FBI in many ways is more like being the CEO of a big company than being the biggest case agent in the FBI, because much of what you need to do is make sure the organization has all the tools it needs to do the investigative work," says Daniel Levin, Mueller's chief of staff during his first year in office. "A lot of that is not exciting, sexy work, but it's extremely important, in terms of technological, record management, and personnel systems and recruiting the right people and having incentives to keep them on board and develop their careers. He took all that extremely seriously."

Like a giant ocean liner, the FBI does not change course quickly. Mueller had to deal with a bureaucracy that often resisted change and did not always give him straight answers. Early on, Mueller removed Sheila Horan as acting director of the Counterintelligence Division. Besides finding that she was generally not on top of the subject, he felt she did not appropriately brief him on a Chinese counterintelligence case involving FBI agent James J. Smith in Los

Angeles and had failed to warn him of problems with the case. Smith eventually pleaded guilty to a charge of lying to the FBI to conceal his affair with Katrina Leung, an FBI informant. Justice Department officials said they believed that Leung was a double agent for China and that she passed classified documents to that country, but she was not charged with engaging in espionage.

Perhaps more than anything else, Mueller's removal of Horan defined the difference between the new director and Freeh. Freeh had the habit of punishing anyone who disagreed with him or brought him bad news. In contrast, Mueller banished those who failed to give him the facts.

Mueller was not a diplomat. Back when he headed the Justice Department's Criminal Division, Mueller would throw office parties at his home. He would signal that the festivities were over by flicking the lights off and on. As a former Marine, Mueller expected his orders to be carried out as given. There would be no hand-holding. At the same time, he would go out of his way to offer condolences to FBI officials when they lost loved ones.

"He comes off as your central-casting ex-Marine—tough, no-nonsense, and not suffering fools gladly," says Michael R. Bromwich, a former Justice Department inspector general.

"In the earlier years, when you didn't have

the facts, he would point out that you didn't have the facts by basically just a machine-gun staccato of questions: 'What about this? What about that?' " says Art Cummings, who wound up heading both counterterrorism and counter-intelligence. "Never a pause for the answer. The point was you don't have this, you don't have this, and you don't have that. And the underlying message was, 'Don't come back here without the right answers next time.' "

Over time, Mueller's cross-examinations became less painful, Cummings says. "But he's still very pointed, very directed." When officials did not meet Mueller's standards or ignored his directives, he quietly forced them out.

Under Mueller, the bureau's mission once again was defined by war.

# Intelligence Mind-set

For someone directly responsible under the FBI director for protecting the country from terrorists and spies, Art Cummings had strange living arrangements.

An agent since 1987, Cummings had worked nearly every kind of FBI case—counterintelligence, violent crime, drugs, child molestation—before focusing on terrorism. The risks involved with being an FBI agent never bothered Cummings. In a way, he was used to taking risks. After graduating from Bowie High School in Maryland, Cummings joined the Navy SEALs, then attended the University of California. All through college and the Navy, Cummings had two motorcycles, a BMW 650 and a Honda 900. When he married his wife, Ellen, in 1982, she made him promise not to ride motorcycles, and he sold them. In the Navy and in the FBI, Cummings had made 160 parachute jumps from airplanes. When he decided to go skydiving for fun, she said, "I'm just going to require one thing: why don't you sit down and write a goodbye letter to each of your kids, just in case?" That was the end of his skydiving.

As an FBI agent, Cummings rose to become deputy assistant director of the Counterterrorism Division, in charge of international terrorism investigations. He spent a year as deputy director of the National Counterterrorism Center (NCTC). There, two hundred analysts from the CIA, FBI, NSA, and other intelligence agencies sit next to one another, sharing intelligence and tracking threats twenty-four hours a day. Cummings also did a stint at Guantánamo Bay, where he personally interrogated prisoners.

In January 2008, Mueller named Cummings to head both counterterrorism and counter-intelligence as the FBI's executive assistant director in charge of the National Security Branch. Cummings maintained his home in the Richmond, Virginia, area, where Ellen and their three teenagers lived. On weekends, he drove nearly two hours to Richmond and back.

During the week, Cummings lived on his twenty-three-foot sailboat, moored near Annapolis, Maryland, about forty-five minutes from Washington. He set his alarm to go off at three-ten in the morning. By four-fifteen, he was working out in the FBI's gym. By six, he was showered and in his office.

Every day, he placed his .45-caliber Glock in a safe. Then he sat down and reviewed briefing books on the latest terrorist threats and develop-ments in espionage cases. The blinds in

Cummings' office on the seventh floor of FBI headquarters are closed as an additional precaution to prevent conversations from being picked up by devices trained on the windows. Even though visitors to the FBI building undergo a background check, no one can enter the executive corridor where Cummings, Mueller, and other top officials have their offices without punching a personal PIN into a security device.

At seven, Cummings met with his staff. At seven-thirty, he saw Mueller in the director's office. Then at eight-thirty, he saw the attorney general. He met with Mueller again at nine. On occasion, Cummings would meet with President Obama, as he had met before with President Bush.

Evenings, Cummings left the office by seven forty-five or eight. He drove back to Annapolis and stopped at a deli near the Chesapeake Bay Bridge, where the counterman knew his standing order: a half pound of tuna salad, a bag of SunChips, and a cold Dos Equis or Sol Brava beer. On his way to his boat, he stopped off at the marina club house, where he brushed his teeth. Then he drove a quarter mile to the dock. On many weekends, breaking cases meant Cummings never got back home to Richmond.

That kind of frantic lifestyle began for Cummings on the day of the attacks on the World Trade Center and Pentagon. At the time, Cummings was running a counterterrorism squad in the FBI's Richmond field office. That afternoon, Dale L. Watson, who was in charge of the FBI's national counterterrorism effort, called Cummings frantically. He considered Cummings a sharp operator who was not afraid to tell his bosses exactly what he thought. Watson needed him in Washington. He gave him until midnight to get there. Cummings arrived at 11:30 p.m. Working fourteen-hour days, Cummings wound up living in a Marriott hotel at Ninth and F Streets, NW, for three months.

All the intelligence pouring in pointed to a second wave of attacks, perhaps within months of 9/11. The Library Tower in Los Angeles was to be one target. The pressure to stop those attacks was enormous.

"Listen, guys, we get another hit, and we're all gone," Pasquale "Pat" D'Amuro, who was in charge of the 9/11 investigation, told Cummings and others at a meeting.

In the days after 9/11, Cummings was only on temporary assignment at headquarters. But after seeing Cummings give a PowerPoint presentation, D'Amuro decided to bring him to headquarters permanently. D'Amuro made Cummings chief of the Document Exploitation Unit, then the Communications Exploitation Section. After that, he placed him in charge of the first national Joint Terrorism Task Force, which brought together dozens of intelligence and law enforcement agencies to go after terrorism. Eventually, the FBI had 106 local Joint Terrorism Task Forces, compared with 35 before 9/11. By March 2003, Mueller had placed Cummings in charge of International Terrorism Operations Section 1 (ITOS 1), which directs operations having to do with al Qaeda.

"The real anxiety [after 9/11] was, 'Okay, if they're here, how do we make sure they don't do another one?' " Cummings says. "We don't have the luxury of time. If they're here, they're already planning. They may have been disrupted with this first wave, but if there's going to be a second wave, we need to get out in front of it."

Now, as the FBI official in charge of counter-intelligence and counterterrorism, Cummings coordinated the bureau's operations with the rest of the intelligence community. Having never granted an interview previously to the press while in charge of counterterrorism or counter-intelligence, Cummings revealed his experiences and thoughts for the first time in a series of interviews for this book.

Before 9/11, Cummings had to fight what he considered the insane policy of separating intelligence from criminal investigations as part of the so-called wall erected by Attorney General Janet Reno. A 1995 interpretation of law by Richard Scruggs, a Justice Department official hired by Reno, had essentially paralyzed the nation's effort to hunt down terrorists before they killed people.

As chief counsel of the Department of Justice's Office of Intelligence Policy and Review, Scruggs decided that when applications were going to be made for electronic surveillance in foreign counterintelligence or counterterrorism cases, information gathered for purposes of obtaining intelligence could not be mixed with information that might be used for a criminal prosecution. The Foreign Intelligence Surveillance Act of 1978 (FISA) had established a court to hear requests for electronic intercepts in such cases. Until Scruggs came along, there had been no problem. John Martin, who headed the Justice Department's espionage section, prosecuted more than seventy-six spies by properly distinguishing between information developed for purposes of intelligence gathering and that gathered for purposes of a criminal investigation.

When advising agents, Martin made the point that while watching KGB officers who have diplomatic immunity as part of a routine counterintelligence investigation, they might very well develop information that implicates a government employee passing secrets to the Russians. FISA specifically recognized that this routinely happens and that therefore a counterintelligence investigation and an espionage investigation were often indivisible. Under court rulings, so long as the "primary purpose" of the initial investigation was to gather intelligence, the evidence collected could be used to support a prosecution without any problem. No prosecution had ever been overturned on appeal.

But Scruggs said that to demonstrate that the primary purpose of an investigation was originally counterintelligence and not a prosecution, those who worked on the case initially should have absolutely no contact with prosecutors.

Asked why he made an issue of contact between the FBI and Justice Department prosecutors in view of the record of success in espionage prosecutions, Scruggs told me a court had held that Justice acted "improperly" in the prosecution of Ronald Humphrey, an employee of the U.S. Information Agency, and David Truong, who turned over secret State Department documents from Humphrey to the North Vietnamese. But that case, brought in early 1978, was before the enactment of FISA. It was therefore irrelevant. Moreover, an appeals court upheld the convictions. Asked about that, Scruggs said he thought the case occurred after FISA was passed. In fact, when Scruggs issued the memo, no court had ruled that intelligence information had been used improperly in an espionage prosecution under FISA.

After Reno and Deputy Attorney General Jamie Gorelick approved Scruggs' memo requiring separation of intelligence and criminal matters when making a FISA application, Scruggs' staff at the Justice Department enforced his dictum by warning that FBI agents could be fired or even prosecuted for a felony if they overstepped. Soon the FBI and CIA overreacted to the warning and began separating information from criminal and intelligence sources even if no application was being made for a FISA warrant. The result was a wall so inflexible that FBI agents on the same counterterrorism squad were prohibited from discussing the case they were working on with one another. Within the FBI, files on the same case were kept separate. What was known as the criminal side of the case was assigned a 65 classification number, while what was known as the intelligence side was assigned a 199 number.

"In practice, the wall crippled our last best chance to catch the hijackers before September 11, 2001," Stewart Baker, a former general counsel of the National Security Agency and assistant secretary of the Department of Homeland Security, wrote in his book *Skating on Stilts: Why We Aren't Stopping Tomorrow's Terrorism*. He was referring to how the wall imposed impediments to the FBI finding Khalid al-Mihdhar, one of the 9/11 hijackers, who was linked by address or data in reservation systems to eleven of the other hijackers.

Scruggs had a "blockage in his thinking, which was accepted by Janet Reno and Jamie Gorelick," Martin says. But few in the FBI had the courage to take on what amounted to a monumental government scandal. Cummings did. He remembers saying to Marion "Spike" Bowman, the FBI lawyer who headed the National Security Law Unit and was in charge of enforcing the wall, "Spike, this is stupid! I can't live with this."

"Oh, you don't have a choice," Bowman replied.

Cummings devised a way around the wall—a subterfuge, really. He told Bowman, "I'm going to open a 199 case. I'm going to work this as an intel case. But I'm going to have a criminal subfile."

"Well, you're supposed to open a 65," Bowman replied.

Cummings said he wasn't going to do that. He didn't have the luxury of adding a second agent to a case so that one could pursue it as a criminal matter and another as an intelligence matter. Adding a subfile was a meaningless gesture to appease Bowman and get around Scruggs' ruling.

After 9/11, the USA Patriot Act broke through the wall, overturning the interpretation of the law that had begun with Scruggs' memo. The Patriot Act also allowed the FBI to wiretap a terrorist suspect regardless of what phone he used. Previously, if a suspect changed from a landline to a cell phone to a pay phone, the FBI had to apply for a new FISA order each time he used a different phone, entailing weeks of delay. Incredibly, the FBI could employ what are known as roving wiretaps in organized crime or drug-trafficking cases but could not use them in terrorism cases, which focused on threats that could endanger the country's survival. But, as the FBI official in charge of counterterrorism, Cummings had a much larger issue to tackle: changing the FBI's culture to make the bureau more prevention oriented.

Two days after the 9/11 attack, Mueller and Attorney General Ashcroft began to brief Bush.

"They talked about how the terrorists got plane tickets, got on planes, moved from one airport to another, and then attacked our citizens," Andy Card, Bush's chief of staff, says. "And the president, while he was very interested in that report, said, 'Mr. Director, that's building a case for prosecution. I want to know what you have to say about the terrorist threats that haven't materialized yet and how we can prevent them.'"

As Bush writes in his book *Decision Points*, Mueller affirmed, "That's our new mission, preventing attacks."

Mueller took the message back to headquarters: instead of simply responding to attacks, interdict them. Of course, the FBI had always sought to prevent terrorist attacks before they occurred. Often the bureau was successful. In the six years before 9/11, the bureau stopped forty terrorist plots before they could be carried out. The FBI foiled an attempt by al Qaeda to blow up the Holland and Lincoln tunnels between New Jersey and Manhattan, the United Nations, and the FBI's New York field office.

But under Freeh's leadership, the FBI tended to treat each incident as a separate case instead of recognizing the larger threat and mounting an effort against the entire al Qaeda organization, as the bureau had done with the Ku Klux Klan and the Mafia.

On top of that, before 9/11, because of relentless media criticism and a lack of clear authority under Justice Department guidelines, the FBI had become so gun-shy and politically correct that even though terrorists were known to hatch their plots in mosques, the FBI was averse to following suspects there. Because he was a cleric, FBI and Justice Department lawyers debated for months whether to open an investigation of Sheik Omar Abdel-Rahman, who was later convicted in the first World Trade Center bombing.

Under the guidelines in place before 9/11, FBI agents could not even look at online chat rooms to develop leads on people who might be recruiting terrorists or distributing information on making explosives. The FBI first had to determine that there was a sound investigative basis before it could sign on to chat rooms any twelve-year-old could enter.

In other words, "a crime practically had to be committed before you could investigate," Weldon Kennedy, the former FBI deputy director, says. "If you didn't have that, you couldn't open an investigation."

"We were told before 9/11 that we were not allowed to conduct investigative activity on the Internet, even though it's public," Cummings says. "Same thing with a mosque. It's a gathering open to the public, but we were absolutely precluded from going into a mosque as an FBI agent. And precluded from having a source in a mosque report on anything in the mosque, or look at anything in the mosque, unless we had a specific target within the mosque."

Focusing on Arab men, as had been suggested by a memo from a Phoenix agent worried about Arabs taking flight training, was a no-no.

"Remember, under the administration of the day before 9/11, the Justice Department was investigating the Pittsburgh police department for profiling," Cummings says. "Profiling was a really, really bad thing back then. Imagine in those pre-9/11 days going to flight schools and saying, 'We want you to give us a list of all your Middle Eastern students.' They would've said,

'Excuse me? Is there a problem with Middle Eastern students we aren't aware of? Why don't you go to the ACLU and American-Arab Anti-Discrimination Committee and talk to them about it?' We'd have had more knocks on our door. In the case of Arab men taking flight training, we would not have been able to justify an investigation."

That changed once Mueller came back from his meeting with Bush after 9/11. Cummings told agents, "The director said, 'We've got this new mission. It's a prevention mission.'"

The FBI's primary goal had always been to lock people up. But Cummings told agents that strategy could actually put the country at risk. Instead of bringing a prosecution, the primary goal should be gathering intelligence to penetrate terrorist organizations and prevent future plots. Cummings considered "intelligence" to be a fancy word for information. The FBI had been using intelligence since it pursued tips to close in on John Dillinger at the Biograph Theater in Chicago. It used intelligence to wipe out the Ku Klux Klan and nearly wipe out the Mafia. But using the word "intelligence" conveys a mind-set that emphasizes the importance of holding off on an arrest.

When an agent would say he wanted to take down a suspect on some alien violations, Cummings would tell the agent: "So you're telling me you've done your job, you know everything there is to know about him, his organization, everything around him, all his travel, all his friends, and all family members? He's not a viable source, and he's not producing any productive intelligence whatsoever?"

Often there would be silence.

Cummings would say to the agent, "This is a deliberate judgment you have to make. Your objective is not to make the arrest. Your objective is to make that suspect our collection platform. That guy now is going to tell us just how big and broad the threat might be. He now becomes a means to collection, instead of the target of collection. I want you to understand his entire universe." Then Cummings would tell the agent, "If he's not a viable source, and his intelligence isn't productive, then knock yourself out and use your law enforcement powers to make that arrest."

Many agents who thought they had joined the FBI to put people in jail scratched their heads.

"There was a communication problem," Cummings says. Agents would say, "I've been working terrorism almost my entire career. What does the boss think we've been doing except preventing attacks?"

The difference, Cummings says, is that when the FBI arrested Ramzi Yousef, the mastermind of the first World Trade Center bombing, the

FBI thought that was the end of the matter and did not take extra steps to develop leads that could uncover future plots.

"Pre-9/11, the first consideration was, I got an indictment in my pocket," Cummings says. "The CIA would have run the other way, rightfully so. They didn't want anything to do with testifying in a court of law. And we ran on the assumption that if you had an indictment, you used the indictment. Slap it down on the table, pick the guy up, you throw him on an airplane. You bring him home, you put him in jail, and you go, 'Okay, I've done a great job today.'"

If that were to happen today, Cummings says, "I would have told my agents they basically just put Americans more in jeopardy rather than less in jeopardy. It's a completely different approach and bears little resemblance to the previous one."

Confirming that point, as an agent for twenty-eight years assigned to counterterrorism and counterintelligence, Nick Abaid remembers, "It was often difficult to get into the heads of administrators and agents that intelligence is a long and often tedious process, but it is the most effective way of gathering the information needed. Misguided deadlines to obtain FISA orders, impatient supervision of the recruitment process, and insistence on arrests and convictions were part of the mentality which controlled the bureau since I could remember. Much of that was attributed to the need for generating statistics so that when we testify before Congress, we could brag about the wonderful things we have done."

Replacing that short-range thinking with the new intelligence mind-set entails risk. In deciding how to handle a suspect, Cummings had to balance the need to gain more intelligence against the need to make sure a terrorist did not strike while under FBI surveillance.

"You make a mistake, there are dead people," Cummings says.

# The Center

The entrance to the FBI's Engineering Research Facility looks a lot like a Roman gladiator's helmet, with square eye holes staring fiercely at all comers. This sleek, two-story reception structure on the grounds of the FBI Academy in Quantico gives access to two taller sections of glass and brick, equally forbidding. Visitors must undergo a background check to enter here.

On the second floor is the heart of the Tactical Operations Section. But the most secret part of the operation—the Tactical Operations Center, which deploys covert entry teams—is at a top-secret, off-site location in Virginia. Agents simply call it "the Center."

Besides building bugging and tracking devices, the Engineering Research Facility develops ways to defeat locks, alarms, and surveillance systems. As one example, the facility has spent a million dollars to defeat Israel's high-security Mul-T-Lock line, which is advertised as pick-resistant and drill-resistant.

To keep up with the latest developments by alarm companies, TacOps agents go undercover to attend schools offered by commercial alarm companies. If they identified themselves as FBI agents, the companies would reject them. They may also go to elevator school and truck-driving school. Besides hiding in office buildings and riding on top of elevators before a covert entry, agents learn to program elevators to prevent them from stopping on a floor where they are busy planting bugs.

In addition to conducting covert entries for the FBI, TacOps carries them out for other agencies such as the Drug Enforcement Agency and NSA when they need help penetrating the communications of foreign embassies or bugging suspects in drug cases. In some cases, with the consent of a foreign country, TacOps breaks into locations overseas when the FBI is going after targets of mutual interest—Russian organized crime, for example.

Occasionally, members of Congress or administration officials with top-secret clearances ask to be briefed on TacOps. The FBI puts them off or, if it must, briefs them but gives few details, as it did with Peter Orszag, President Obama's director of the Office of Management and Budget. But with the approval of the FBI director, executive assistant director Louis Grever arranged interviews for this book with those now in charge of the operation: J. Clay Price, chief of the Tactical Operations Section, and the agent who is assistant section chief in charge of the Tactical Operations

Support Center. Because he works undercover, he is referred to here as Jimmy Ramirez, a fictitious name.

One interview took place in a conference room on the second floor of the west wing of the Engineering Research Facility, where bugging devices are built and systems to defeat alarms and computer security systems are developed. The newer east wing focuses on interception of communications and emails and on defeating telecommunications encryption. In contrast to the stern exterior of the building, the inside is airy, light, and spacious.

In his fourteen years on TacOps, Ramirez says he conducted more than five thousand covert entries. Now that he heads the operation, he occasionally participates in especially challenging ones.

"I would so much rather be out there doing entries," Ramirez says.

Going up against foreign intelligence agencies is the biggest challenge because they set traps to detect entries. When a hostile intelligence officer was visiting the United States, the FBI wanted to copy the hard drive of his laptop, which agents believed he kept in his hotel room. While intelligence officers should not retrieve or save anything sensitive on an unprotected computer, they are human and sometimes slip up. Or they may delete sensitive material before entering the country. In that case, the FBI can reconstruct it.

In targeting the hostile intelligence officer, the FBI rented another room in the hotel. Ramirez got the word from the surveillance team that the target was away from his room attending a conference in the hotel, and he gave the green light to go in.

Agents began by searching the man's luggage. As one way to detect an intrusion, intelligence officers may tie a rope around their luggage and knot it in a certain way. Or they may leave a zipper partially open. The agents had to make sure everything was put back exactly as they had found it.

"We have a team of guys, the 'flaps and seals' guys, who will photograph the item first," Ramirez says. "They will look for hairs and fibers—traps we would call it, tradecraft—on that specific item. Before we move the computer, we've got to make sure we can put it back the same way. He could have placed his glasses against it in a certain way. The method doesn't need to be sophisticated. It just needs to be effective."

Agents were taking photographs when Ramirez heard a noise at the hotel room door.

"I walk over to the door, look out the peep-hole, and there's a person fitting the description of the target," he says.

Ramirez asked the case agent to take a look.

"That's my f—— guy," the agent said, meaning the man was the target.

"Impossible," Ramirez said. "I'm hearing on my earpiece right now that surveillance has him on a train."

The surveillance team had somehow missed him. In FBI lingo, surveillance teams are called "keyholder teams." They are supposed to keep keyholders "in pocket." If the team loses them, agents say they are "out of pocket." In this case, the target was definitely out of pocket.

"Either they got him mixed up with someone else at the conference and legitimately thought they still had him, or they didn't want to tell anybody that they lost him," Ramirez says. "They may have thought that at any moment they would pick him up, and on an operation like this, they didn't want to admit on the radio that they had lost him. I tell them that it's okay to lose him, but we need to know. Please do not hold that back on us. Because now he's going to be in my room."

The intelligence officer continued to try his key in the lock, but Ramirez had placed a device developed by the Engineering Research Facility on the door so it could not be opened. Meanwhile, Ramirez radioed to a Hispanic agent who was in the hotel. He told him to pretend to be a hotel maintenance man who happened to see the intelligence officer having difficulty. He said he should speak mainly in Spanish to further confuse the intelligence officer.

"In broken English, the agent told him the hotel was having trouble with that set of locks," Ramirez says. "He asked him to please not contact management or he would lose his job. He apologized and offered to buy him a cup of coffee. That's the kind of guys that we have on our team. He got him away long enough to let us evacuate."

To gain entry, agents may introduce loud static on the target's phone line from a telephone pole or an underground vault. When the target calls to report the problem to the telephone repair service, agents see this on a pen register, which displays numbers dialed. Agents then answer the call themselves, pretending to be telephone company personnel. They promise that a repair team will be dispatched immediately. When the bogus repairmen arrive wearing telephone company uniforms, they install a bugging device in the phone in question or in a nearby telephone line box.

In a Mafia case in Brooklyn, Ramirez and Price, who had done two hundred entries, were trying to figure out how they could get access to the apartment of the target. The man lived on the second floor of a three-story brownstone. Three days before Christmas, they noticed that he began making trips to the basement to retrieve

Christmas ornaments. They timed his movements and installed microphones when he was making one of his forays to the basement. But the microphone they installed on his phone was causing interference on the man's telephone line.

"We're picking this up because he'd get on the phone and start bitching and cursing, saying his phone's not working," says Price, who is forty-nine.

The Mafia figure called the telephone company, and the FBI was glad to help out.

"When he called, we intercepted the call, and he was speaking to us," Price says.

"Yes, sir, can I help you?" an agent asked.

"Yeah, my goddamn phone doesn't work," the Mafioso said.

"We'll be right out there," the agent replied.

"We go in our fabricated telephone company uniforms in our fabricated telephone company truck," Price says. "This guy's standing right there next to us. We say we'll take it apart. So we took it out, put a new mic in, fixed his phone."

"Youse guys are the best," the man said.

When the FBI later arrested the Mafia figure, "he immediately cops an attitude," Price says. " 'You've got nothin', screw you.' "

The agents played him snippets of his recorded conversations.

"He ends up confessing and cooperating," Price says.

Before deciding how to handle a dog, agents test it. Dogs that are not police or military dogs may bite, but not as ferociously as dogs that are trained to bite. If the dog is ferocious, the FBI will tranquilize it.

"When I'm doing the assessment, I've got to be very accurate on the weight of the dog," Ramirez says. "Because if I give him too much drug, you're going to have to try to resuscitate him during the entry. If I don't give him enough, some of these dogs go into a rage and become even more aggressive. Of course, he's just doing his job, protecting his family."

Rather than drug them, agents prefer befriending dogs or training fire extinguishers on them. They don't want to harm them. A dog that has been drugged may experience side effects, such as diarrhea, and agents don't want to give targets any reason to be suspicious.

When assessing the home of an organized crime figure in Las Vegas, agents reported that he had a thirty-five-pound schnauzer. But when Ramirez went out to do his own assessment, he found the man had a seventy-five-pound Bouvier des Flandres, which looks like a giant schnauzer. When testing the dog in Las Vegas and setting up sensors around the house, Ramirez fed him a Burger King Whopper.

"He loved Whoppers," Ramirez says. "At first, he would bite the chain-link fence and actually pull it back with his teeth. But he'd much rather have a Whopper. After two days of Whoppers, he came to the fence to see me and didn't bark anymore."

When Ramirez and Grever finally broke into the house, the dog was expecting a Whopper, and Ramirez gave him one. Instead of attacking Ramirez, the dog began licking his face. After that, fellow TacOps team members called Ramirez "Dog Man."

Ramirez was doing a job in the Washington apartment of a foreign intelligence officer when a cat greeted him.

"This cat looks at me and realizes I'm not the owner," Ramirez says. "Something's not right here. He takes off for the back door. The back door is a six-foot-long sliding door. He runs smack into that glass door, to the point where he's lying knocked out on the carpet."

Ramirez was trying to figure out how to resuscitate the cat so as not to tip off the target to an intrusion.

"Finally, the cat gets his act together," Ramirez says. "I guess it just stunned him. He gets up and looks back at me and takes off for the bedroom. We never saw the cat again during the entire entry."

When entering the home of a Russian organized crime figure, Ramirez listened for an alarm system to go off. Before it could alert the alarm monitoring service, he would suppress it electronically. But nothing was happening, making him think that the alarm had not been set because someone was still in the house.

"Now we want to make sure there's no one there," Ramirez says. "So we ease through the house wearing night vision gear and we hear, 'Hello?' "

The agents froze and looked at each other, their guns drawn. Just then, the parrot that had said hello began talking some more. The bird was in a solarium and had the run of the house.

"He spoke better than our lock guys," Ramirez jokes.

To make sure nothing goes wrong, Ramirez will clue in a police officer who is on a joint task force with the FBI. Agents rarely inform the police chief. The police department or individual officers may be the actual target of an investigation.

In one case in Washington, everyone in a home was away. But a little girl who lived across the street was sleeping over at a friend's house in the neighborhood. She apparently got into a fight with her friend, so at two in the morning she decided to walk home with her dog, who had gone with her to the sleepover.

"We have two lock guys and myself at the back door of this house," Ramirez says. "We felt like we could stay there all night long. And this young lady comes by, and her little dog probably smelled us from when we had walked into the back gate. He kind of nudges her. She gets a glimpse of two of our guys, and now we hear on the radio that there's a pedestrian walking toward the house across the street."

Having spotted the two suspicious men on the grounds of the house, the girl wisely continued to walk down the street into her house, where she woke up her father and told him people were breaking in across the street.

"He calls the police, and we pick up the dispatch on our scanner," Ramirez says. "But instead of the officer coming out, we have our task force officer come out. He checks out the place, goes over and sits down and pretends to interview this young girl," Ramirez says. "We backed off that target for several months."

In this case, the task force officer working with the FBI was able to cancel the dispatch. In the event officers are dispatched, agents will show their credentials and say they are "working." That is enough.

Agents sometimes dress as police officers, but that can be risky.

"You've got to be careful with your ruses, because if I'm trying to fool another police officer, he knows everybody on that shift, and you're not fooling anybody at that point," Ramirez says. Agents never enlist the aid of a police officer who is a neighbor because he could be a friend of the target or even could have been corrupted by him.

In one case, a neighbor in an apartment across a courtyard saw something suspicious during an entry and called 911. The man told the dispatcher he had a gun and could go over and confront the burglars.

"Of course, the police department doesn't want you to do that," Ramirez says. "The dispatcher gave good advice to sit tight, and thank God for everybody concerned, he took that advice." By the time the police showed up, "our guys had bailed out."

In carrying out its mission, TacOps shares techniques with the intelligence services of Great Britain, Australia, New Zealand, and Canada. In terrorism cases, agents work closely with Great Britain's MI5.

"They're much more risk-averse than we are," Ramirez says. "We do in two weeks or three weeks what they would take months or years sometimes to plan."

Each field office has technical agents who may work with the TacOps Center on specific entries. In rare cases, after assessing the risks and intelligence on a target, TacOps may give a local field office the go-ahead to perform an entry on its own.

Special agents in charge of field offices sometimes demand that TacOps perform an entry immediately without the necessary surveillance.

"We'll get these calls on Friday night, and they'll make up all these reasons why you got to come out this weekend to do it," Ramirez says. "We know nothing about the target. And that's the scariest."

TacOps evaluates the risk versus the reward of the operation. If the target is a terrorist who may be on the verge of detonating a bomb or deploying a chemical weapon, TacOps will comply, bringing in more agents for surveillance if necessary. In such a case, "we're going to do whatever we have to do. We'll take whatever necessary risks to get you in there," Ramirez says.

If there is no imminent danger, TacOps agents may gently suggest that if a problem were to arise, the SAC's career could be in jeopardy. The SAC quickly backs off.

If no covert entry is involved, local field office technical agents perform jobs on their own. For example, in Cincinnati, local technical agents began installing a Global Positioning System tracking device in the Mercedes-Benz owned by Gerardo Mulato on April 26, 2007. An illegal immigrant from Mexico, he was a suspected member of a gang that shipped black-tar heroin from Mexico to Cincinnati. Since the GPS device was being installed on the exterior of the car under its floor, it was not technically a covert entry.

Mulato parked his car in a lot at his apartment house at 1995 Waycross Road. To guard against theft, he had installed a surveillance camera with a microphone in a window overlooking the parking lot. It beamed images and sound back to the bedroom in his apartment at the rear of the building.

Awake at 4:20 a.m., Mulato saw men crouching around his car. He grabbed his 9-millimeter Ruger pistol and rushed outside. Wearing a T-shirt and a pair of shorts, he confronted the strangers, who were FBI tech agents from the local field office.

"He saw these guys messing around with his car," Price says. "He pulls out his huge revolver, walks down there to see what the problem is. He points his gun at an agent. The agent says, 'FBI! Drop the gun!' He did not drop the gun, and the agent killed him."

Because of that tragic outcome, the FBI has changed its policies for what it calls "slap-on" installations.

"We now require notification of local law enforcement, unless a compelling reason is cited," Grever says. "The tech agents are required to wear body armor and have readily available official identification. There must be a documented operations plan that addresses contingencies. Interdiction teams must be at the ready and close enough to keep a subject from confronting exposed and vulnerable agents."

Now, instead of taking place on a street or in a parking lot, such operations are conducted in what Grever euphemistically calls a "controlled environment." For example, if the bureau is wiretapping a target's calls under a court order, agents will hear when he is planning to bring his car in for servicing. If they trust the auto repair company, they may enlist its cooperation and install a GPS tracking device when the car comes in.

"Another option is to steal the car," Grever says. "Of course, we are not technically stealing the car, as we will obtain a court order authorizing the FBI to seize the vehicle long enough to implant any device that we have lawful authority to install." On second thought, Grever says, "Maybe a better word is 'borrow.' When we borrow a car, we will usually park an exact duplicate of the car in the same spot for the brief time we have the vehicle, should the subject or an associate happen to check on the car."

In one case in New York City, the target showed up and looked in what he thought was his car, then drove off in his wife's car. His car was actually down the street in the bay of a fire station having a tracking device installed. But to allay suspicion in such a case, "as part of our tradecraft, we always remove visible items from the subject's car, such as bags or briefcases, and place them in our look-alike car," Grever says.

TacOps has considered rekeying the locks and ignition in the substitute car to match the target car, but drivers would probably notice that the substitute car had a different telltale squeak or smell. Luckily, says Grever, "no one so far has tried to take one of our look-alike cars for a joy ride."

# The Hunt

After 9/11, the reflexive criticism became that the FBI and the CIA had not connected the dots. The implication was that the two agencies could uncover plots simply by moving a cursor around on a computer screen. But in no way would that have uncovered the kind of carefully compartmented scheme devised by Osama bin Laden and a few of his top lieutenants.

To be sure, collating all the existing data and analyzing it properly likely would have led to more aggressive investigations that could have uncovered more leads. Whether those investigations would have stopped the plots is anybody's guess. But it is a certainty that such investigations are necessary to uncover future plots.

The problem before 9/11 was that the information that would uncover the plots was not there in the first place. There were few dots to connect.

Art Cummings' job was to develop intelligence that would uncover those dots. In Cummings' mind, counterterrorism came down to a hunt.

"I know he's there, I know he's trying to kill somebody. How do I find him?" he would say. "It's about understanding the behavior and the activity, what the bad guy looks like and smells like and breathes like, and then actually putting a system together to go hunt for that."

Early on, Cummings set up the FBI's interrogation operations at Guantánamo and learned first-hand how to get terrorists to cooperate without using coercive methods. When Cummings first showed up at Guantánamo, the American general in charge said, "I don't know why you are here. You're not going to arrest any of these guys."

"General, you have a fundamental lack of understanding of what the FBI does for a living," Cummings told him. "We're not going to come here with handcuffs. My job is intel collection. I need to get what's in their head out of their head."

When Cummings and other agents observed egregious conduct during interrogations at Guantánamo, they reported it back to FBI head-quarters. In October 2002, a Marine captain squatted over a copy of the Koran during intensive questioning of a Muslim prisoner. That same month, interrogators wrapped a bearded prisoner's head in duct tape because he would not stop quoting the Koran. One interrogator bragged to an FBI agent that he had forced a prisoner to listen to Satanic black metal music for hours, then dressed as a Catholic priest before "baptizing" him. Such conduct was not condoned by military policies.

Coercive techniques were nothing new to Cummings. During training as a Navy SEAL, Cummings had been subjected to such techniques, including waterboarding, that might be used on him if he were captured. But he argued that coercive and degrading techniques likely wouldn't work on hardened Islamic militants.

"Okay, let me understand this," he would say. "You are going to somehow coerce a young jihadist who has just traveled a thousand miles through desert and unfamiliar territory to go put his ass on the line to die in really austere, dirty, nasty, rocky conditions, wholly untrained. And you think you're going to somehow make this guy uncomfortable? You found this guy in a cave starving and drinking only water, and what are you going to do to this guy that will compel him to do anything except hate you more?"

On the other hand, "if you're going against Johnny down the street, who was brought up in middle-class America, yeah, it would probably work," Cummings says. "When talking about a jihadist, maybe it would work, maybe it wouldn't."

Cummings concedes that coercive techniques may elicit information faster. But he says, "You may actually encourage deception. So whatever it takes to get my head out of that bucket of water, I'm going to tell you something that's going to make that happen."

Cummings knew what does work. Maybe others couldn't understand how FBI agents turned murderers into cooperative sources without using aggressive tactics. But the fact is, says Cummings, "we've had case after case after 9/11 of genuine, real, true-to-life bad guys who have sat down in hotel rooms with us, for weeks on end, just pouring it out."

While the FBI likes to think it takes the moral high ground, "that's not really the driving reason," Cummings says. "The driving reason's, frankly, because we think we as an organization are much more effective working that way. And it doesn't take that much time. It's something you learn as you go. You work with somebody, you see what resonates with him. Is it family that drives him? Is it children that drives him? Is it career that drives him? Is it freedom that drives him? What is it that motivates him and keeps him motivated?"

The approach is the same as in working a criminal case.

"You have a drunk driver, you work everything from rationalization to all kinds of different themes," Cummings says. "You say, 'I know you didn't mean it. Of course you didn't. You left the scene, it was kind of stupid, we've all done that,' when really it's not the case. When you see a little sparkle, then you work that theme."

On the other hand, the CIA could point to

plots that were rolled up because of leads to individual terrorists developed through coercive interrogation techniques. CIA officials say that, regardless of what techniques are used, they try to corroborate any information gleaned from a terrorist. Even intercepts of conversations are not infallible, they note. A conversation could be a setup, so the CIA has to try to verify any information it obtains.

In seeking cooperation from a terrorist at Guantánamo, Cummings would try out different themes.

"You try to understand the kid, whoever he is," he says. "Most of them are very young. You try to find out what's driving him, what's important to him based on his culture. It could be marriage and children."

Cummings would say something like: "You're never going to see your mother again." He explains, "Kids will be tough, but one of the values that should never be lost is compassion. You're never unkind for the sole purpose of being unkind. Not because we're just a bunch of great people, but because compassion actually works. We will sit down in front of a bank robber and tell him his life is completely off track, and if he ever wants to live the life of a normal human again, he needs to get it back on track. It's a compelling argument."

Cummings found that what drives terrorists to

respond most is a look into their future.

"You understand, you're going to die in this steel box," Cummings would say. "And when you're dead, your life is nothing. You will die, and you will be nothing to anyone. When you die, you will be in an unmarked grave, and no one will know how you died, when you died, or where you're buried."

Cummings would look for body language that would tip him off to whether his approach was working. If not, he might take another tack.

"I saw one kid who was sitting there, not moving," Cummings says. "The tears were coming down by the gallons when I started talking to him about never having a child," he recalls. "He wasn't blubbering, but I knew I had him. Maybe it takes a couple days. But I'm not going to slap him on the side of the head. All that does is steel him—steel his courage. It reinforces why he hates me so much."

Instead, Cummings would offer hope: "If you ever want me to make the argument for you, I'm the conduit that gets you out of here," he would say. "I'm it. Look at me directly in the eyes. I'm it! No one else in the world. That's it. You'll have to help me out, and I'll help you out."

Most are susceptible to creature comforts as well.

"That's the one thing plenty of time will always give you," Cummings says. "Eventually, these guys just get tired of living in austere conditions, and the government offers them different accommodations based on different levels of cooperation. I got this guy who was in Guantánamo Bay and had tried to go on a jihad. He saw a little snuff on my lip—I don't dip anymore. He asked for some, so I said, 'Sure.' I gave him some."

The doctors at the base "went nuts because I was giving him snuff," Cummings says. "I said, 'Okay, enlighten me here. What's the problem?' 'Well, it's not healthy.' "

"The only reason he's talking to me is because I'm supplying him with snuff," Cummings told the doctors. "So I'm going to be bringing a tin of Copenhagen every time I interrogate this guy," Cummings said. "And I guarantee you that every time before he starts talking, he's going to put a big ol' mighty healthy dip in his lip."

The terrorist wound up talking to Cummings.

When Cummings returned from Cuba, Mueller asked what he had learned.

"What we got was a general understanding of this whole mind-set," Cummings told him.

"Are we getting any tactical answers?" the director asked.

"Well, tactical stuff is only good for a week or two weeks after they're captured," Cummings said. "These guys have been in for months. But they can teach us everything about how the organization moves its money, moves its people, where did they get their education, when did they get radicalized, when did that happen, at what age?"

Cummings found that religious fanaticism was not necessarily the driving force among all terrorists.

"Islamic extremism was a factor," he says. "But a lot of these guys were young and adventure-seeking. A lot of them were pressured by their families to go check that box: they wanted the jihadi badge of honor. But believing that when they died they would have seventy-two virgins waiting for them and that this was just a wonderful thing to die in the service of Allah was not the driver."

As with detainees, Cummings looked at suspects as collection platforms. That approach worked well back in 2002 with Iyman Faris, who had been tasked to take down the Brooklyn Bridge by Khalid Sheikh Mohammed (known as KSM), the architect of the 9/11 plot. The Pakistanis were about to arrest a relative of Mohammed's, but Cummings asked the CIA to get the Pakistanis to hold off until surveillance could be put in place on others who could be expected to react to the man's arrest.

The Pakistanis "gave us four hours, total," Cummings says. "We basically identified that guy's associates in the U.S. in four hours—we knew about some of them—and basically put collection [electronic surveillance] in place, leading to Faris."

After a FISA application was approved, the FBI began wiretapping Faris.

"Faris was someone who had gone overseas and reached out for al Qaeda," Cummings says. "He had some connections in Pakistan. He met KSM, who tasked him to come back into the U.S. and study how to drop the Brooklyn Bridge."

Faris "actually was looking at some cutting devices for cutting the cable," Cummings says. "You can imagine some idiot sitting up there straddling an eighteen-inch cable with a cutting torch, trying to cut the cable," Cummings says. "He would have been tackled and probably beaten to death by the New Yorkers before he got very far. But he was looking at a number of other things at the same time. The problem was, he was a research conduit for al Qaeda central, directly. So eventually he probably would have gotten to a point where they would have given him something useful. He also knew a lot of people."

Before 9/11, Cummings says, "we would have indicted him, taken him to jail, and worked with his lawyers to see if he wants to cooperate. Absolutely. After 9/11? No way. We approach him, using smart agents with lots of experience to convince him that it's in his best interest to work with us."

Faris quickly agreed to cooperate.

"We worked him for over a month—worked him and worked him and then worked him some more," Cummings says. "We had the agency and military and everybody on board with us."

In June 2003, Faris pleaded guilty to providing material support and resources to al Qaeda and to conspiracy for providing the terrorist organization with information about possible U.S. targets. In October, he was sentenced to twenty years in prison.

Cummings applied the same approach to Mohammed Junaid Babar, an American citizen who was based in London but traveled periodically to the United States and Pakistan. The FBI became suspicious of him when NSA found he was emailing al Qaeda operatives from a New York City library. Attorney General Ashcroft later cited the Babar case as an example of why the FBI needed to be able to monitor computers in libraries. Meanwhile, the Brits picked up intelligence on a plot to blow up locations in London. Clues from that cell led to Babar.

"We were working with them, and they gave us intel about the cell that they had in the U.K. and the ties to Babar," Cummings says. "We took all of that, and we began to run it through all of our systems—CIA, FBI, NSA. We then tracked him. He was flying into the U.S. There was an initial impulse on the part of the community at large to react directly to him coming to the U.S. They said, 'Okay, what are we going to do about this guy right now? We can't let him come in.' "

Cummings argued that the FBI should use him as a collection platform.

"Everybody stay back, stay away from this guy," Cummings would say. "We got his picture, we know when he's coming in, what flight he's coming on, we've got all of that. It does the U.S. government and the counterterrorism mission no good to take him off the street. It does nothing for us. I don't know why he's coming here, I don't know what his connections are. But I need the opportunity to spend as long as I need to spend collecting against him."

Working with the other agencies, the FBI did just that.

"New York had the case, and headquarters micromanaged the daylights out of it," Cummings says. "We worked everything we could possibly work against Babar. We surrounded him with everything—a full net of collection. Technical, physical, airplanes, surveillance teams, everybody." He points out, "A lot of it seems like overkill, but it's not. Babar was an operator. He had sent some guys through training, and they were now going to murder some people."

Cummings needed to give the attorney general

and the director confidence that the FBI had this under control and could work Babar on the street while agents collected against him.

"It was that balance that's weighed every single day on an operation like this," Cummings says. "The daily discussion was: 'What's the current intel on Babar? What's the current threat? And can we tell the attorney general and director that we have 100 percent confidence that he's not going to get away and kill somebody?' We could only assure a confidence level of 99.9 percent. There's always a chance that something is going to happen."

Once the FBI knew everything about Babar, agents moved in. In April 2004, the FBI, working with the New York Joint Terrorism Task Force, arrested him on Long Island. Facing the possibility of life in jail, he quickly flipped and agreed to cooperate.

"Babar just wanted to save his ass," Cummings says. "Babar plainly and simply knew that he was going to die in an American prison. And a deal is what we have to offer, right? You have to offer an incentive to talk."

Babar pled guilty to five counts of providing, and conspiring to provide, money and supplies to al Qaeda terrorists fighting in Afghanistan against U.S. international forces. In March 2006, Babar testified against the men accused of plotting bomb attacks in London in March 2004, a plot rolled up in what was known as Operation Crevice. Because of what prosecutors called his "extraordinary" cooperation with the FBI, he was released from prison in December 2010.

# Armed and Dangerous

The FBI Academy sits on 547 acres of land off I-95 in Quantico, Virginia. Pink and white begonias bloom beside the tree-lined entrance road and around the pleasant campus of twenty-one tan brick buildings. In the shade of a passageway between buildings, a tiny spotted baby doe awaits its mother's return.

From a rise just beyond the parking lots, volleys of gunfire ring out like the sound of a firing squad. No one flinches. Trainees and staff walk purposefully through the 9/11 Memorial Courtyard, inured to the barrages coming from firearms training at the range. At the FBI Academy, the sound of bullets is as common as birdsong.

On the wall in the leadership development corridor, a hand-lettered sign offers a gentle reminder: "Be kinder than necessary, for everyone you meet is fighting some kind of a battle."

Going back to the Hoover era, that has been the FBI's approach: treat suspects with respect, then lock them up. But Hoover would not recognize today's academy and its twenty-week training program that turns ordinary men and women into FBI agents.

As one of his first acts, Robert Mueller ordered a training program for analysts at the academy and more training in data mining and leadership. In 2008, he created the FBI School of Intelligence, where "prevention" is the watchword. Trainees are taught the importance of "not only knowing what we know but knowing what we don't know," says agent Jeffrey Mazanec. "It's knowing what you don't know so you can collect against it. We have to be proactive; we don't have the privilege of reacting."

Each year, seventy thousand apply to be new agents. Fewer than a thousand are accepted and graduate from the training program. The average age is thirty, and for most, this is a second career. Most of the trainees have law degrees or other advanced degrees.

While in training, new agents live in dormitories. They are taught how to arrest the bad guys in a fake little town with an alarming crime rate. It's known as Hogan's Alley, where the sign "Hogan's Alley Have a Nice Day" welcomes unsuspecting visitors.

A big feature is the Bank of Hogan, which has the reputation, unproven, of being the most held-up bank in America. If the bank is not robbed twice a week, it could go out of business. And there's a mailbox. It is sealed shut because people used to deposit their mail, and since it's a fake town, no mail carrier would ever pick it up. Still, with all the shoot-'em-ups going on around it, you might well expect a dead letter box.

Visitors pass the Tall Pines area, a park named for the bureau's first encounter with the notorious bank robber John Dillinger in 1934. While agents surrounded Little Bohemia Lodge in Wisconsin, where he was staying, Dillinger escaped through the tall pines. But three months later, special agents Clarence Hurt and Charles Winstead shot and killed Dillinger on July 22, 1934, in front of Chicago's Biograph Theater. At the Biograph replica in Hogan's Alley, the marquee always advertises "Manhattan Melodrama" with Clark Gable and Myrna Loy. The show never closes because it was the last movie Dillinger ever watched.

In this mockup of a little town, there's also a handful of faux boutiques and bars, a deli that sells real sandwiches, and Pollitt's Computer Repair Center. The slogan painted on the store window speaks to all computer-plagued passersby: "It Is What It Is."

At the moment, explains John Wilson, the mayor of Hogan's Alley, also known as the practical applications manager, an extortion money drop is happening at the motel. Trainees are expected to take down the bad guys. The suspects are armed and dangerous. Tires screech, sirens wail. Crime scenarios are staged all day long in Hogan's Alley, and many of them conclude at the motel, where instructors and a legal expert evaluate agent trainees on how they respond.

Hogan's Alley is growing, now sprawling over seven acres, as evidenced by the three tactical houses recently built on Memorial Drive. At 102 Memorial Drive, a matronly white-haired woman sits on a sofa in the living room and leafs through a pile of magazines. Polly Raines, an actor hired by the FBI, leans back with a Mona Lisa smile. She has been handcuffed and shot at. She says her husband also role-plays, and she shares with her visitors that "he's a bad guy today. He has been arrested thousands of times."

Around the corner is the big motel where no one ever checks in or out and guests don't have to check their guns. As the extortion money scenario wraps up, shots are fired and a ne'er-do-well collapses outside his room. The blue weapons that the trainees carry shoot blanks, but the acting is good.

Another bad guy yells, "Somebody call an ambulance!" The trainees ignore him. Could be a diversionary tactic. Meanwhile, lying facedown on the concrete, the ne'er-do-well doesn't move. His friend yells again: "Get a f—— ambulance!" No ambulance arrives. The scenario ends in arrests, then evaluations begin.

Meanwhile, over at the Tactical and Emergency Vehicle Operations Center, agent Stanley Switala, wearing a baseball cap and sunglasses, shows off how agents are trained to drive through rough terrain. As he starts out driving in a 4 x 4 all-terrain Jeep Grand Cherokee Laredo on a strip of grass, you realize this isn't going to be any ordinary ride in the country. When he mentions "front end swing" and "rear wheel cheat," he's talking not about infidelity but about the ins and outs of tight turns.

Switala drives up a twenty-five-degree slope into a woodland, where young elm, maple, oak, tulip poplar, beech, and pine trees crowd the muddy tracks of the off-road course, which stretches more than a mile. This is what Switala calls "tight quarters driving," where "you realize the four corners of the vehicle." There's no breathing room on either side, but he negotiates it as though he does it every day, which he probably does.

"In the woods, your depth perception is off," because of all the trees and the sunlight's dappling effect at certain times of day, he says. "I find it's even better without my sunglasses on off-roading," he says as he turns sharply at a trail marker.

He talks about the bridge he is crossing, made of poles. You look back behind you, and it is literally two poles, one for each tire. The gentle ride under the green canopy turns into a stomach churner, up hillsides at a cockeyed angle, like the breathless climb on a roller-coaster before it plummets.

The off-road training is for tactical units like the Hostage Rescue Team and SWAT teams, but all agent trainees must drive an obstacle course with FBI sedans. This obstacle course is a giant playground dotted with orange cones close together in serpentine lines. Every cone knocked down costs the trainee a deduction of 5 points from a starting score of 100. Passing is 75. Another exercise requires trainees to drive the same course of tight turns with a Bu-car in reverse the whole time.

Trainees must also pass collision avoidance, where the trainee is supposed to drive safely while reading maps, getting questioned over the radio, and looking out the window to identify characteristics of a bad guy—actually a manne-quin—on the street.

Inside a classroom that houses the Firearms Training Simulator, trainees watch different arrest scenarios on a large screen. As the inter-active video plays on the screen, the agent trainees act as though they're in the scenario, making life-or-death decisions in a situation that is quickly unraveling. They are ready to shoot their digital pistol if necessary. Is a suspect going for a gun or a cell phone? Trainees don't have to know for sure, but they have to have a reasonable belief before they fire. They can't wait until the bad guy shoots them.

For future agents, the Firearms Training Simulator is stress inoculation: to keep your head when others are losing theirs. Beware the sympathetic reflex—keep your finger off the trigger until you're ready to fire. And if you must fire, go for the center mass or head shot.

And watch out for "Tina," a tricky scenario where the suspect on the big screen is a woman in a plaid shirt and jeans working in a warehouse. You and another agent are attempting to question her. As her anger grows, she knocks down your partner and comes at you with a karate kick. It's too late for talk. To your surprise, she takes your service weapon and shoots you.

"We use deadly force to eliminate an imminent threat," agent Jonathan Rudd says. "We continue application of force as the threat continues. We don't fire warning shots, we don't shoot to disable. Shooting at the chest area gives you the best chance for incapacitating. Just because we shoot someone in this center mass area doesn't mean it's going to kill them."

Along with physical and firearms training, recruits are schooled in ethics.

"When you mow the lawn, you're still the FBI," as agent James T. Reese puts it. Agents may be asked by neighbors to intervene in situations they should avoid. "You should tell them to call the police," Reese says. "What you do is give them a logical explanation for why we are not Batman."

The training program uses role players to teach trainees how to conduct interviews. Secretaries, agents, and cooks are enlisted to play the bad guy—or gal. But until Hogan's Alley was built in 1987, trainees chased FBI agents who posed as criminals at the academy. One day, Vincent P. Doherty, then the academy's feisty comptroller, was showing the facilities to official guests. Doherty happened to match a description given to a training class of the perpetrator of a bank fraud. A trainee spotted Doherty and gave the usual warning: "Freeze, FBI!"

Saying he was giving a tour, Doherty said, "Get lost."

Whereupon she flipped Doherty, who found himself lying on the carpet.

About 2 percent of agent trainees flunk out, are kicked out for rules infractions, or decide being an agent is not for them. Often that's because they recognize that they may have to take another human life, and they simply cannot ever see themselves doing that.

Recently a trainee was kicked out because he was arrested for driving while intoxicated while attending training. When he was assistant director over training, James D. McKenzie was walking through the academy when he saw a trainee buy a candy bar from a vending machine, rip it open, throw away the candy, and eat the wrapping. McKenzie called him into his office.

"I was walking down this hall, and I saw you buy a candy bar, throw the candy bar away, and eat the paper," he said to the trainee.

"Yes," the man said.

"What did you do that for?"

The trainee said that when he was a small child, his parents would not let him have candy in his room, so he would sneak it. "I would eat the candy, and then I would eat the paper so there wouldn't be any evidence. After a while, I started to like the paper," he told McKenzie.

"Now, can you imagine this guy being an FBI agent?" McKenzie says. "This guy is out on a surveillance and gets hungry and eats the surveillance log. The guy is a couple of bubbles off center. Naturally, people like that don't become FBI agents. He resigned based on that."

At the end of their training, newly minted agents are issued the .40-caliber Glock 23 they have trained on, along with a Colt M4 carbine, a Remington 870 12-gauge shotgun, and a Heckler & Koch MP5 10-millimeter submachine gun.

"This is actually a calling I felt since undergraduate days," says Ryan, a trainee from Indianapolis who is about to graduate. "This is something that I feel will make a difference, by helping to protect America."

# 23
# Preaching Jihad

As the agent in charge of counterterrorism, Art Cummings, backed by Mueller, put out the word that no lead would be overlooked. Prior to 9/11, if an email came in saying that somebody was going to bomb the Sears Tower, "we would've looked at it and said, 'This is just not realistic,' " Cummings says. "Now we begin knocking on every door. A lead may seem to be 99 percent absolute garbage. But we have no tolerance for the one-tenth of 1 percent. That could get somebody killed."

Hundreds of leads came in about Arab men acting suspiciously—talking in a bar about a terrorist operation, for example.

"Now, is it realistic that Arab men, speaking English, drinking beer, would talk in public about an operation where people can overhear them?" Cummings asks. "I'd love to be able to say, 'No, sorry, nothing's going on in there.' But maybe, just maybe, someone had a foolish moment, talked about something they were actually planning. No way would most of our counterparts go out on that. It may or may not make us better. Makes us busier. Because none of those kinds of leads has panned out."

Still, even as critics called the FBI broken and its agents dumb cops, the bureau began rolling up terrorists every few months. Cummings found that jihadists who were simply inspired by bin Laden rather than controlled by him were becoming more common. For example, Ali Al-Timimi, a spiritual leader at a mosque in northern Virginia, encouraged other individuals at a meeting to go to Pakistan to receive military training from Lashkar-e-Taiba, a designated foreign terrorist organization, in order to fight U.S. troops in Afghanistan. When they returned to the United States, the FBI had them under surveillance.

On September 13, 2002, the FBI arrested five more homegrown terrorists in Lackawanna, New York, for providing material support to al Qaeda. A sixth man was rendered from Bahrain. The case began with an anonymous letter to the FBI, followed by the development of a source within the group, which professed to support bin Laden.

The men were U.S. citizens of Yemeni descent who lived in a tight-knit rural community. The group flew to Afghanistan in the summer of 2001 to train at Osama bin Laden's al-Farouq jihad camp. There, they studied how to make explosives, rocket-propelled grenade launchers, land mines, and other military equipment.

Nobody suspected them of terrorist activities. Indeed, Yasein Taher had been voted the friendliest person in his 1996 high school graduating class. A former captain of the high school soccer team, he married his high school sweetheart, a former cheerleader. Another of the men arrested, Sahim Alwan, was a counselor at the Iroquois Job Center in Medina, New York.

"There was a lot of rhetoric, but you know rhetoric's rhetoric," Cummings says. "Jihadi bravado, we call it. But in terms of law enforcement, jihadi bravado doesn't get you anywhere other than show someone thinks that way. But that does give us enough predication to take a look at them." As the FBI began investigating further, however, the bureau found that they were deadly serious.

"They really wanted to do something," Cummings says. "They went to training camps overseas, they came back, they lived in very, very austere conditions, lived in trailers. But they were second-generation Americans."

In March 2003, the suspects all agreed to plead guilty and cooperate with the FBI. They were sentenced to prison terms ranging from eight to ten years.

While the writer of the letter tipping off the FBI to the Lackawanna case never came forward, he clearly was a Muslim who was a friend or family member of the terrorists. In another case of a Muslim providing leads to the FBI, the father of Mohamed Osman Mohamud tipped off the FBI to his son's extremist proclivities. It turned out the son intended to wage violent jihad by blowing up a 2010 Christmas celebration in Portland, Oregon.

The FBI has outreach programs to try to develop sources in the Muslim community and solicit tips, but Cummings has found little receptivity. He found that while Muslims have brought some cases to the FBI, Muslim leaders in particular are often in denial about the fact that the terrorists who threaten the United States are Muslims.

"I had this discussion with the director of a very prominent Muslim organization here in D.C.," Cummings says. "And he said, 'Why are you guys always looking at the Muslim community?'"

Cummings began laughing.

"Okay, you know what I'll do?" Cummings said. "I'll start an Irish squad, or how about a Japanese squad? You want me to waste my time and your taxpayer's dollars going to look at the Irish? They're not killing Americans. Right now, I'm going to put my money and my people in a place where the threat is."

Then Cummings told him to take a look at the cells the FBI had rolled up in the United States.

"I can name the homegrown cells, all of whom are Muslim, all of whom were seeking to murder Americans," Cummings said. "It's not the Irish, it's not the French, it's not the Catholics, it's not the Protestants, it's the Muslims."

In response to such points, Muslim groups have told him he is rough around the edges.

"I'm not rough around the edges," Cummings tells them. "You're just not used to straight talk."

They respond by getting angry at him.

While Muslims will occasionally condemn al Qaeda, "rarely do we have them coming to us and saying, 'There are three guys in the community that we're very concerned about,'" Cummings says. "They want to fix it inside the community. They're a closed group, a very, very closed group. It's part of their culture that they want to settle the problem within their own communities. They've actually said that to us, which I then go crazy over."

On one hand, "they don't want anyone to know they have extremists in their community," Cummings says. "Well, beautiful. Except do you read the newspapers? Everyone already knows it. That horse has left the barn. So there's a lot of talk about engagement, but realistically, we've got a long, long way to go."

At one meeting, a Muslim group suggested having a photo taken of their members with Bob Mueller to show their community isn't a bunch of terrorists and that they are partners in the war on terror.

Cummings responded, "Let me make a suggestion: When you bring to my attention real extremists who are here to plan and do something, who are here supporting terrorism, and I work that based on your information, then I promise you, I will have the director stand up on the stage with you."

To Cummings' amazement, the answer was, "That could never happen. We would lose our constituency. We could never admit to bringing someone to the FBI."

"Well, we've just defined the problem, haven't we?" Cummings told them.

After 9/11, says Cummings, imams in as many as 10 percent of the two thousand mosques in the United States preached jihad and hatred of America. About a quarter of the Muslims in America ages eighteen through twenty-nine believe that suicide bombings can be justified, according to a Pew Research Center poll. But in more recent years, "preaching jihad and hatred of the U.S. overtly has become more unusual and happens more in private," Cummings says. Instead, "Radicalization on the Internet has risen to fill the void," Cummings says.

"If you look at the websites of the Council on American-Islamic Relations, the Muslim Public Affairs Council, or the Arab-American Anti-Discrimination Committee, you see a passive, almost obligatory approach to condemning terrorism," Cummings says. "The most prominent crisis for the Arab and Muslim communities is this perception that they're terrorists, when only a small fraction of them are. Why wouldn't you have a very loud, active program that says murder of anyone is immoral, illegal, and not consistent with Islam, and anyone who supports terrorism or harbors a terrorist is a problem?"

To be sure, some individual Muslims have brought leads to the FBI. That led to FBI cases in Lackawanna, New York; Lodi, California; and Atlanta, Georgia.

"But I don't see the community doing that," Cummings says. "I talked to a very prominent imam in the U.S. We would have our sweets and our sweet tea. We would talk a lot about Islam. I would say we understand Islam and where they're coming from. We'd tell him what our mission is, trying to keep people from murdering Americans, or anybody else for that matter."

Months later, the FBI found out that the man's mosque had two extremists who were so radical that they kicked them out. Clearly, those two extremists would have been of interest to the FBI. If they only engaged in anti-American rhetoric, the FBI would leave them alone. More likely they were planning action to go with their rhetoric.

Cummings asked the imam, "What happened?"

"What do you mean?" the imam asked.

"Why didn't you tell me about this?" the agent said.

"Why would I tell you about this?" the imam said. "They're not terrorists. They just hate the U.S. government."

Despite the FBI's success in rolling up terrorists and preventing another attack, Cummings encountered a new threat: a growing movement to do away with the FBI's counterterrorism effort and replace it with a new terror-fighting agency similar to the British MI5. Such an agency would have investigative powers but no law enforcement powers, as the FBI has.

The idea was first floated by William E. Odom, a retired general and former head of the NSA. In a *Washington Post* op-ed headlined "Why the FBI Can't Be Reformed," Odom wrote that the FBI's shortcomings in fighting the terrorist threat are systemic.

"No one can turn a law enforcement agency into an effective intelligence agency," he said. "Police work and intelligence work don't mix. The skills and organizational incentives for each are antithetical. One might just as well expect baseball's Washington Nationals to win football's Super Bowl as believe the FBI can become competent at intelligence work."

These and other similar proposals to break up the FBI came from people who had never investigated terrorism cases and seemed to have no idea how the FBI investigates terrorism post-9/11. That did not stop members of Congress from endorsing the idea, giving them another chance to go on TV.

In fact, the MI5 idea made little sense. It meant creating a new wall that would bifurcate the counterterrorism effort. In Great Britain, when an arrest must be made, MI5 presents the case to a police agency such as the Metropolitan Police, based at New Scotland Yard. MI5 then has the task of trying to persuade that agency to pursue it. Thus, rather than tearing down walls that impede cooperation and sharing of information, an American agency patterned after MI5 would create a new wall.

More important, without law enforcement powers, MI5 cannot use the threat of prosecution to try to elicit cooperation and recruit informants. Because terrorists often finance their activities by smuggling cigarettes, selling stolen designer clothing, or dealing in drugs, the FBI's structure makes it easy for the bureau to pass along leads from agents pursuing these cases to agents focused on counterterrorism.

During creation of a new agency, the country would be vulnerable to attack as investigators are recruited and trained and as they try to develop relations with counterparts in foreign countries. The well-publicized chaos at the Department of Homeland Security, which combined twenty-two agencies and departments, is an illustration of what can happen initially when a new agency is created.

The beauty of the FBI is that its focus on violations of criminal laws keeps its agents from violating civil liberties. Without that framework, agents might begin to stray into investigating political beliefs or dissent or even gathering personal information for the purpose of blackmailing political leaders, as they did when J. Edgar Hoover was director. In doing so, they would lose their compass, forgetting what their target is and botching investigations because of a lack of proper focus.

Cummings considered nutty the idea of handing over such awesome powers to a new agency not trained in law enforcement. Cummings and other agents who worked with MI5 in Great Britain knew that the British officers' work was constantly impeded by their lack of law enforcement powers, although recent changes have improved coordination between MI5 and the police.

"I find it astounding that anyone would take the position that what you want to do is essentially strip away the law enforcement powers and say, 'Now go fight terrorism,' " Cummings says. "To think that you're going to develop a domestic intelligence service from the ground up and do it in anything short of a decade before they can even crawl, let alone walk, is crazy. And then to think that they could do that and still have the organization grounded in the Constitution and the civil liberties that go with that, I think is crazy as well."

Fanning the movement to create an MI5, Richard A. Posner, a U.S. appeals court judge who wrote a book on intelligence, said in a *Washington Post* op-ed that the FBI is oriented toward "arrest and prosecution rather than toward the patient gathering of intelligence with a view to understanding and penetrating a terrorist network."

"The day we arrest someone is the day I can't collect against him anymore," Cummings observes. "I don't know anything about him, I'm operating in the blind. And the day I take somebody off the street, leaving someone on the street who's going to kill me tomorrow, that is the day I haven't done my job."

"The FBI model of combining intelligence and law enforcement responsibility is the envy of allied services, including the British," says John Martin, who, as chief of the U.S. Justice Department's Counterespionage Section for twenty-five years, had extensive dealings with MI5.

"Indeed," he adds, "MI5 is constantly impeded by its inability to quickly translate intelligence operations into arrests and prosecutions. Setting up an MI5 in the United States would create a significant and unnecessary barrier to fighting terrorism and espionage at a time when this country needs to enhance its communications among agencies and to quickly react to terrorist threats."

# 24
## Year of the Ponzi Scheme

After 9/11, Mueller shifted 2,000 agents who were working criminal cases to counterterrorism. That doubled the number of agents pursuing terrorists to 4,000 of the bureau's then complement of about 11,000 agents. He also increased the number of supervisors working counterterrorism at headquarters from 30 to 850. As a result, good criminal cases involving white-collar crime or political corruption were not pursued.

"I've been in meetings with U.S. attorneys where they were screaming for more agents for fraud cases," says Thomas Fuentes, a former FBI assistant director in charge of international operations.

Agents—many of whom did not like change to begin with—grumbled about Mueller's leadership. But as the economic downturn exposed shaky banks and other financial firms that had been cutting corners, Mueller began increasing the number of agents assigned to criminal work. He was able to do that because the number of agents within the bureau increased each year.

Heading that effort was Thomas J. Harrington,

the executive assistant director in charge of the FBI's Criminal, Cyber, Response, and Services Branch. Harrington had wanted to become an agent ever since he took his FBI agent father to his kindergarten class in Fitchburg, Massachusetts, as part of show-and-tell. He saw how impressed and excited his classmates were.

An accountant by training, Harrington moved up the bureau ladder supervising counterterrorism and financial fraud and becoming involved in improving FBI management and computer systems. In Denver, he put together an FBI undercover operation that took two FBI-controlled companies public to uncover corruption within the penny stock market. Harrington led a team of investigators to identify cases of abuse of prisoners at Guantánamo Bay and, on behalf of the FBI, wrote a letter to the Pentagon objecting to some of the harsh interrogation practices used.

As chief of the FBI's criminal side, Harrington has seen close up the effects of the recession on financial crime.

"The economy, unfortunately, began to fall apart on us," Harrington says. "The last couple of years have been the year of the Ponzi scheme. We've had one huge investment fraud after another. I think Warren Buffett probably said it best: you don't realize who's swimming naked until the tide goes out. And that's exactly what happened."

After his two sons turned him in, Bernard Madoff, seventy, admitted to two FBI agents who met with him at his Manhattan apartment that the investment arm of his firm was "basically a giant Ponzi scheme" and that it had been insolvent for years. The firm took in $22.5 billion but claimed in statements to investors that their accounts were worth $60 billion. Madoff's undoing was the plunging stock market, preventing him from honoring requests by investors for their money. It was the biggest known Ponzi scheme in history, wiping out the life savings of thousands of investors. Instead of being worth millions, many found they had to subsist on social security payments.

"These folks trusted this man because of who he was within his community," says Patrick Carroll, the supervisory agent in charge of the investigation. "The victims lost a tremendous amount of money and their dignity because they felt they didn't need to look into who he was. They trusted him."

Cases involving financial fraud are the most time-consuming, Harrington says. "The average bank failure case involving fraud is at least two years, from the time we open it to the time we can get to a charging document."

The size of the companies involved has also grown.

"On 9/11 the number of cases under $100,000

was probably 70 percent of our workload," Harrington says. "It's totally flipped around. In fact, I barely have any cases under $100,000 in financial institution fraud. Sixty-eight percent of mortgage fraud work involves cases well over a million apiece."

The FBI's response to the rising number of cases was to develop a more targeted approach when deciding which cases to pursue.

"We've become more strategic, not necessarily mapping individual events per se but rather looking for the threats in a particular territory," Harrington says. "You sit down with an SAC, and they clearly tell you what threats are in their territory. Previously, they would have tried to tell you about their cases. Today, if you ask them about gangs, they'll talk about the size of their territory and how many gangs are present in that territory, how many gang members, what areas of the city they control, and then the case is a tool that they're using to infiltrate or penetrate that organization and eventually disrupt and dismantle it."

The meetings are held with Mueller. "When he hears things he doesn't like, he brings it up and challenges them," Harrington remarks.

"I still have agents who will say, 'When I joined the outfit I wanted to lock people up.' They feel they're spending too much time on these other things," Harrington says. "The response typically from me is, 'Well, what is the threat that you're working? If it's violent crimes, is it better today?' Most will tell you it's worse. And my thought is, 'Okay, then our strategy has to change, and we have to be more focused.' You can't just arrest everybody who commits crimes. We're going after the worst of the worst, trying to improve these communities as best we can."

Today, the FBI has sixty thousand ongoing criminal cases on everything from kidnappings to the Mafia. Responding to bank robberies is left largely to local police. Instead, cybercrime has become one of the highest priorities, both on the criminal side and on the national security side.

"Some of that is illustrated most recently by Google, which has publicly come out and told folks about losing source code, and believing they'd lost it to Chinese operatives," Harrington says. "There is a challenge on the national security side. Every day, government computers are being attacked by agents of foreign powers or criminal networks trying to seize as much data as possible, and then using it to their advantage."

Criminals who take control of tens of thousands of home and office computers through what are known as botnets are a dramatically growing threat. A botnet—short for "robot network"—

allows a criminal to command any number of computers by introducing malicious programs such as spyware, viruses, worms, or Trojan horses into each computer through its Internet connection.

With a single command, the master of the botnet can instruct each slave computer to contact a particular computer network, bringing it down because of the sheer demand on its ports. A company may lose millions of dollars in business. If the target is a police department or hospital, shutting down its computer system can jeopardize public safety or health.

In addition, slave computers can be used to compromise still more computers for the botnet or to engage in phishing schemes, inducing people to give up their personal information in response to phony emails supposedly sent by banks.

Harrington cites a group that looted the Royal Bank of Scotland of $9.5 million by stealing customers' ATM card numbers and PINs. A flaw in the bank's computer security allowed the intrusion.

"We believe the numbers were then turned over to organized crime elements in Eastern Europe, and they then produced ATM cards," Harrington says. "Within twelve to twenty-four hours, they took literally millions of dollars out of hundreds of ATM machines in dozens of countries. The currency was then reaggregated at some point and paid back to the organized crime syndicates."

Another new cybercrime involves locking down a company's computer system and demanding cash in return for the key to unlocking it.

"We've had some extortions recently where people have broken into a corporate system, and then basically locked the system down, password-protected it," Harrington says. "So the corporation couldn't even get access to its own data. And then the extortion begins with a request for a payment for the password."

Some companies have paid up. In other cases, the FBI's Cyber Division has been able to break the codes and unlock the system.

In 2009, the criminal side of the Cyber Division conducted investigations into 2,600 computer intrusions and 7,300 crimes committed with computers, leading to 1,900 convictions.

At the same time, the FBI has seen an explosion in public corruption cases. Harrington cites the investigations of former Illinois Governor Rod Blagojevich and former U.S. Representative William J. Jefferson, a Louisiana Democrat, who kept $90,000 in cash in his freezer.

Referring to such cases, Harrington says that unfortunately, "public servants sell out their services to the highest bidder in many cases." The FBI has "more agents assigned to public corruption today than we've ever had in the history of the bureau," says Harrington, who subsequently was named associate deputy director of the FBI. "We have thirty-four hundred investigations pending, and over seven hundred agents are currently working public corruption matters. Which I guess cuts both ways. It's good that we're out there and we're doing this; it's unfortunate that it's a target-rich environment."

Despite the explosion in current cases, Mueller decided to back an effort started by agent Cynthia Deitle to try to prosecute Ku Klux Klan members who killed blacks as far back as the 1960s. The effort had its genesis with the FBI's success in reopening its investigation into the September 15, 1963, bombing of the Sixteenth Street Baptist Church in Birmingham, Alabama.

That day, Denise McNair, eleven, and Carole Robertson, Cynthia Wesley, and Addie Mae Collins, all fourteen, were dressed in white party dresses and patent leather shoes for a youth service. Nineteen bundled sticks of dynamite concealed under a stairwell exploded inches from them. All four died, and another girl, Sarah Collins, was blinded in one eye. The bombing shocked the country and contributed to passage of the 1964 Civil Rights Act.

No one was charged back then, but because of the FBI's more recent efforts, former Ku Klux Klan members Thomas E. Blanton Jr. and

Bobby Frank Cherry were convicted in 2001 and 2002, respectively. The case was brought to a successful conclusion by the ingenuity and persistence of FBI agent William L. Flemming. Flemming worked the case after G. Robert "Rob" Langford, the SAC in Birmingham, decided to reopen the bombing case and start a fresh investigation.

Since 2007, Deitle, who heads the FBI's Civil Rights Unit, and her agents have investigated 122 cases from decades ago. About 20 percent turned out not to be murders or were not related to race. In many other cases, no state or federal laws existing back then could be applied, the suspects had already been cleared by all-white juries, or the evidence was just too thin. Even with a fresh murder case, developing evidence is difficult. But Deitle managed to refer six cases to state authorities for possible prosecution, and she expects to refer another six eventually.

"A lot of these guys were tried and acquitted by an all-white jury back in the day, so they can't be retried because it would be double jeopardy," Deitle says. "Even if no prosecutions are possible, we still tell the family what we found."

Reactions have been mixed, ranging from gratitude to open hostility. Some question the thoroughness of the FBI's investigation. Others cannot accept that a suicide or an auto accident was not a hit job by the Ku Klux Klan.

"We've had everything from 'We appreciate your work, thank you' to family members who say they don't want our letter explaining why the case was closed with no prosecution," Deitle says.

# Trip Wires

To hunt down terrorists, the FBI devised what Art Cummings calls "trip wires," which might tip off the bureau to terrorist activity. For example, chemical supply companies are urged by the FBI to develop profiles that pinpoint large or suspicious purchases of chemicals that can be used to make explosives.

To supplement that, Cummings initiated a $350,000 project to, in effect, reverse-engineer a terrorist operation. It looked at a potential terrorist incident and then worked backward to pinpoint all the elements a terrorist might require to achieve his goal, so that the FBI could be on the lookout for those clues.

"We set these trip wires, and when people come across them, we have abilities to report that, wait a minute, someone is buying dual-use technology or the precursors to make nerve gas or industrial-strength peroxide," Cummings says. "Someone does that, boom! We have an alert, either a HUMINT [human intelligence] alert from an individual or a technical alert."

To be a terrorist, "you need communications strategy, you need to be able to raise money, you need to be able to move money, you need an organizational structure that allows for that to happen, and you need communications that go back to the mother ship," Cummings says.

So, he says, the FBI looks at people caught by Customs with cash in excess of $10,000.

"I'm going to correlate this person who is leaving the country with money with his communications," Cummings says. "If he is raising money for Hamas and is communicating with the occupied territories, that is of interest."

Then, he says, "you get the personal transaction reports from the bank and find he is depositing or withdrawing funds just under the $10,000 reporting requirement. You find he is a guy who is Palestinian, goes to a mosque that is dominated by Hamas supporters and Palestinians, and is wiring money on a regular basis to the occupied territories. Right there, I've just built a picture of a Hamas fund-raiser."

In the same way, the FBI has asked beauty shops and beauty supply stores to contact an FBI office to report purchases of chemicals such as hydrogen peroxide in high concentrations.

"They are asked if they have any suspicion of any kind whatsoever about people buying large quantities of such chemicals in industrial strength to make a phone call to the FBI," Cummings says. "Our guidelines are such that we're not going to violate anybody's civil liberties simply because they bought a certain amount of hydrogen peroxide."

News outlets reported that the FBI got onto Najibullah Zazi, who had plotted to blow up New York City subways for al Qaeda, through such purchases. But the case actually began with a combination of intelligence from the CIA and the rest of the intelligence community, Cummings says.

"You've got the people working overseas who did exactly what they were supposed to do, but we caught it at the tenth, eleventh hour," Cummings says. "Zazi was already making explosives. That's cutting it way too close."

On top of that, the New York City Police Department jumped the gun.

"The intelligence division of the NYPD went out and asked some questions, showed some photographs, and that person told Zazi's father and said, 'Hey, they're looking at your son,'" Cummings says. "The father called Zazi. But Zazi's antenna was already up because he may have already detected some surveillance."

While Cummings did not think any malice on the part of the police was involved, "there was an agreement between the New York City Police Department and the FBI New York that any action based on the information we provide has to be coordinated," Cummings says. "And in this case, that just didn't happen."

The press got hold of the story and let Zazi's family know about the investigation, requiring the FBI to make arrests sooner than Cummings desired.

"The press blew us out of the water," he says, and adds, "I'm a very strong believer in the free press. But I also believe it should be more responsible than it is. I hear all the time the public has a right to know. And I look at what they're claiming the public has a right to know, and I just go, what does this do for the public? We regularly have to race the press on an operational strategy. We find out the press is on something and we have to completely change our strategy, because we know a story is going to break on something, and when it breaks we'll lose collection. And when we talk to most of the mainstream press on this, some work with us a little bit but not that much. That makes our job tougher and could jeopardize lives."

The Zazi case involved more than a thousand FBI agents. That included running bomb-detecting dogs through storage facilities. As he did during other fast-breaking cases, Cummings slept on the black leather couch in his office, surrounded by photos of his wife and three kids.

Trip wires led to the arrest of Khalid Ali-M Aldawsari, a twenty-year-old college student from Saudi Arabia who allegedly was planning to blow up the Dallas home of former president

George W. Bush. The FBI received a report from Carolina Biological Supply on February 1, 2011, that Aldawsari had tried to buy large quantities of concentrated phenol, which can be used to make a high explosive. The order was sent to a freight company, which called police in Lubbock, where Aldawsari lived, and the police also notified the FBI.

In two covert entries of his Lubbock apartment, a TacOps team found a hazmat suit, chemicals for making explosives, and bomb-making paraphernalia. In his journal, the team found this entry: "And now, after mastering the English language, learning how to build explosives and continuous planning to target the infidel Americans, it is time for Jihad." The journal said he obtained a scholarship and came to the United States with the intention of carrying out jihad.

The subject line of one email message Aldawsari allegedly sent to himself said "Tyrant's House" and included Bush's Dallas address. Other emails listed "nice targets," including reservoir dams, nuclear power plants, and hydroelectric plants. In addition, he emailed himself ways to construct an explosive device and convert a cellular phone to detonate an explosive device. The suspect posted jihadist sentiments on an extremist blog he created and made it clear he had been inspired by Osama bin Laden.

Besides pinging in on trip wires, the bureau changed the paradigm for declaring that a lead or tip was not valid. Now if a lead turns out to be useless, the FBI requires agents to conclude that "information has been developed to indicate they're not a threat, as opposed to we couldn't verify the information," Cummings says.

Whenever an agent closes a case, he or she is asked the reason.

"The answer better not be 'I didn't find anything to show they were a terrorist,' " Cummings says. "Instead, the answer better be 'I made an informed judgment, based on my collection, that they're not a terrorist. No phone links to terrorists, no finance links, no family links, and I've explained the contacts specifically.' " That, Cummings says, is quite different from saying, "I can't find it, so therefore it's not there."

With the new paradigm, "the labor involved goes up by a factor of five or ten," Cummings says. "To have to continue collecting until you make your own judgment that they're not a terrorist? When basically there's no CIA records, there's no NSA records, there's no FBI records. He doesn't appear to be in a position to be a terrorist. He looks like a regular guy. He's a life insurance salesman, and he's never been out of the country."

In one example of the new approach, when the FBI investigated a report of a man buying chemicals that could be used for explosives, it could have dismissed the purchases as innocent because the man was buying the supplies from a swimming pool company, and his business shipped pool supplies.

"That explanation wasn't good enough," Cummings says. "It's not okay to say, 'It looks like pool supplies, we're done.' You don't finish there. Who at the pool company, specifically, did he buy them from? What specifically was the transaction, and what happened from there? Is it a friend, is it an associate, is it somebody who wants to do us harm? There was a day we would have said, 'It's a commercial transaction, don't worry about it.' Each and every lead is followed all the way down to the most minute detail."

Taking those extra precautions—which never would have been followed prior to 9/11 —frustrates agents.

"They say, 'Come on, it's a pool supply company—the guy ships pool parts,'" Cummings says. "We say, 'Great. Go see the company records, find out who bought what, where it was shipped, what was the item exactly, does it have dual-use possibilities? And when you've finished all that, then we can make an informed judgment.'"

Before 9/11, "it's unlikely the Aldawsari arrest would have happened," Cummings says flatly.

Cummings credits new Justice Department

guidelines developed under Attorney General Michael Mukasey in 2008 with giving the FBI the freedom needed to look for potential terrorists before they strike. The FBI must have a proper purpose before conducting surveillance, but suspicion of wrongdoing is not required.

"As they were written before, the guidelines did not allow FBI agents to look for that which in effect hadn't been seen yet," says Cummings, who pushed for the changes. "Sure, investigations spider out significantly, and leads take you in many different directions. But they start with a lead, they start with tangible information—be it from financial or operational planning or from a telephone call or a source or an informant—telling you this person is involved in terrorism."

The guidelines, in turn, bolstered the new paradigm of prevention, "allowing us to collect before we see the problem," Cummings says.

As FBI general counsel Val Caproni puts it, "The guidelines allow us to look to see if we have a problem, rather than waiting for someone to tell us about it, before bodies start falling."

As with the Zazi case, Cummings says, "The whole mission is complemented by a suite of tools. We could not function as a prevention organization on terrorism without NSA on collection. Could not. Absent that, we'd be blind in what constitutes everything but the United States."

When an arrest occurs, "what you don't see is

the CIA and the broader community hand," Cummings says. "When you see a terrorist plot disrupted in Germany, or you see a terrorist plot disrupted in Austria or Switzerland or Norway or Italy, name it, the CIA's hand is on most of those."

Before 9/11, "I used to battle NSA," Cummings says. "If there was an American's name attached to any of it, and he was going overseas, they wouldn't give it to us."

President Bush's NSA intercept program changed that, giving NSA more flexibility to intercept calls from overseas to Americans. However, the initial program was so broad that it uncovered nothing of value, FBI officials say. As time went on, the program was refined and became more focused on potential terrorists, uncovering useful leads. Congress incorporated that program into the existing FISA statute.

As lone wolves become an increasing threat, trip wires have become especially important. Lone wolves have no ties to existing terrorist organizations or networks. With lone wolves, "you don't have financial networks that if you look really, really closely you see a thousand dollars going to an operator somewhere," Cummings notes. "We don't see it, because there isn't someone sending that lone wolf a thousand dollars. This is very difficult, so we rely heavily on trip wires and HUMINT. These are the eyes and ears on the street. And we rely heavily on the lone wolves' breaking out of that complete and absolute isolation. Human nature being what it is, they do. We've caught several recently who were pretty isolated, but they still wanted to talk and share their ideology with people."

That was what led to the arrest in October 2010 of Farooque Ahmed, thirty-four, of Ashburn, Virginia, for conspiring with people he thought were al-Qaeda operatives to carry out terrorist bombings at stations in the Washington Metro subway system. Agents posing as Islamic radicals began meeting in April with Ahmed, a naturalized U.S. citizen born in Pakistan. At the meetings, held in northern Virginia hotels, he allegedly agreed to conduct video surveillance of the stations and suggested the best time to attack and the best locations to place explosives to maximize casualties.

Still, problems remain. The FBI would have targeted Nidal Malik Hasan, the U.S. Army major who shot to death thirteen people at Fort Hood, if it had known everything the Army knew about his activities and sympathies, Cummings says.

For example, Hasan told colleagues that sharia law trumps U.S. law and lectured other doctors that nonbelievers should be beheaded and have boiling oil poured down their throats. The FBI was in the dark about that, while the Army was fully aware of Hasan's threatening comments and extremist beliefs. In fact, despite his statements in meetings, the Army gave him good performance ratings.

"People say, 'Why didn't you stop him when he was talking to radical cleric Anwar al-Awlaki? Clearly he's a terrorist,' " Cummings says. "Well, no, it's not clear he's a terrorist. There's a continuum between having sympathies and being a militant."

On the surface, it appeared that Hasan was in contact with al-Awlaki, the radical imam in Yemen, to conduct research on Muslims in the military within the context of the war on terrorism, Cummings says.

"His contacts with al-Awlaki to ask him for certain advice appeared to anyone looking at it to be research consistent with the paper he was writing on behalf of, and funded by, the U.S. military," Cummings says. "His questions were probing: 'Well, what about this, and how do you justify that?' So where was the snapping point?" he asks. "Where was it when he moved to being a militant?"

What apparently pushed Hasan over the edge were his orders to deploy to Afghanistan, where he would be fighting fellow Muslims.

To this day, Cummings says, because the Army is conducting the prosecution of Hasan, it has not turned over to the FBI records that would have raised red flags about his beliefs and sympathies.

# Yacht Party

On a crisp fall day, a half dozen gorgeous young women showed up for a champagne party on board a yacht cruising the Eastern Seaboard. The men at the party were the bad guys in an organized crime case; the female guests, all undercover FBI agents.

The men were on board at the invitation of another undercover agent who had befriended them. The idea was to divert the men while TacOps performed a covert entry at two organized crime businesses. In this case, the yacht belonged to the FBI, which had confiscated it in a drug operation and transferred it to the bureau's Stagehand program.

For the yacht party, the female agents flew in from a field office on the West Coast to lessen the chance they would be recognized. If any of the men tried to leave the party by boat, the agents were to send a prearranged coded electronic message to a command center, which would warn TacOps agents conducting the covert entries to leave immediately.

Both covert entries, to plant bugging devices and copy hard drives, went off flawlessly. But there was one hitch: the men were so smitten with the friendly female agents that they insisted on partying long after the TacOps agents had finished their work for the night.

"To keep our subjects comfortable and unsuspecting, the party had to go on for several more hours, even after the TacOps teams had cleared the two targets," says Louis Grever, who participated in one of the entries. "This episode ended up being one of the rare instances where the entry crew was able to get to bed in our hotel rooms before all the surveillance and undercover teams were able to head home."

Given the explosion in ways people communicate, bugging a room would seem less important than in years past. But the growth in communication methods and the availability of encryption software has made it harder for the FBI to ping in on conversations. As a result, bugging devices have become even more essential.

"One of the by-products of this connected world is sometimes we can't collect intelligence on the outside even if we have the authority to do so," Grever says during an interview at FBI headquarters. "The data is encrypted, we're hard pressed to find out what kind of communications path they're using, they hide in the noise and the clutter of modern-day communications. So consequently we have to go to you and install a microphone to catch your communications."

Grever walks over to his desk and returns with a state-of-the-art FBI bug, which he places in my hand. It's a circuit board that is the size of a postage stamp and the thickness of two stacked quarters.

"It's a transmitter and a stereo recorder," Grever says. "It records for about twenty-one hours, and it will transmit to a local receiver in encrypted form. Lots of times the transmit function would not be enabled. Why transmit when it's just another thing that could potentially expose the penetration? This is actually big in comparison to some of our bugs."

Grever shows how the bug can be concealed inside the rechargeable battery of a cell phone. Alternatively, the FBI could program a cell phone to record and transmit conversations.

While bugs are made in the FBI's Engineering Research Facility, they are secreted inside what TacOps agents refer to as a "host" or a "concealment" by the off-site TacOps Center. It could be a battery, a plaque, a calculator, or even a book. To allay suspicion, the center portrays itself as an industrial testing company.

"We make it look like a functioning company with people driving in and out and machines going all the time, so the mailman, the delivery person, the county inspector will come by and think it's a legitimate company," Grever says.

Besides TacOps agents, the center has a staff

of fifty engineers, woodworking specialists, machinists, and other support personnel. There's a machine shop, a high-speed engraving machine, and a stereolithography machine for making plastic items such as a mug that could conceal a bug in its base. The Tactical Operations Section, which includes the center, has a budget of $62 million a year out of the FBI's annual budget of $8.3 billion. The FBI section receives some additional funding from the National Intelligence Program.

To hide TacOps agents as they defeated the lock on a Baltimore townhouse, agents first photographed the brick exterior of the house. The TacOps Center then imprinted the image on a tarp that would cover the entryway and surrounding areas. One side of the tarp was coated with plastic, and the other side had a cloth finish, on which the image was printed. The tarp was attached to light plastic tubing so it could be folded and opened like an umbrella. Agents carried it in an elongated gym bag. In the middle of the night, they erected it two feet in front of the entryway. Then they worked from behind it to make a key to the house without being noticed by passersby.

"Our TacOps machine shop made lightweight frames to hold the façade, and our TacOps print shop created a life-size drapery of the front of the townhouse," Grever says. "We practiced hanging the façade several times to get it right and get it up fast. From twenty feet away in dim light, you could not tell it was simply a picture. The operation went like clockwork, and the many people who passed by that night were none the wiser."

For another job involving an organized crime target in Las Vegas, the TacOps Center created a bush to camouflage two TacOps agents so they could defeat the locks on a garage door and plant bugs in the house. An image of a bush was imprinted on cloth. As with the image of the townhouse, it was attached to plastic tubing and could be opened and folded like an umbrella. When unfolded, the bush was shaped like a cup turned upside down. Working on a dark night, the agents inched toward the garage door while shielding themselves from any passersby on the street, which was about a hundred feet from the house. While the agents could have hidden themselves inside the bush, they preferred to hold it in front of them so they could run away quickly if challenged.

"The only difference between this bush and others around the target that night was that every few minutes, when all was quiet, the bush would grow legs and walk ever so slowly closer to the building," Grever says. "Thank goodness no one saw us. We might have ended up on *America's Funniest Home Videos*."

Before planting bugs in a yacht, agents practice breaking into an identical model. In penetrating supersensitive places such as embassies or other foreign government installations, TacOps agents may proceed in phases.

"You may break into the first set of doors and take pictures of those," Grever says. "You'll do measurements, and then the next night you'll try to go a little bit farther and locate sensors. We'll wait weeks between phases just to make sure there's no commotion."

While the easiest way to gain entry is with the help of an inside source, that source may be a double agent.

"That's a balancing act the case agents will evaluate," Grever says. "Am I going to try to develop a source, or am I going to do everything covertly? There are instances where we would do both. We would develop a source inside, and then the entry operation is really to validate that source, to make sure that source is telling us everything he knows and to verify his information."

TacOps checks weather forecasts to help choose the right night for an entry.

"We try to work when the weather's bad, believe it or not," TacOps chief Jimmy Ramirez says. "We like fog, cold, rain, and snow because people aren't walking around having a good time."

But snow poses a special problem. "You have to be careful not to leave what we call bunny tracks going in and out of the target," Ramirez says. "If it's snowing hard and we're going to leave evidence that we were there, we would abort the mission. If it is imperative that we get in, then we would make arrangements to have the streets and sidewalks plowed first."

Pretending to be good neighbors, FBI personnel will shovel the walks of a target home and the walks of adjoining homes.

Another challenge is working with agents from the local field office.

"I'm real careful when I work with a guy that I don't know," Ramirez says. "Is he going to leave a strip of wire on the ground? Is my lock guy going to leave some filings from a file when he was working on a key?"

The last man out has the greatest responsibility.

"You're responsible for resetting the alarm, locking the doors, making sure that nobody left screwdrivers and wires," Grever notes. "You have a lot of responsibility, you're doing it sometimes in a short amount of time with very little sleep. I might not have slept all night, and now it's four o'clock, five o'clock in the morning. That can be scary."

TacOps agents consider the greatest threat to be what they call the "Mrs. Kravitz factor."

"We know from a technical aspect that we've

got this equipment that we're going after, and we have the equipment to attack it," Ramirez says. "But you can't plan for Mrs. Kravitz getting up in the middle of the night and looking across the street and saying, 'Something is not right with the Joneses' house tonight.' "

By 4:30 a.m., agents had finished a job in a single-family home in the San Francisco area and were ready to leave. "The two neighbors on each side of the house came outside and began doing t'ai chi, their morning ritual," Ramirez says.

Another complication is a neighbor who decides to do yard work early in the morning, perhaps trimming his hedges.

"We may go to their front door and ring the doorbell, and ring and ring and ring, and that gets him away from the hedge or stops the neighbors doing their t'ai chi just long enough to get the final guys out of there," Ramirez says.

Agents plan ruses carefully because they can easily unravel. Thinking it's an innocuous statement, an agent may tell someone that he's a high school teacher.

"They're going to either be a high school teacher, or they're going to know a high school teacher from the school where you said you were teaching, and now you've got to lie more," Ramirez says. "So you've got to be really careful with your cover story. You've got to think about it. Because if you don't, and you kind of stutter

315

and stammer, it's not going to be believable."

TacOps may send an agent to a home posing as a pizza delivery man. When the front door is opened, he can see if the home has an alarm keypad and what kind it is.

"They didn't order pizza. But what if they decide they want some?" Ramirez says. "You can't just have a cardboard box. You better have pizza in it or they'll become suspicious."

Posing as a telephone repair crew can be a problem if real workers show up.

"One time we were at a telephone company outside box, and some phone company guys showed up," Ramirez recalls. "Fortunately, we were in New York, where one of the guys on the team knew the security guy for that area. The security person basically told them, 'You guys just get the hell out of here,' and they did."

In assessing a target, agents try to come up with a ruse that cannot be traced back to anyone. "We'd carry around posters with photos of a lost dog," Clay Price says. "The dog could be one of ours. If anybody ever came up and asked, 'What are you guys doing around here?' we would say, 'We lost our dog. Have you seen this dog?' Then we just get lost."

In some terrorism or counterintelligence cases, TacOps may assess the target for as long as two years. It may take another two years before a case comes to fruition. In a kidnapping or missing-child case, the results are more immediate. TacOps microphones have picked up two parents discussing how they disposed of their child's body.

In the case of a motorcycle gang in Reno, it was too risky breaking into their club. Agents waited. Eventually a member was killed in a traffic accident.

"They all went to the funeral, giving us an opportunity to do their clubhouse. They left no one behind," Ramirez says.

Similarly, in a mob case in Cleveland, agents planted bugs while the target was attending his daughter's wedding at a nearby church.

Still, TacOps agents experience close calls. In an entry in New Haven, the surveillance team had missed the fact that a restaurant owned by an organized crime figure received nightly deliveries of bread.

"We get there, we're in, we've got the alarm shut off, and the bread delivery guy shows up at four a.m.," Ramirez says. "The owner trusts the bread delivery guy, gives him the key, gives him the alarm code."

When they heard the bread man enter the restaurant, the agents ran to hide. When he left, he reset the alarm. Heat and motion detectors would sense the agents coming out of their hiding places. But the agents had picked up electronic information from the alarm control panel and were able to turn it off remotely through wireless technology. Then they finished installing microphones in the Mafia figure's office.

In a spy case in San Francisco, a cleaning service crew walked in while agents were installing bugs in an office building. The agents pretended that they belonged there, and the cleaning people did their work and left without becoming suspicious.

Before entering a store in Cleveland, agents had to open a heavy steel roll-down door covering the front. Obtaining the key was no problem. But when agents rolled down the door, it made a racket. Surveillance thought nobody was in the apartment upstairs, but that turned out to be wrong. The neighbor stuck his head out a window and yelled, "What in the hell is going on down there?"

A supervisor yelled up, "Police business. Just go back inside." The neighbor was involved in the case and reported it to the bad guy, saying he thought the men might have been serving a search warrant.

As a result of the call, Ramirez says, "the subject got so nervous that he hired an attorney and walked into the local FBI office and says, 'I want the best deal I can get. I know you guys have me. I know you've got recordings of me.' He got so paranoid he went in and coughed up the whole story."

At a Mafia social club in New York, a pad-locked steel gate protected the front door. A problem arose in extracting the cylinder of the lock, and agents had to pound on it, making a noise. In this case, the FBI was already monitoring the Mafia figures in an apartment above the store, where they were playing cards. The Mafia men heard the noise.

"We got them on tape saying, 'Well, it can't be the FBI. They wouldn't make that much noise breaking into a place,'" Ramirez says.

The men continued playing cards.

Back in the Hoover days, the program for break-ins in counterintelligence cases was code-named Anagram. When breaking into one Soviet-bloc embassy, an agent had a heart attack and died in the ambassador's office. Agents carried him out, but his bowels emptied on an oriental rug in the office. The agents took the carpet to a dry cleaner that operated all night and had it cleaned. However, it was still wet when they replaced it, so they applied paint to the ceiling above to make it look as if the ceiling had been leaking.

Agents find their surveillance sometimes picks up crimes in progress. In a chilling episode, an FBI bug picked up the sounds of Zein Isa, a Palestinian American, murdering his sixteen-year-old daughter. For two years, the FBI had been listening to the conversations that took place in the tiny St. Louis apartment he shared with his wife, Maria. The bureau believed Zein Isa was involved in terrorist activities.

Isa disapproved of the fact that his daughter Palestina had gotten a job at Wendy's and, without his permission, was seeing a young man. When the girl, nicknamed Tina, arrived home from work on the evening of November 6, 1989, her mother asked in Arabic, "Where were you, bitch?"

"Working!" Tina shot back, according to the FBI tape.

"We do not accept that you go to work," Isa interrupted.

"Why are you doing this to us?" her mother asked angrily.

"I am not doing anything to you," Tina said.

"You are a she-devil," her father hissed. "Listen, my dear daughter. Do you know that this is the last day? Today you're going to die?"

Realizing he was serious, Tina let out a long scream. There was a crash, and Tina's screams became muffled. Her mother held her down as Isa began stabbing Tina in the chest with a seven-inch boning knife.

"Die! Die quickly! Die quickly!" her father shouted, panting from his exertion.

Tina screamed one more time. By then, Isa's knife had punctured her lungs. Only the sound of the girl's breath being expelled could be heard.

When the tape was translated the next day, the FBI called in the St. Louis police. They arrested the couple. The tape even picked up Isa calling 911, claiming he had killed his daughter in self-defense.

Contrary to the impression created by the tape, Isa killed his daughter because she was rebellious and knew too much about his group's activities. One of the other terrorists had suggested he kill her to keep her from talking. Her father agreed, telling a relative, "This one should live under the ground."

Based on the tape, Isa and his wife were convicted of first-degree murder and sentenced to die by lethal injection. While he was on death row, Zein Isa and three others were indicted for allegedly plotting to kill thousands of Jews, blow up the Israeli embassy in Washington, and smuggle money to members of the Abu Nidal terrorist organization.

Zein Isa died on death row of diabetes. His wife's death sentence was commuted to life imprisonment without parole.

In another case in Philadelphia, agents installed video cameras in an organized crime figure's restaurant. Fifteen minutes after they left, a rival Mafia gang broke in and shot the man. It was all captured on videotape.

Breaking into Mafia-owned Italian restaurants has its advantages. At one such establishment in

Brooklyn, a TacOps agent admits he sampled some delectable shrimp scampi from the refrigerator.

Burglarizing homes and offices may require courage, but one agent was afraid of dogs and refused to go into locations where they would be encountered. Another agent would not fly to a job in Houston over New Year's Eve 1999. He was afraid that computerized instruments would fail when the new century began. Other TacOps agents covered for both agents.

In monitoring bugs and wiretaps, agents often encounter illicit affairs. In one case, they opened a linen closet and found $2 million in cash. In another case, agents saw the suspect—an organized crime figure—having sex with his young daughter.

"The surveillance team across the street broke in, forced their way in, took custody of the child, and waited for the police," Grever says.

But the greatest payoff is when an entry by TacOps stops a terrorist plot in progress, as happened with Khalid Ali-M Aldawsari, who was planning to blow up the home of former president George W. Bush. Similarly, Najibullah Zazi was already mixing chemicals to make explosives to blow up New York City subways when TacOps agents obtained enough evidence to lead to his arrest. That included nine pages of notes they found on his laptop in his rental car with formulations and instructions on the manufacture and handling of initiating explosives, main explosives charges, explosives detonators, and components of a fusing system.

While conducting surreptitious entries at Aldawsari's Lubbock apartment was a no-brainer for TacOps, "the biggest obstacles were limited intelligence about the internal layout of the targeted apartment and unknowns such as how friendly and attentive were his neighbors and how alert he might be to possible surveillance," Grever says. "He had a very erratic pattern of life—typical for subjects of his age—and the entry team had to remain on standby in close proximity to the targeted apartment for several days."

TacOps also played a crucial role in the arrest of 120 alleged Mafia members from seven East Coast organized crime families in January 2011. The largest FBI crackdown on the Mafia in history, the arrests proceeded after two court-authorized covert entries by TacOps teams.

Like other FBI agents, TacOps agents are often amused by the difference between what they see in the media and what is really going on in the FBI. Ramirez, Grever, and a few other TacOps agents and their wives went to see the movie *Breach*, which gave support employee Eric O'Neill all the credit for cracking the Robert Hanssen spy case.

"We had a blast together," Ramirez says. "It was funny because we knew what really happened and what didn't happen."

But being a burglar takes its toll.

"Some agents eventually leave the unit because it's too much stress," Ramirez says. Those who stay usually have tremendous support from their families. "When you have a wife who will say, 'I don't know what you were doing out there, but I support you,' that's the only way we're able to make it," Ramirez says.

Because the work is secret, agents can't be given awards by the attorney general. "You can't write it up, because you would be exposing so many things," Price says.

"We have stopped many, many bad things from happening in this country," Ramirez says. "And we don't want credit for it, we don't get credit for it, we don't need credit for it. A lot of times the SACs will call me and say, 'Your team was out here the other night, and they were gone before I had a chance to say thank you.' That's because they're either on to the next entry or they haven't slept in two or three days. We don't need that kind of stroking. But these guys and gals are the best in the business."

# 27
# Christmas Day

After learning of Umar Farouk Abdulmutallab's attempt to blow up a Northwest Airlines plane, Cummings arrived at his office at FBI headquarters in the afternoon. On the hallway door leading to his office, Cummings had hung a three-by-five-foot photo of the American flag being raised at the World Trade Center site. Even though he never used it, a blue FBI raid jacket hung on a rack near his desk.

Abdulmutallab had tried to blow up the flight with a bomb whose components included pentaerythritol, also known as PETN, and triacetone triperoxide, also known as TATP, both high explosives. The bomb was sewn into his underpants near his crotch and was designed to allow him to detonate it at a time of his choosing.

If successful, Abdulmutallab, a Nigerian citizen, would have killed all 253 passengers and 11 crew members on board. However, because he somehow fumbled triggering the device, the bomb failed to explode. When passengers saw the flames and smoke, they subdued and restrained him.

After talking with Mike Leiter, a former federal

prosecutor who heads the National Counter-terrorism Center, on a secure phone, Cummings, who was once a special agent bomb tech, put together a secure video conference. On the call along with Leiter were John Brennan, the counter-terrorism chief at the White House, and Jane Lute, deputy secretary of the Department of Homeland Security, among others.

Based at the NCTC, the secure video tele-conferences—known as SVTCs, pronounced "sivitz"—take place in a room straight out of *Dr. Strangelove*. On an oak oval table, which seats at least twenty, are mice belonging to eight invisible computers. A command on a touch screen orders the computers to rise like Atlantis from somewhere at the center of the table. On a wall at the head of the table, the requisite clocks show the time in New Delhi, Stockholm, Shanghai, Sarajevo, Jerusalem, Paris, Teheran, and New York.

At the other end of the table are plasma screens. During daily SVTCs, they show certain high-level, security-cleared members of the intelligence community at the FBI, CIA, NSA, Pentagon, and Department of Homeland Security, as well as the White House.

The secure video conference on the attempt to blow up the plane began just after agents gave Abdulmutallab a Miranda warning. The conference lasted two hours and covered "what we knew, who was doing what, who we needed to interface with, who needed to be briefed," Cummings says. The subject of a Miranda warning never came up during the conference, he says.

Brennan later said that he fully briefed Republican congressional leaders—Senators Kit Bond and Mitch McConnell and Representatives John Boehner and Peter Hoekstra—on Christmas night about the arrest and subsequent handling of Abdulmutallab.

"None of those individuals raised any concerns with me at that point," Brennan said on NBC's *Meet the Press*. "They didn't say, 'Is he going into military custody? Is he going to be Mirandized?' They were very appreciative of the information. We told them we'd keep them informed. And that's what we did."

But according to all four leaders, Brennan merely said that Abdulmutallab had been arrested, with nothing about how the case would be handled. Some of the Republican leaders pushed for such cases to be presented to a military tribunal, obviating the need to read a foreign suspect rights guaranteed to American citizens.

Cummings says that what was unusual about the case was that, in contrast to most FBI cases, Abdulmutallab had already been taken into custody by U.S. Customs and Border Protection officers. The FBI therefore did not have the luxury of questioning him before he was in custody. However, based on the Supreme Court's 1984 *New York v. Quarles* decision that permits such warnings to be put off if the public safety might be threatened, a Miranda warning was delayed.

"Usually, what you would do is just not arrest a suspect," Cummings says. "We'll have a chat, explain the facts of life to him, where his life is headed. It happens regularly, and therefore we don't have to sit down and say, 'You have a right to this, you have a right to that.' "

In the case of the twenty-three-year-old suspect, he talked freely at first. "In the first hour, he gave us really good information on the front end," Cummings says. " 'Yep, I did this on behalf of al Qaeda. Yep, it was in Yemen.' " He gave up names, places, training camps. Then he was transported to the University of Michigan Medical Center for a medical procedure. After that, he started to clam up.

"He was under the influence of painkillers, and they'd scrubbed the skin to remove the burnt skin," Cummings says. As the narcotics wore off, two new agents went in to see him. They were instructed to deal with conditions on the ground as they saw them.

The agents saw the Nigerian the day after his arrest. He was praying. They began by asking elementary questions he had already answered. "He either lied or didn't give them the answer,"

Cummings says. "And at that point, they were like, 'He's done.' So then they gave him Miranda."

Over the next five weeks, the FBI worked on him. The focus was on finding out what he cared about. "Is it his mother, is it his family, is it his future?" Cummings says. "Is it shame upon his family? We offer them the possibility that instead of dying in an American prison, maybe sometime in their lifetime they will actually be able to go home and see their family, and they won't be executed and die at the hands of this nation they hate so much."

As with failed Times Square car bomber Faisal Shahzad, Abdulmutallab was a self-initiated terrorist enabled by al Qaeda.

"So it really gets to the point of what the heck is going on?" Cummings says. "What really is happening to influence a young man [Shahzad] who in this case was essentially raised in the United States to take this path? It's not terribly far from youths who join violent gangs. Instead, these guys are moving toward combat in al Qaeda."

Cummings sent two agents to Nigeria to learn everything they could about Abdulmutallab's background and family. "They engaged his family and explained, 'This is really, really serious, and it's in the best interest of your son that we cut a deal of some sort,' " Cummings says.

One agent moved in with Abdulmutallab's uncle, then flew him to Detroit. Later, his father flew to Detroit as well. Both told Abdulmutallab it was in his interest to listen to the agent. Meanwhile, agents told the suspect, "You have a long life to live, there are a number of conditions you can live it in," Cummings says. "It's all up to you."

Five weeks after he had stopped talking, Abdulmutallab was cooperating again.

Cummings says that while the public safety exception allows a relatively brief delay in giving a Miranda warning, it may be helpful to enact legislation that would allow an even longer delay than currently permitted. But he says that in many cases, the FBI does not have to worry about giving the warning because the individual is not in custody. If the suspect is in custody, Cummings says the FBI can obtain the information it needs in most cases after a Miranda warning so long as agents have unfettered access and can offer incentives for cooperation.

"Frankly, I can't remember a case where a guy didn't talk to us in a terrorism case," Cummings says. "You let them know what it's all about, and then you tell them what their rights are, and you say, 'But just sign here, and we can just continue our discussion.' Most cases they're willing to sign the waiver and continue talking. The question usually is not whether or not we can get them to talk. The question is how long it takes."

If the FBI arrests a suspect in the United States, Cummings sees no need for a military tribunal. He points out that Jose Padilla, a Brooklyn-born man who converted to Islam, was initially held as an enemy combatant in military custody.

"No Miranda, no rights, no lawyer," Cummings says. "They got nothing from him."

Padilla was eventually transferred to the civilian court system. He was convicted of conspiring to help Islamic jihadist fighters abroad. Some other high-ranking FBI officials privately favor tribunals.

Even though it is within the purview of the FBI, Janet Napolitano, secretary of homeland security, maintained that her department should have a vote on whether or not to Mirandize a suspect, Cummings says. "It's the insanity of Washington when representatives of Homeland Security believe they might have a say in whether or not the FBI Mirandizes or doesn't Mirandize somebody," Cummings says. "They should not be getting involved in tactical CT [counterterrorism] operational decisions."

Under Bush, the Department of Homeland Security (DHS) did not try to become involved in such issues. However, under Michael Chertoff, Bush's secretary of homeland security, it did push to join local Joint Terrorism Task Forces, a move the FBI resisted.

"Their mission is infrastructure protection, and no one else does it," Cummings says of DHS. "Shore up the dam, shore up the power plant, shore up the chemical plants, deny the target to the enemy. No one else is doing it, and frankly, I'm not convinced they are focused on it."

The NCTC determines whether an individual should be added to the Terrorist Identities Datamart Environment, or TIDE, which lists about 550,000 individuals, addresses, and objects such as cars and weapons. From that list, the FBI develops the Terrorist Screening Database (TSDB), from which consular, border, and airline watch lists are drawn. The list has 430,000 names. The Transportation Security Administration maintains its own no-fly list of about 4,000 people who are prohibited from boarding any domestic or U.S.-bound aircraft. Another list has about 14,000 "selectees" who require additional scrutiny but are not banned from flying. Each list is used for different purposes and is based on differing criteria. The TIDE list is broadest and includes anyone who might be suspicious. The no-fly list includes only the most clear-cut threats. In placing individuals on these lists, intelligence officials receive constant pressure from the American Civil Liberties Union (ACLU) and other civil liberties advocates who complain that there is something inherently insidious about the number of names on the lists. Timothy Sparapani, the ACLU's legislative counsel for privacy rights, has called the numbers "shocking."

Abdulmutallab's father had warned U.S. officials in Nigeria that his son had fallen prey to radical Islam and had said he would never see his family again. Consequently, Abdulmutallab was on the TIDE list—but he was not on the more select lists that would have subjected him to additional screening.

"The Abdulmutallab case was really a convergence of missed opportunities," Cummings says.

Getting the State Department to deny a visa based on an FBI request is almost impossible, Cummings says. Cummings and the FBI constantly tried to get both the Bush and Obama administrations to change the visa policy, to no avail.

"In this country, if you're a student and you come to the U.S., and the FBI has you under investigation for being a terrorist, we can't get your visa pulled," Cummings says. "And I say what, do they have a right to be here? When did that happen? When did the privilege become a right?"

But Cummings applauds the Obama administration's new guidelines for screening passengers on airplanes. Instead of using nationality alone to determine which U.S.-bound international air travelers should receive additional screening, the government now selects passengers based on how they match up with known intelligence on possible threats, including their physical descriptions or travel patterns. Previously, passengers were subjected to extra screening if they came from one of fourteen countries. With the new guidelines, extra screening is applied based on the latest intelligence.

In his FBI role, Cummings met with White House officials on a regular basis. Several times he met with Bush and later Obama. The FBI agent saw little change between the two administrations and no increase in what may have been politically motivated direction. "Frankly, we would not have responded to such direction," Cummings says.

What most frustrated him was the additional bureaucracy that the Office of the Director of National Intelligence (ODNI) imposed. While the 9/11 Commission originally envisioned the office as having several hundred employees to coordinate the intelligence community, it has ballooned to an agency of 1,500 employees. A small segment of those employees work for the NCTC, which is vital, but the rest of the agency produces little that Cummings could see to enhance the intelligence effort.

That point was symbolized when the director

of national intelligence, James R. Clapper Jr., admitted in a December 2010 interview with ABC's Diane Sawyer that he was unaware of the arrests of twelve terrorists in London. It had been all over the news for most of the day. Cummings regarded Clapper as by far the most qualified DNI to have held the post. But the embarrassing lapse spotlighted the folly of creating a bureaucracy on top of operational agencies that must be alert to terror threats.

"The intelligence community operators are doing a good job," Cummings says. "It's the massive bureaucracy around them that slows things down and frustrates the effort. You have this big planning machine generating endless meetings. We would walk out of the meetings shaking our heads."

# 28
# Suitcase Nuke

By 2010, Art Cummings was starting to see a turnaround in the war on terror, largely because of increased cooperation by the Pakistanis and others and an increase in strikes by Predator drone aircraft.

He traces the changes to August 2006, when British authorities disrupted an al Qaeda plot to explode nine American airliners in flight from London. Cummings was then deputy assistant director of the Counterterrorism Division. In that capacity, he issued orders for wiretaps and physical surveillance of terrorist suspects in the United States. The objective was to pick up clues from how these suspects reacted when they heard the news of the impending arrests in Great Britain.

After that plot was rolled up, the Bush administration began to intensify pressure on the Pakistanis to cooperate. At the same time, Bush ordered a threefold increase in the number of drone aircraft. Because it takes several years for such aircraft to be produced, it was not until 2010 that Predators began knocking off top al Qaeda leaders on a regular basis.

Before increased pressure was applied, Cummings had a chart on the wall tracing multiple scary plots.

"Everybody was going, 'Holy s——,' " he says. "There were ongoing plots all around the world, all emanating from different al Qaeda strongholds in the FATA or other parts of Pakistan. The Pakistanis knew back in 2006 that if they didn't do something, we're coming in, because it was getting that bad."

Now, he says, "They're getting the crap kicked out of them. I believe that absent the Predator program, we'd be in a ground war in Pakistan. Because this country would in no way tolerate successful al Qaeda plots inspired and hatched in Pakistan. Our frustration level was so high that al Qaeda was training people, and there just didn't seem to be anybody who really had the capacity to do anything about it."

Yet as the FBI and the United States changed their approach, so did al Qaeda.

"Al Qaeda in the Arabian Peninsula has moved from an internal focus on Yemen and Saudi Arabia to a focus on both the Arabian Peninsula and the United States," Cummings says.

Al Qaeda in the Arabian Peninsula was behind the failed efforts to bring down planes with bombs on Christmas Day 2009 and in October 2010, when two package bombs were shipped from Yemen to the United States. Even though Saudi intelligence pinpointed exactly where the bombs could be located in the planes, explosives-sniffing dogs failed to detect them. The radical cleric Anwar al-Awlaki, who is a leader of al Qaeda in the Arabian Peninsula, also inspired Nidal Malik Hasan, the U.S. Army major who shot to death thirteen people at Fort Hood.

While al Qaeda has suffered big losses, it is becoming more sophisticated and effective in its recruiting, using Facebook and YouTube to enlist new terrorists.

"Their media machine is really effective," Cummings says. "Hence, they are getting volunteers from around the world. Something is working. Their communications strategy to those young men mainly and some young women now who are off on the wrong path speaks to them loudly and effectively."

Despite the diffusion, al Qaeda would love to release biological, chemical, or nuclear weapons on the United States. But when it comes to nuclear weapons, "while they aspire to use them, when it comes down to limited resources, limited capacity, and being always on the run, where are they going to put their money?" Cummings says. "They're going to put their money in five thousand pounds of ammonium nitrate and not in a nuclear warhead."

While some say obtaining a nuclear weapon

would not be that difficult, both acquiring such a weapon and keeping it secret carries with it "very high risk with a very high likelihood of failure," Cummings says.

A terrorist bent on detonating a nuclear weapon would have to negotiate successfully a series of steps, according to Dr. Vahid Majidi, the FBI's assistant director in charge of the Weapons of Mass Destruction Directorate. The terrorist would have to find an expert with the right knowledge. He would have to find the right material. Such a terrorist would have to bring the device into the country, and he would have to evade detection programs.

"While the net probability is incredibly low, a ten-kiloton device would be of enormous consequence," Majidi says. "So even with those enormously low probabilities, we still have to have a very effective and integrated approach trying to fight the possibility."

Besides an investigative and an intelligence approach, that entails using a forensic approach, including use of detectors and other technology, Majidi says. "You have to bring the three approaches together, and each one of them will bring you a certain amount of information at a given time," he says.

While TV shows such as *24* feature suitcase nuclear devices, Majidi—who confesses he never misses an episode—says that is a fantasy.

"One of the smallest weapons that we have had in our arsenal is the special atomic demolition munition, which weighs about a hundred fifty pounds and is designed to take bridges out," Majidi says. "That is like carrying seventeen gallons of milk. So that's the kind of weight we're talking about. That's one of the smallest weapons that we have that is full-up," meaning it is self-contained.

To be sure, stealing a nuclear weapon from a country would be easier than building one. Iran, for example, is "like a rabid dog, absolutely unpredictable," Cummings says. "You just don't know what they're going to do, and they have capabilities."

Currently, Majidi is working on ways to detect development of new organisms that could be used in a biological attack. By definition, there would be no way to detect a new organism or to develop an antidote before it is unleashed.

"We are not sitting on our hands waiting to predict what will happen based on what happened yesterday," Majidi says. As an example, he says, "you can design an organism de novo that never existed before. While there is no known articulated threat, this is something that we feel is a technology or science that potentially can be misused, either accidentally or on purpose."

Among other methods, the FBI is working with the synthetic biology community to develop ways to zero in on any hint that someone could be developing such an organism.

"We're not there to stop the science but to integrate our activities within their portfolio so that when the threat does develop or may develop over a long arc of time, we are ahead of those issues," Majidi explains.

Another "huge" potential threat, says Cummings, is the explosion by an enemy of a nuclear weapon high in the atmosphere to unleash an electromagnetic pulse (EMP). The electromagnetic pulse generated by the blast would fry all electronics in North America. Because everything relies on microchips—computers, financial records, furnaces, refrigerators, police dispatchers, hospitals, telephones, cars, trains, and planes—such a blast would send America back to the 1300s.

In the event of an EMP attack, either by terrorists or more likely by a foreign power, the electrical power grid would be destroyed because its computers would be inoperative. Transformers critical to it would take years to replace. Only a few countries build the transformers, which take more than a year to make.

The vast majority of Americans would die from starvation or disease or would freeze to death, according to Dr. William Graham, who was chairman of the bipartisan congressional Commission to Assess the Threat to the United

States from EMP Attack. While the military is largely protected from an EMP attack with shielding, the government has done virtually nothing to address the effects of such an attack on the civilian sector, Graham says.

# CSI

Above the grassy hills and woodlands of Quantico rises the new FBI Laboratory building. The long rectangular box with sparkling windows resembles an office building, but the ventilation towers on the roof make it look more like a processing plant. What they're processing here is evidence: stains and human remains, codes and ciphers, paints and polymers, bullets and bombs.

Witnesses are notoriously unreliable, and documents can lie. Skillful defense lawyers can twist videotapes of crimes to cast doubt on a defendant's guilt. But physical evidence found at a crime scene—a spent bullet, a shard of glass, a drop of semen or blood—is the surest kind of proof, one that is least susceptible to differing interpretations. It can cut either way, sending a suspect to jail for life or exonerating an innocent person.

The FBI lab started in 1932 with a microscope, some ultraviolet light equipment, a drawing board for firearms identification, and a Packard sedan that agents called "Old Beulah" for speeding to crime scenes. Hoover decided to create the lab after scientific crime analysis had been used successfully in several cases, including the kidnapping of Charles A. Lindbergh Jr. In the Lindbergh case, local police were able to show that a wooden ladder Bruno Richard Hauptmann used to climb into the Lindbergh baby's bedroom had been fashioned from struts from Hauptmann's attic.

The main entrance to the FBI lab is very quiet. A pond with a trickling fountain and a silent-but-full parking garage break up the expansive lawn. A walkway, lined with manicured bushes, clumps of begonias, and crape myrtles in full bloom, leads from the garage to the entrance. Now and then someone walks into the building.

By contrast, at the busy back entrance on Laboratory Road, a continuous fleet of FedEx trucks arrives throughout the day, delivering boxes of evidence. Every seam on every box is sealed with translucent yellow plastic tape. The Laboratory Division conducts more than a million forensic examinations a year for both the police and FBI.

Inside the building, the beige corridors, a quarter mile in length, are empty. While the building has about eight hundred employees— 10 percent of them special agents, and the rest laboratory technicians, scientists and chemists, forensic examiners, and support personnel—the hallways are silent. Windows into the labs show the technicians hard at work in white coats, in their warrens of beakers and vials, sinks and microscopes.

In the Evidence Control Unit, lab techs remove the yellow plastic tape, which ensures the integrity of the evidence. Then they open the boxes. They triage the evidence, from a femur to a shirt to a car door, and assess it guided by the communications from the field that they read on computer. One of the evidence bays can accommodate an eighteen-wheeler.

Behind the windows of an evidence bay marked "Inventory in Progress—Do Not Enter," a lab tech wearing purple gloves and protective goggles places a piece of cloth carefully on brown paper spread on a table. There is a stain on the cloth. You begin to understand the silence.

But if the FBI personnel here jumped up and down every time they solved a crime, "they'd be doing that all day, because they're always discovering things," says Dr. D. Christian Hassell, who is the FBI assistant director in charge of the Laboratory Division.

The new building, which opened in 2003, occupies 463,000 square feet, doubling the space the lab previously took up at headquarters. Every office has sunlight—if your office doesn't have a window, you can look out the window across the hall. No more working in a dark basement, as many technicians did when the lab at headquarters was divided between the third floor and the first basement level.

To minimize cross contamination in an emergency or accident, the new building has two intake systems, one for either side of the building, the offices being on one side and the labs on the other. Along a wall in a corridor, there is another reminder that processing the evidence itself can be a dangerous business: where a drinking fountain would be, there is an eye-wash station and an overhead shower with a pull that delivers an emergency deluge of water.

In September 2003, during his tour of the new lab facilities, President George W. Bush reached up and asked what the pull was for. The lab director frantically yanked back his arm. On hearing the explanation, Bush was reported to have said, "I guess that's why the Secret Service makes me carry an extra suit."

Dr. Hassell, with his wire-rimmed glasses, buzz cut, and fireplug build, is a chemist, not an agent. The only thing he's packing is a Black-Berry. Years back, agents headed the laboratory. But as Louis Freeh transferred personnel out of the laboratory, the case backlog stretched to a year, and the work suffered. Frederic Whitehurst, an FBI chemist and supervisor in the lab, alleged to the press in September 1995 that not only was the lab doing shoddy work, its examiners had committed perjury and fabricated evidence.

After an investigation, Michael R. Bromwich, the Justice Department's inspector general, determined that none of those charges involving perjury and fabricated evidence had any basis in fact. But he found instances of errors in court testimony, substandard analytical work, and problems with record management. As many as fifty cases going back years might have been mishandled. With six hundred thousand examinations being conducted each year, that was not a large number. Despite claims by defense lawyers that thousands of cases would be affected, no case was ever overturned as a result of the problems found at the lab. But procedures clearly needed tightening.

Like the rest of the FBI, the lab had always resisted outside scrutiny. There was a need to bring the lab into line with procedures used by other forensic laboratories. The FBI lab is now accredited and inspected by the Laboratory Accreditation Board of the American Society of Crime Laboratory Directors. Now a scientist, not an agent, is in charge of the lab. And while he is a scientist, Hassell is skilled at translating his difficult subject, the science of crime, into a layperson's terms.

One way or another, the lab becomes involved in every major tragedy that occurs in the United States and even abroad. Because of the possibility that criminality was involved, the lab

347

worked on the investigation of a crash on Washington's Metro that killed nine people. It examined evidence in the Fort Hood and Holocaust Museum shootings. For trials or incident reconstruction, it built models of the Twin Towers and Pentagon and of the trunk of the car used by the Washington snipers. FBI evidence response teams directed by the lab helped locate the engines from the U.S. Airways plane that ditched in the Hudson River.

The lab doesn't do everyday cause-of-death determinations. "We deal more with human remains, people who have been gone for a long time," Hassell says. The remains of Caylee Anthony, a toddler who disappeared in Orlando and was found dead in 2008, were sent here. "We did the DNA extraction," he says. The lab coordinates the evidence response teams at all fifty-six FBI offices. "You work for the Milwaukee office, but we provide the training here."

One thing Hassell is quick to point out: television's *CSI* version of forensics bears little resemblance to that of the FBI Laboratory Division. For instance, to identify hidden stains, the lab techs here "don't use special glasses and a flashlight like on TV."

On the public tours that used to be conducted at headquarters, the Firearms and Toolmarks Unit was a big draw. Moved over to Quantico, the weapons collection now numbers six thousand items, from automatics to artillery to cane guns that were sold in the 1935 Sears, Roebuck catalog. The centerpieces are guns that belonged to Bonnie and Clyde, Ma Barker, Baby Face Nelson, and John Dillinger.

The weapons are worth millions but are uninsured. "We have pretty good security," Hassell says, deadpan.

In this unit, bullets are analyzed to see if they were shot through a particular gun. Similarly, wire cutters are tested by cutting a wire to see if the striation patterns left are the same that appear on the evidence—a wire used in making a bomb, for example.

The FBI's unique collection of duct tape was moved from the downtown lab, as was its inventory of sample paint panels. Paint panels can be critical in solving a crime or accident. "That's how they knew in France that Princess Di's car was hit by a white Fiat," Hassell says.

Over at the Cryptanalysis and Racketeering Records Unit, Dan Olson, the unit chief, describes his work simply: "We break codes." Not those generated by computers, but rather the old-fashioned kind, which can be just as challenging. Many of the codes are written by spies, gangs, and members of organized crime. Mail bomber Theodore Kaczynski kept encoded diaries referring to his exploits and thoughts about his crimes.

The unit has twenty employees, running the gamut of expertise in intelligence, business, computers, and mathematics. There's a vice cop and a former narcotics officer. "I want a real wide range," Olson says. "Pool that knowledge, those experiences."

At any given time, the unit is trying to decipher fifty items. The typical cipher comes in by BlackBerry, Olson says. A typical question: "Just found this in a cell in a prison in California. Is he planning a murder or is it a love letter?"

Nine out of ten messages are decoded the same day they are received. "We either figure it out very quickly, or it's not a code. The rule of solving a cipher is it's usually very quick or never," Olson says.

Some of the toughest nuts to crack are from criminals who know history. They may look back to a code that hasn't been used since the Civil War, or employ a system developed during the Napoleonic Wars. "With the Internet," Olson says, "all you have to do is Google 'cipher hard to break.'"

Just as the FBI has its list of the Ten Most Wanted, it has its Top Ten Unsolved Ciphers. Number one is a cipher used by the Zodiac killer, who operated in Northern California in the late 1960s and early 1970s and whose identity remains unknown.

In the Explosives Unit demo room, Greg Carl,

the unit chief, goes over how the bureau solved recent cases that have been in the news. He's been with the bureau since 1987, and that includes having worked the Pam Am bombing over Lockerbie, Scotland.

Carl says the Explosives Unit is unusual at the Quantico lab because it has "a good mix" of scientists and agents. In fact, he says, "now the scientists kind of think like an agent and the agents think like a scientist."

A sign of the times, explosives experts from the Russian SVR now meet with FBI experts from the lab to compare notes. They may be helping each other, but the FBI is still on guard. The meetings take place at the FBI Academy, not at the secure lab.

In the display of fragments, fuses, replicas, and mockups in a demo room is a two-foot-long sole of a sneaker. It's a cross section that shows the lining of shoe bomber Richard Reid's footwear. A self-admitted member of al Qaeda, he tried to take down American Airlines Flight 63 flying from Paris to the United States on December 22, 2001.

Reid placed his bombs in the waffled air pockets within the rubber soles in his shoes. Because the bombs were secreted in both shoes, no anomalies presented themselves to X-ray screeners.

But Reid was so disheveled-looking that red

flags went up at the airport in Paris. Security delayed his boarding for so long that he missed his flight to Miami and had to wait until the next day. Meanwhile, Reid kept his sneakers on too long. His feet sweated. In short, he didn't keep his powder dry.

"The time fuse he used is Pakistani," Carl says, "not that it's not any good, but it uses cotton fibers inside the fuse." Because cotton absorbs moisture, a lot of explosives manufacturers use synthetic fiber instead. The fuse was inside the shoe, coming out of it was a piece of time fuse, and Reid's sock was on top of that. The result: the explosive black powder for the bomb became damp.

On the flight Reid also tried to use matches, instead of the lighter he had carried the previous day, which made it harder to light the now-damp fuse and black powder. A flight attendant smelled the burning match, accused him of trying to smoke a cigarette, and soon Reid was in custody.

The bomb secreted by Umar Farouk Abdulmutallab, the Christmas Day bomber, also did not go off, but he wasn't as dumb as he might appear. By stitching the bomb into the crotch of his underpants, he avoided detection.

Carl wonders aloud "why you might choose to hide a bomb on your person, in your crotch, knowing you could very well be searched." He answers his own question. "Security people feeling uncomfortable grabbing in that area."

One of the things the Explosives Unit does is to test how bad things might have been had a terrorist attempt been successful. For the Shoe Bomber, the unit first detonated a mockup of the shoe. It vanished. But that wasn't the same thing as a plane at thirty-seven thousand feet depressurizing with a hole blown into its side.

The unit discovered that if Reid's shoe had been against the wall of the cabin when the bomb went off, it would have taken a smaller quantity of explosives to damage the aircraft's aluminum skin. When it starts to rip, the aluminum continues to peel back, or "petal." The hole just gets bigger and bigger, as happened with the Pan Am plane that exploded over Lockerbie.

Ahmed Ressam, the Millennium Bomber, might have slipped into the United States successfully and detonated explosives in Seattle, but he was nervous. When his rental car came off a ferry on the evening of December 14, 1999, he presented his Costco card as identification to Customs at Port Angeles. That triggered questioning, and he tried to flee.

In the spare-tire well of his car were 110 pounds of urea, four black boxes that contained time-delay fusing systems, and bottles labeled as olives, Tylenol, and zinc tablets. Whenever agents would move the olive bottle, the thirty-three year-old Algerian would duck.

Says Carl: "That's what we call in law enforcement a clue."

When investigators searched Ressam's apartment in Montreal, they found a pair of pants with acid burns in them. They called the prison where Ressam was being held and asked them to check the suspect's legs for burn marks. The answer came back positive. The information was presented as part of the evidence against him in court.

What was in the bottles? Surely not olives, Tylenol, and zinc tablets. Instead, the FBI lab found HMTD, a primary explosive that can be initiated by a heat source; RDX, not quite as sensitive, but it causes the next explosive to detonate; and EGDN, ethylene glycol dinitrate, or dynamite.

In the demo room is a backpack similar to one used by Eric Rudolf, the Centennial Bomber, at the 1996 Summer Olympics in Atlanta. Inside the base of the pack, Rudolf assembled the equivalent of a timed military Claymore mine, which is designed to propel shrapnel when it goes off. He positioned the backpack so that when the bomb exploded, it would shoot at least five hundred nails into the crowd at Centennial Park. But kids discovered the pack and tried to steal it. When they decided it was too heavy and put it down, they reoriented the bomb so that it didn't fragment into Rudolf's planned kill zone. Instead of the dozens who might have been victims, one person died.

Like Art Cummings, Carl talks about trip wires. In making bombs, hydrogen peroxide is used in higher concentrations than found in the medicine cabinet. Beauty supply outlets sell an 18 percent solution; and pool supply outlets, a 30 percent solution, compared with 3 percent at your local drugstore. Suspicious or large purchases of such chemicals should be reported to the FBI or the local Joint Terrorism Task Force.

"It's important to get trip wires in place," Carl says. "It's not your father's FBI," he adds. "It's not reacting. A lot of it is preventing."

#  Spy Swap

As the chief of counterterrorism and counter-intelligence, Art Cummings was responsible for protecting the country against spies and cyber-threats from foreign countries as well as from terrorists. When Mueller appointed Cummings, Mueller told him that he had a reputation for having "sharp elbows" and that he needed to be more diplomatic.

"You need to know how to play in the sand-box a little bit better," Mueller said.

"You don't pay me to not have sharp elbows," Cummings responded. "You personally have no tolerance for a lapse in carrying out our respon-sibilities or for consensus on everything. Consensus is absolutely an avenue to failure. I'm not looking for a watered-down solution that everyone can agree upon. I'm looking for informed information and a final decision that's the right decision, taking everything into account but discarding much of it."

In this new position, Cummings was in charge of a new Presidential Threat Task Force created to gather, track, and evaluate assassination threats that might be related to domestic or international terrorism. First disclosed in a new chapter of the paperback edition of my book *In the President's Secret Service*, the task force consists of twenty representatives from pertinent agencies, including agents from the FBI and Secret Service and operatives from the CIA, NSA, and the Defense Department, along with analysts.

Each day, more than ten thousand attempts are made by foreign governments such as China's to penetrate U.S. military and commercial computer networks.

"We are being flooded, absolutely flooded by predominantly Chinese cyberattacks," Cummings says. While they originate both with the Chinese government and with Chinese companies, the government has a great ability to conceal their source, Cummings notes.

Besides cyberintrusion, China makes use of Chinese who work in the United States and are loyal to China, Cummings says.

"You have tens of thousands of vulnerabilities where Chinese and other foreign nationals are working on high-dollar proprietary information or intellectual property with the expectation that they're going to take it back to China," Cummings says.

As a result of economic espionage, foreign companies are stealing U.S. technological break-throughs. "Secrets, proprietary information, and technology are just flying out of the U.S.," Cummings says. "If we lose the manufacturing rights and we're not producing items, we've just lost hundreds of millions of dollars in tax revenue."

Until he replaced Tom Harrington as head of criminal investigations, Shawn Henry had run the FBI's Cyber Division and then briefly the Washington field office. Although Henry has the trademark furrowed brow and crinkly eyes of the fully engaged, he is warm and relaxed. He has a dimple in his left cheek, and he's Bruce Willis bald.

"There are terrorist groups that would like to have the same impact on this country through an electronic attack as they did by flying planes at the buildings ten years ago," Henry says. "To disrupt communication systems, to impact our critical infrastructure. We know for a fact that they have an interest in doing that. Even if they don't have the capability, they can lease the capability because there are people who have the skill set who are willing to rent their services. So the threat that we face today from foreign intelligence services, terrorist organizations, and organized criminal organizations is substantial."

Terrorist groups tied to the jihadist cause have in fact tried to launch cyberattacks, Henry says. "They're interested in disrupting our way of life. They've looked at our critical infrastructure—

electrical power grids, water treatment plants."

At the same time, dozens of foreign countries "have an electronic collection plan in place as part of their arsenal" to learn U.S. military and corporate secrets, Henry says.

While the United States has a national cyber-strategy, "I'm not so sure it's effective," Cummings says. "I would advise companies that with anything they really care about, take it off the Internet. Put it in a closed system. If it's attached to the Internet, know you can't protect against its loss. If it's attached to the Internet, then you're stating, de facto, you can afford to lose that information."

With the exceptions of Great Britain, Canada, Australia, and New Zealand, nearly every country in the world with any power spies on the United States, and the United States spies on those countries. In particular, the Russians are just as active now as during the Cold War.

That became evident at the end of June 2010, when the FBI arrested ten Russian spies who had been trying to ferret out intelligence about U.S. policy and secrets by making connections to think tanks and government officials. An eleventh spy was detained by authorities in Cyprus. The Russians were so-called illegals, officers or assets of an intelligence service sent to spy on another country without diplomatic cover or any overt connection to their government.

In November 2010, the Russian newspaper *Kommersant* reported that an SVR official, identified only as Colonel Shcherbakov, was responsible for giving up the spies and had left Russia shortly before they were arrested by the FBI. An unidentified Russian government official was quoted as issuing death threats against him. However, it turned out that the individual in question was actually Colonel Alexander Poteyev, deputy director of Department S within the SVR, the unit that coordinates the work of illegal agents. He had been recruited by the CIA.

What did not come out was that the case had started back in 2001, when a CIA operative was able to recruit Poteyev, the SVR official who had knowledge of the spy network, which extended to other countries besides the United States. The CIA operative was under nonofficial cover (NOC), meaning that if he had been arrested, he would have had no diplomatic immunity from prosecution and could be executed.

In the end, the Russian spies obtained no classified information. Indeed, the Russians could have learned more secrets at less cost by going on the Internet. But the FBI kept the case going in part because it did not want to jeopardize the NOC and his source, and in part because watching the spies enabled the bureau to track Russian methods.

Because the Russian spies never obtained anything valuable, they were only charged with failing to register as foreign agents or with money laundering instead of with espionage. The maximum jail sentence would have been twenty years.

But just after their June 27 arrests, CIA director Leon Panetta called his counterpart, Mikhail Fradkov, the head of the SVR, to propose a spy swap. Since becoming CIA director, Panetta had been dealing with Fradkov, who was appointed by Russian prime minister Vladimir Putin in 2007, and had developed a good relationship with him. Over the course of a week, they exchanged more calls and worked out a deal.

On July 9, 2010, the United States traded the Russians at the Vienna airport for four individuals who had been imprisoned in Russia for spying. While some criticized the deal as lopsided in favor of the Russians, two of those freed from Russian prisons—Aleksandr Zaporozhsky and Gennady Vasilenko—were incredibly valuable.

An SVR colonel who became deputy chief of the American Department, Zaporozhsky gave up Aldrich Ames, the CIA officer arrested on February 21, 1994, for spying for the Russians, according to intelligence sources.

In 1997, Zaporozhsky moved to the United States with his wife and three children and went into business. But in 2001, former KGB colleagues lured him back to Moscow for what they promised would be a festive KGB anniversary party. Zaporozhsky thought the SVR did not realize he had been working for the CIA. He ignored FBI advice not to return.

"The last two Americans who met with Zaporozhsky to talk him out of returning to Russia were Steve Kappes from the CIA and myself over lunch in northern Virginia just prior to Hanssen's arrest," says Mike Rochford, who acquired the code name "Professor" within the Federal Security Service (FSB), the Russian equivalent of the FBI. "We told him that information about his identity had been given to the Russians by Hanssen in his drop of November 13, 2000, but he refused to believe us and returned anyway."

Upon arriving in Russia, Zaporozhsky was arrested at the airport. He was convicted of espionage and sentenced to eighteen years in prison.

Vasilenko, the other critically important asset swapped by the Russians, helped uncover Hanssen. Before Rochford recruited the SVR intelligence officer who gave up Hanssen, Vasilenko introduced him to a retired CIA officer. The retired CIA officer then introduced the SVR source to an American businessman, who set him up so that Rochford could make a cold pitch to him on the streets. Rochford is now retired from the FBI, but the Russian FSB still believes—wrongly—that when he travels abroad, he is developing assets and making pitches.

Russian guards savagely beat Zaporozhsky and Vasilenko while they were in prison, reportedly on the direct orders of Aleksandr Zhomov of the Russian Federal Security Service. An FSB general, he runs the American Department and is obsessed with uncovering the assets who gave up Ames and Hanssen.

"Zhomov took it personally that the FBI recruited a source who fingered Hanssen," says an intelligence source. "He blamed Zoporozhsky and Vasilenko for this because he could not get his hands on the source who had given Hanssen up to the FBI. Zhomov picked on the two he could hurt and made sure that both Zoporozhsky and Vasilenko would suffer while in jail. Intelligence sources reported that he ordered them beaten regularly by guards before and after they were convicted and at each of five prisons each served in. Both likely would have died at the hands of their guards if they had not been traded back to us."

In addition to these details, what never came out is that during the negotiations, the Russians tried to include Robert Hanssen and Aldrich Ames in the swap. The United States firmly rejected that idea.

In the summer swap, the United States got a

good deal, according to John Martin, the former chief Justice Department spy prosecutor. Martin's credentials for evaluating the spy swap are unparalleled. As part of his job, Martin helped arrange six previous spy swaps. The most notable occurred in 1986, when Soviet dissident Natan Sharansky and others were released and Karl and Hana Koecher, the two Czech Intelligence Service spies, were sent back to Prague.

Martin says the United States was able to swap the Russian illegals for four individuals of far higher quality. The Russian illegals who were swapped were pathetic spies: they never obtained any classified information. FBI counterintelligence officials wondered if that meant the SVR was losing it and was a diminished agency compared with its predecessor, the KGB.

"These eleven people charged with spying were useless appendages of a shattered regime," Martin says. "They are a hangover from the old Soviet Cold War days. As part of the proceedings, they were fully exposed; they had to identify themselves by true name in open court. All of their assets—their homes, their cars, their banking accounts—were seized, and they were packed up with their children to go back to Mother Russia, never to reenter the United States again."

Martin points out that in the event the administration had proceeded with a trial, the political climate in Russia could have changed, and Russia might not have agreed to a swap at that point. "You strike when the iron's hot," Martin says.

"At the beginning of the investigation, the FBI didn't know what they had," Martin observes. "Why were the Russians running it? I don't know, because no one from Montclair, New Jersey, can get close to someone in Washington, D.C., who has access to secrets, and apparently none of these people did get close to anyone."

But, Martin says, "you've got to understand the paranoid Russian mentality. Remember, one of the things that they instructed all of their people to look out for were any signs of war. So maybe they were looking for a primitive early-warning system. That would have been part of their training."

The operation is an example of government bureaucrats trying to make themselves look good to their bosses, Martin says.

"It is art for art's sake," Martin says. "They were running it because they could run it. Because it's in their blood, it's in their bureaucracy, it's in the system. And they can show their bosses they're doing something. Boss, they can say, we've got these people, they haven't ever been detected or caught, and they're all over the place," Martin says, suggesting that other illegals probably have not been caught.

"The Russians started this; the FBI didn't," he

says. "The Russians trained and embedded their citizens, except for one defendant, into U.S. society, using false names, false documentation, and equipped with all of the old spycraft, but spycraft never really gets old."

To its credit, the FBI got on to them. Of the eleven individuals charged, one jumped bail in Cyprus, so only ten spies were swapped.

In deciding whether to swap the ten spies immediately, "the question the administration faced was, are you going to have ten people standing trial in three separate jurisdictions under three different sets of judges, trying these cases?" Martin says. "And what do we get in return? These people have no criminal records, they have not had access to secrets. A number of them could get probation, others could get very light sentences, but the administration knew we're not going to get a very big bang for the buck."

Holding trials would have meant that "we're going to go through ten lengthy trials, showing all of the ways we got this information, all of the information regarding FISAs and surreptitious entries, and our techniques for surveillance, because not all of that stuff could be subject to secret proceedings," Martin says.

In this case, "the quality of the people that we got out of Russian prisons far outweighs the quality of people that we sent back," Martin says.

As for the attempt by the Russian government to include Hanssen and Ames in the swap, Martin calls it unprecedented. In past trades, the Russians have wanted to include Russian intelligence officers or illegals who had been arrested. But they had no interest in the fate of the Americans they had recruited to spy.

"The Russians have always looked upon Americans who spied on their behalf as expendable and of no value," Martin says. "The fact that during those discussions the Russians asked for the return of Aldrich Ames and Robert Hanssen suggests to me that the Russians feel they still have some value. The Russians would want them back to explore how they were captured and how they were detected, arrested, and prosecuted, in order to clean up any doubts about how they were compromised. They would want to know if there were other moles in the Soviet system still working for U.S. and allied intelligence services who could have compromised Hanssen and Ames."

In fact, the FBI learned in the late 1990s that the SVR "was planning on contacting Ames in jail, using one of its co-opted Russian media correspondents," Rochford says. The FBI also believes that the Russians played along with a request for money from Harold James Nicholson, a former CIA officer convicted of espionage, "because the SVR thought that he could provide information, even from his jail cell, that would help them find another internal mole inside Russia," Rochford says.

Given the Russians' efforts, the FBI put a permanent clamp on media requests to interview Ames. On the assumption the Russians would also try to contact Hanssen, the bureau extended special administrative measures that include a lockdown for all but one hour a week to both convicted spies, Rochford adds.

The Russians' effort to trade them is the death knell for both of them, Martin says.

"Should they pursue any case in federal court, such as an appeal seeking to get them released from prison in the U.S. or an effort to seek parole at any time or to seek executive clemency, the government now can argue that they should not be released because they still have value to the Russian intelligence service," Martin points out. "So, unwittingly, the Russians have put the final nail in Ames' and Hanssen's coffins, and they will never get out. That would normally be the case, but, should they feel in the future that the political atmosphere has changed so they could be released, the Russians have foreclosed that forever."

# Geronimo

In December 2010, the CIA informed the FBI that it had honed in on what the agency believed was a high-value terrorist target. To maintain the highest security, the FBI was not initially told the identity of the target. However, from National Security Council meetings, Mueller knew the target was Osama bin Laden. From then on, FBI agents played a key role in helping to train U.S. Navy SEALs for their mission, focusing on the commandos' task of scooping up evidence about al Qaeda once inside bin Laden's compound.

The trail leading to bin Laden's hideout in Abbotabad, about thirty-five miles from Pakistan's capital of Islamabad, went back to when Abu Zubaydah was waterboarded in 2002. He gave up information about bin Laden's couriers as well as information leading to the capture of Ramzi bin al-Shibh, a member of bin Laden's inner circle. After being subjected to coercive techniques, Abu Faraj al-Libi, a top al Qaeda facilitator for bin Laden, provided more detail on the couriers. In turn, clues from Abu Zubaydah and bin al-Shibh led to Khalid Sheikh Mohammed, the architect of the 9/11 plot. After being waterboarded, KSM confirmed knowing bin Laden's main courier, but he denied the man was connected to al Qaeda, creating suspicion that he was indeed important.

Working with those leads and others that would materialize, the CIA zeroed in on bin Laden's main courier, who used the pseudonym Abu Ahmed al-Kuwaiti. Finally, in 2010, the courier took a cell phone call that allowed NSA to pinpoint his location. Using surveillance teams and RQ-170 stealth drone aircraft, the CIA then tracked him in August 2010 to the compound where bin Laden had been hiding since 2005.

As a matter of course, Navy SEALs and Delta Force teams work closely with the FBI's Tactical Operations Center, which helps equip them with devices for entering premises quickly and detecting threats such as radiological, chemical, or biological weapons.

"The SEALs don't have much time on the objective," Louis Grever says. "They're in hostile territory, typically. So we will try to make things that they can take in pretty quickly, covertly, with less risk."

In Afghanistan, FBI agents trained SEAL Team 6, which had been selected for the assault, on what to look for when the commandos went in and how to handle the material they seized. By now, the FBI's Counterterrorism Division knew the identity of the target.

"They would quick grab an item, bag it, tag it, drop it into a bin, zip it up, put it on the aircraft," an intelligence official says. By the time the SEALs hit the target, "They'd already practiced and done this literally hundreds of times," he says. "They could do it in their sleep. They knew to pick up those things they thought were really important." However, "They did not have time to dig into every drawer and look for hidden crevices," he says.

Sending in a ground team to capture or kill bin Laden was considered, but the CIA and SEALs decided that going in by helicopter was the safest course.

"They flew in by helicopter because they wanted to get a lot of forces on the objective very quickly, and they had to have a very quick evacuation capability," a counterterrorism official says. "They could very easily have snuck in, but arguably, we probably couldn't get that number of forces all the way that deep in Pakistan clandestinely to execute an assault like that."

If the American assault was from the ground, bin Laden's people could have repelled the SEALs by flooding the entryways with gasoline and igniting it. "So the decision was, it was better to come in overhead by fast ropes, and then also have the ability to evacuate everybody very quickly," the official says.

The raid took place at 1 a.m. Pakistan time on

May 2, 2011. During the raid, one of the Black Hawk helicopters stalled, forcing a hard landing that disabled the helicopter. The two dozen SEALs had to abandon their plan to rappel down into the main building. Instead, they assaulted the compound from the ground after all, blowing up walls to enter. The burst of light and sound helped to stun and disorient the occupants.

Under a covert action finding signed by President Obama, the SEALs were to kill bin Laden "unless he was completely in a surrendering posture," the official says. "He was going to look for any crack at all to escape, and I'm sure he had no reservations about taking SEAL team members with him. The outcome was in the hands of UBL [the intelligence community designation for Usama bin Laden], and he did not surrender himself to capture."

After a SEAL shot bin Laden in his left eye and in the chest, the team notified the White House that Geronimo—the code name for bin Laden—had been killed. Four others were also killed, and one of bin Laden's wives, who rushed to protect him in his third-floor bedroom, was shot in the leg.

During the thirty-eight-minute raid, SEALs took fingerprints of bin Laden with scanners that transmitted the data back to the FBI. They also took fingerprints the old-fashioned way, rolling his fingertips onto an ink pad. The FBI thought it might have bin Laden's fingerprints on documents it had obtained, but it turned out they were not his. Therefore, the identification of bin Laden was accomplished solely by matching his DNA profile with that of his relatives and by identifying his face with facial recognition software. After he was shot, his wife who was with him identified him at the compound as well. Al Qaeda later issued a statement vowing revenge for the loss of its leader.

After 9/11, the FBI took on the role of safeguarding any material seized in U.S. counterterrorism actions around the globe. That preserves the chain of custody if a prosecution is brought in the United States or in other countries. In addition, the FBI is the premier agency for analyzing fingerprints, DNA traces, and handwriting.

The FBI Laboratory took custody of more than one hundred items seized in the raid of bin Laden's compound. They included documents such as letters and handwritten notes from bin Laden, shoulder weapons and handguns, digital thumb drives, laptops, computer hard drives, CDs, DVDs, and cell phones. In pages, the material would constitute a small college library. On the DVDs were videos of bin Laden watching clips of news coverage of himself on television.

Among the seized DVDs, the outtakes of his propaganda videos showed them to be heavily scripted affairs. He dyed and trimmed his beard for the cameras, then shot and reshot his remarks until the timing and lighting were to his liking. At the CIA's direction, the FBI distributed copies or photographs of the material to the CIA Counterterrorism Center and to other agencies poring over the treasure trove of leads.

"The documents could have fingerprints on them," a counterterrorism official says. "The loose media can have fingerprints, they can have DNA on them. Many people actually transfer DNA when they handle something."

"At the end of the day, it was the CIA's operation," the intelligence official noted days after the raid. "It was their opportunity, and they're going to make the judgments about how you action things. For the most part, anything that has a domestic nexus or U.S. interest nexus is going to get optioned into the FBI or Department of Homeland Security (DHS) if it's threat-related. If it's going to be an overseas or 'get' action, it will be handled by the CIA or by the State Department for disclosure to a friendly service: We don't want something bad to happen in Norway or the Philippines or whatever. Anything that happens in the theaters of operation where the combined commands have an interest or an active role, you get action to the military."

Sewn into his clothes, bin Laden had five hundred euros, the equivalent of $715, along with two telephone numbers. When the discovery of the phone numbers leaked to the press, intelligence officials became more cautious about parceling out the material to different agencies.

"The disclosure of the two telephone numbers potentially undermined an opportunity for us to exploit," the official says. "You want time to track and follow the people who have those numbers. The one thing about phone numbers; they're usually easy to get rid of and cut all your ties to them."

Besides the FBI and CIA, the NSA and Defense Intelligence Agency (DIA) had copies of the materials and ran down leads.

"These agencies are scrubbing the data against their databases," an intelligence official says. "Are there indicators; has this number shown up before? Has this name shown up before? And then they come back together and coordinate every day. They found this, this is what we found, and the CIA is taking a lead role in this and making sure what is then disseminated in the form of IRs—intelligence reports—is coordinated, is controlled, and is disseminated so that the appropriate agency, such as the FBI, could properly take action."

Al Qaeda's Achilles' heel turned out to be its need to communicate. Analysts poring over the cache of material found that to avoid detection, bin Laden would download his instructions to al Qaeda operatives to tiny flash memory computer drives. Couriers delivered the electronic material to others, whose job it was to transmit the messages by email or by other electronic means to the intended recipients.

"As effective as it was to bar any electronic communications from his compound, it still proved to be their vulnerability," an intelligence official says. "If you want to be an organized group, you have to communicate. Bin Laden would draft an instruction in his compound, and couriers took it out on electronic media and then transmitted it in the form of an email or some other communication."

While some recipients would question whether they had received a legitimate message from their leader, "They had no choice but to act on it," an official says.

Now, with the seized material, analysts from a range of intelligence agencies are able to trace messages back to specific individuals who will be placed under surveillance.

"We have real leads, telephone numbers, and digital data that we can link up to where we had some small piece of information from an intercept or human intelligence," a counterterrorism official says. "Now we can link it back to bin Laden, and we are seeing the connections come together. We did not appreciate how effective the couriers were. They took out the information electronically and then put it online."

Almost immediately, DHS alerted law-enforcement agencies to a plot being considered by bin Laden against the rail sector on the tenth anniversary of the 9/11 attacks.

"We will develop more sources, and they will develop more intel on targets, and they will develop new targets of opportunity, and it might take months or potentially years before we realize that what we refer to as this Sensitive Site Exploitation (SSE) resulted in this action two years down the road," the counterterrorism official predicts.

The process is similar to the one that led to bin Laden.

"Much like the information that came out from some of the interrogations early on, maybe the information doesn't thread together initially," the official says. "But over time, it builds a picture. In this case, by identifying couriers, it led to our objective."

Two days after the raid, CIA director Leon Panetta confirmed to NBC's Brian Williams that the CIA obtained some of the intelligence that led to bin Laden from enhanced interrogation, including waterboarding.

The raid left al Qaeda with no unifying leader, jeopardizing its future.

"I don't think there is any charismatic leader to replace Osama bin Laden," says Art Cummings. "In the long term, this could really degrade the future of the organization." Now, he says, "You end up with a much more distributed system than a centralized system all around the world for planning for a big operation. Al Qaeda has pulled back, and their ambitions are much more modest."

# The Biggest Threat

Looking back on his ten years as FBI director, Robert Mueller remembers the concerns he had when first taking the job. As head of the Justice Department's Criminal Division, he often had difficulty getting the information he needed from the bureau because the FBI's computer systems were such a disaster. The shortcomings evidenced at Ruby Ridge and Waco troubled him. And, upon becoming director, he was told that none of the popular software such as Microsoft Word could be used at the FBI.

Yet that was nothing compared to what he encountered on September 11, 2001, when he found the FBI knew little about possible terrorists and had an information system that was still largely paper-based.

"Whatever I anticipated was sort of set aside by September 11," Mueller tells me in a rare interview. "So what I thought I would be doing was not necessarily what I ended up doing. I knew coming in that we had information technology issues that had to be addressed. I had concerns about how we handled issues like Ruby Ridge or Waco, in terms of having a clear chain of command. I had some concern that we had not always put the best players in the playing field on cases of major national significance. I knew that terrorism was an issue but not the issue it would become several days later."

In the conference room adjoining his seventh-floor office at FBI headquarters, Mueller conducts an interview in his shirt-sleeves, a G-man-white oxford cloth with a subdued Brooks Brothers tie. While he is handsome, what impresses most is his commanding presence. He has the demeanor of an FBI agent combined with a prosecutor, which he once was.

After 9/11, the priority became changing the FBI's mind-set to prevent attacks first and worry about prosecution later.

"While the American public believed we were good at investigating terrorist attacks after they occurred and had prevented some attacks, the only metric now was preventing terrorist attacks," Mueller says. "Instead of reacting, we had to know where the threats are, identify the gaps, and then fill those gaps with sources or intercepts in anticipation of a possible attack."

In doing so, the FBI needed to have better liaison with the CIA and NSA. Today, Mueller notes, the FBI has more than a hundred agents detailed to the CIA. In turn, the CIA has attached officers to every FBI field office and Joint Terrorism Task Force.

Going back to 9/11, Mueller cites the CIA's success at rolling up Khalid Sheikh Mohammad and Abu Zubaydah as making a "huge difference in terms of the security of the United States." Intelligence from the CIA has led to FBI arrests in the United States, he notes.

Today Mueller says the greatest threat is an attack with weapons of mass destruction (WMD).

"The possibility of a nuclear attack is relatively remote, but you can never dismiss it, because of the devastation that would occur," Mueller says. "A radiological attack is not so remote, because it's relatively easy to get radiological materials and have some sort of radiological improvised explosive device. Although the damage would be far less than from a nuclear detonation, the threat is still there today."

In fact, Dr. Vahid Majidi, the chief of the FBI's Weapons of Mass Destruction Directorate, says the probability that the United States will be hit with a WMD attack at some point is 100 percent. Such an attack could be launched by foreign terrorists, lone wolves who are terrorists, or even criminal elements, Majidi says. As Mueller suggests, it would most likely employ chemical, biological, or radiological weapons rather than a nuclear device.

As it is, Majidi says, American intelligence picks up hundreds of reports each year of foreign terrorists obtaining WMD. When American forces invaded Afghanistan, they found that al Qaeda was working on what Majidi calls a "nascent" WMD effort involving chemical and biological weapons.

In every other case so far, the reports of foreign terrorists obtaining WMD have turned out to be unfounded. However, Majidi's directorate within the FBI investigates more than a dozen cases in the United States each year where criminals intend to use WMD. For example, in 2008, the FBI arrested Roger Bergendorff, who was found to have ricin and anarchist literature. Ricin kills cells by inhibiting protein synthesis. Within several days, the liver, spleen, and kidneys of a person who inhales or ingests ricin stop working, resulting in death.

"The notion of probability of a WMD attack being low or high is a moot point because we know the probability is 100 percent," Majidi says. "We've seen this in the past, and we will see it in the future. There is going to be an attack using chemical, biological, or radiological material."

Even a WMD attack that does not kill a great number of people would have a crushing psychological impact. "A singular lone wolf individual can do things in the dark of the night with access to a laboratory with low quantities of material and could hurt a few people but create a devastating effect on the American psyche," Majidi says.

That possibility is what Mueller says keeps him up at night. "The biggest threat comes from individuals who have had some association with the United States, understand the United States, can move either individually or with others relatively freely into the United States and within the United States," Mueller says.

A major cyberattack that could take down America's infrastructure is another concern.

"Sooner or later, I think probably somebody will get through and take down an electrical grid by attacking power company computers," Mueller says. At the same time, "The exfiltration of information from U.S. government entities and nongovernment entities by a number of countries, including China, Russia, Iran, and others out there, is the wave of the future."

In his ten years in office, Mueller says the FBI has "come a long way toward understanding and becoming a part of the intelligence community, both in terms of learning about it and bettering ourselves, developing intelligence and analyzing it and disseminating it."

The bureau still needs to do more to develop its leaders by exposing them to the rest of the intelligence community.

"It's important for persons who are doing terrorism throughout the United States to understand how the CIA works, what kind of information they have, how you get that information,"

Mueller says. "Same with NSA, same with the Defense Intelligence Agency."

High-ranking FBI officials were amazed that for this book, Louis Grever opened a window on how the FBI conducts covert entries. In fact, during one interview with Grever, who is on a level just below the deputy director, an FBI agent assigned to public affairs interjected and asked whether he should be revealing these secrets.

Grever responded by saying the capabilities of some bugging devices may not be as sensitive as they seem. He later said that besides Mueller, he consulted with other high-ranking FBI officials before deciding to reveal the TacOps story.

"It would be hard, if not impossible, for our targets to counter our attempts to penetrate their space based solely on the information revealed in the book," Grever said. "The American public has a right to know what their government services are doing—where they're investing money, why it's important that you have this kind of capability."

Asked why he approved Grever's proposal to reveal these most closely guarded secrets, Mueller said jokingly, "Already he's told you too much, that's what my thinking is." But then he added, "I'll go along with whatever he told you. . . . He has a wide degree of discretion."

Within the FBI, Mueller was known to think

highly of President Obama's intelligence and commitment to counterterrorism. At the same time, he wondered whether he should go along with Obama's directive that he fly to Tucson to take charge of the investigation into the shooting of Representative Gabrielle Giffords in January 2011. Not since the Hoover days has a president injected himself that directly into FBI operations, risking a perception that the bureau is subject to White House influence that could be political in nature.

Mueller himself had no experience or interest in directing FBI investigations. His presence meant FBI agents who were conducting the investigation had to divert their attention to briefing him. While Mueller did not object to Obama's order, he and other top FBI officials did keep their distance from Janet Napolitano, the secretary of homeland security, whom Mueller considered too political.

Two problems arose during Mueller's tenure. One was poor supervision of the process for issuing national security letters, which are used in international terrorism and espionage investigations to obtain data on where and when telephone calls and emails are sent and received. Contrary to reports in the press, national security letters do not authorize the FBI to wiretap calls or to see the contents of emails.

In an audit, Justice Department inspector

General Glenn A. Fine found deficiencies associated with 22 of the 293 national security letters he examined from 2003 to 2005. In some cases, the letters were issued after the authorized investigation period, or an agent had accidentally transposed digits in the telephone number of a person under investigation.

Fine specifically found that the FBI had not intentionally violated any rules. He determined that, with the exception of situations where the recipient made an error, the FBI in most cases had obtained information to which it was, in fact, entitled.

By the time the report came out, Mueller had taken steps to correct the problems, including installing a Web-based data system to keep better track of national security letters and instituting new review processes and additional training.

"I did not know that we were not following the appropriate administrative protocols to make certain that we were dotting the $i$'s and crossing the $t$'s to obtain those records," Mueller says.

Mueller's biggest failure was the FBI's case management computer system, which was supposed to replace paper files. Like most government agencies, instead of beginning with off-the-shelf software, the FBI decided it had to reinvent the wheel and start from scratch. The FBI never had a clear idea of what it wanted and kept changing its requirements.

In December 2008, Mueller hired Chad Fulgham as the FBI's new chief information officer. "We had three hundred twenty FBI people working on the program," Fulgham says. "I had never heard of that. There were too many cooks in the kitchen."

Fulgham streamlined the procurement operation and halted development while key issues were straightened out. He expected the kinks to be worked out so that the system would be fully operational by the end of 2011.

"With the first go-round on the virtual case file system, I didn't ask the hard questions," Mueller says. "With the latest iteration, the problems did not come to my attention until the contractor was due to give us the fully operational phase two of the system. I'm pretty comfortable that we're on the right path now."

That failure aside, Mueller successfully turned the FBI around to make it a powerful weapon against terrorism. Every few months, the FBI announces new arrests of terrorists. In many cases, instead of waiting years to nail them with terrorism-related charges, the FBI will charge terrorists with lesser crimes that put them away for years or result in deportations. At the same time, no abuse—meaning an illegal or politically motivated act—was ever found during Mueller's tenure.

Unlike J. Edgar Hoover and William Sessions,

Mueller never used his position improperly. Unlike Louis Freeh, Mueller never presided over fiascoes that undermined FBI investigations and credibility. While William Webster improved FBI investigations of spies and the Mafia, no director since Hoover has had a greater positive impact on the bureau than Mueller.

Because of Hoover's abuses, Congress in 1968 enacted a law requiring that future FBI directors be nominated by the president and confirmed by the Senate. Their terms were limited to ten years. Mueller is the first director to serve all ten years of his term. He served longer than any FBI director except Hoover.

Prior to the expiration of his term in September 2011, at President Obama's request, Mueller agreed to a two-year extension of his term to be approved by Congress. Mueller was said to be shocked that he had been asked to stay beyond the ten-year term. After considering it for several days, he agreed to continue.

Within the FBI, some agents were unhappy because they had hoped that a new director would rescind Mueller's policy of requiring supervisors in the field to transfer to headquarters after seven years or give up their supervisory status. As in any organization, some agents think first of their own well-being and second about the organization as a whole. But most agents looked at the bigger picture and credited Mueller with the FBI's success at rolling up plots and keeping the country safe since 9/11.

When I first interviewed Mueller six months after he took office, his black hair was just beginning to gray. Today it is silvery. He still has ramrod-straight posture. I asked him what advice he had for future FBI directors.

"Learn the organization," Mueller says. "You're not going to find a more patriotic, dedicated, hardworking, knowledgeable professional organization to be a part of. Ask very hard questions, and then surround yourself with competent and capable people."

# Acknowledgments

My wife, Pamela Kessler, is my partner in writing and in life. A former *Washington Post* reporter and author of *Undercover Washington*, about the spy sites of the nation's capital, Pam accompanied me on key interviews at FBI headquarters, the FBI Academy, the Washington field office, and the FBI Laboratory. She contributed vivid descriptions that are the best writing in the book. She then preedited the manuscript. I am fortunate to have her love, wise judgment, and unwavering support.

I am grateful for the love and support of my grown children, Rachel and Greg Kessler. My stepson, Mike Whitehead, is a loyal and endearing part of that team.

As with my previous book, *In the President's Secret Service: Behind the Scenes with Agents in the Line of Fire and the Presidents They Protect*, Mary Choteborsky, publishing manager at Crown, contributed excellent suggestions and edited the final manuscript brilliantly. When it comes to book publishing, Mary and her team are without peer.

I am lucky to have my agent, Robert Gottlieb, chairman of Trident Media, on my side. Since

1991, Robert has guided my book-writing career and has been a source of staunch support and wisdom.

The FBI gave me unprecedented access for this book. I am grateful to FBI director Robert S. Mueller III. Michael Kortan, assistant FBI director for public affairs, and Susan McKee in FBI Public Affairs went out of their way to help.

The Society of Former FBI Agents made available its collection of one hundred thirty-five oral histories with agents going back to the Rudolf Abel case. I am grateful to Sean McWeeney and Craig Dotlo.

Hundreds of current or former FBI agents contributed their experiences and shared their insights for this book. They have my appreciation.

**Center Point Publishing**
600 Brooks Road ● PO Box 1
Thorndike ME 04986-0001 USA


**(207) 568-3717**


**US & Canada:**
**1 800 929-9108**
www.centerpointlargeprint.com